The Ch

SRHE and Open University Press Imprint
General Editor: Heather Eggins

The Changing University?

Edited by Tom Schuller

The Society for Research into Higher Education
& Open University Press

Published by SRHE and
Open University Press
Celtic Court
22 Ballmoor
Buckingham
MK18 1XW

and 1900 Frost Road, Suite 101
Bristol, PA 19007, USA

First published 1995

A catalogue record of this book is available from the British Library

ISBN 0 335 19420 6 (pb) 0 335 19421 4 (hb)

Library of Congress Cataloging-in-Publication Data

The changing university? / edited by Tom Schuller.
  p. cm.
 Includes bibliographical references and index.
  ISBN 0-335-19421-4. (hb) ISBN 0-335-19420-6 (pbk.)
  1. Universities and colleges—Great Britain. 2. Education,
Higher—Great Britain—Aims and objectives. 3. Educational change—Great
Britain. I. Schuller, Tom.
LA637.C43 1995
378.41—dc20

                   95-19419
                     CIP

Typeset by Graphicraft Typesetters Limited, Hong Kong
Printed in Great Britain by St Edmundsbury Press Ltd
Bury St Edmunds, Suffolk

Contents

Contributors

Stephen Brookfield is currently Distinguished Professor at the University of St Thomas in St Paul, Minnesota, and the author or editor of seven books on adult learning, critical thinking and teaching. He has taught in England, Canada and Australia and was formerly Research Director for the Advisory Council for Adult and Continuing Education (England and Wales).

Thomas Owen Eisemon is a Senior Education Specialist in the Education and Social Policy Department at the World Bank. He is also Professor and Director of the Centre for Cognitive and Ethnographic Studies at McGill University. Dr Eisemon has published extensively on science and higher education in Africa and Asian countries.

John Field has been Professor of Continuing Education and Head of the Division of Adult Education and Community Development at the University of Ulster since June 1994. Previously he was Director of Continuing Education at the University of Bradford; before that he taught at the University of Warwick where he was the founding director of the Continuing Education Research Centre. He is Secretary of the International Network of the Universities Association for Continuing Education. Among his publications are *European Union Policies on Vocational Education and Training* (Longman 1994) and *Learning through Labour: Unemployment, Training and the State, 1890–1939* (Leeds University Press 1992). He is currently working on a study of the European Union's policies in the field of employment.

Alison Girdwood is an administrator at the University of Edinburgh, working on quality assurance and university policy on teaching. She is currently Chair of the World University Service (UK) and undertaking part-time research on aid to universities in Sub-Saharan Africa.

Christine King is Vice-Chancellor of Staffordshire University, having taken up the post in September 1995. Professor King is well known for her research and publications on the history of religion and in particular the plight of Jehovah's Witnesses in the Third Reich. She has also researched and published on topics as diverse as women in management and Elvis Presley.

Alistair MacFarlane was trained as an electrical engineer at Glasgow University and Metropolitan-Vickers, Manchester, then worked as a radar system designer before becoming an academic. As Principal of Heriot-Watt University he has taken a deep interest in educational technology, was a Commissioner in the National Commission on Education, and chaired the working party of the Committee of Scottish University Principals which produced the report *Teaching and Learning in an Expanding Higher Education System*.

Craig McInnis is a Senior Lecturer in the Centre for the Study of Higher Education at the University of Melbourne. His current research activities include a national survey of the academic profession and senior non-academic administrators. He is also conducting a study of the undergraduate experience in Australian universities.

Ian McNay heads the Centre for Higher Education Management at Anglia Polytechnic University, which offers bespoke courses, consultancy, organization development and research services in the UK and overseas. Professor McNay has worked as an academic and administrator on both sides of the former binary line, and in Belgium and Spain.

Robin Middlehurst is the Director of the Quality Enhancement Group of the Higher Education Quality Council. She has experience of teaching at all levels of education, from primary to adult, and has worked in other areas of the public sector before joining higher education in 1986. Postgraduate study at the University of Reading, four years of research work at the University of Surrey, three years of teaching, research and consultancy at the Institute of Education resulted in *Leading Academics*, published by the Open University Press in 1993.

Radim Palouš received his doctorate in philosophy from Charles University (Prague) in 1948, but was then expelled for political reasons. He returned to education as a chemistry teacher, first in high school and then at university, but in 1959 was again banned. Having published several works in the 1960s he suffered further persecution in 1969. Neither this nor several further arrests stopped him becoming a signatory of Charter 77, publishing a book on Comenius' approach to education and other works on the philosophy of education, and teaching philosophy clandestinely. In 1990, he became Rector of Charles University on the first free vote of the Academic Senate, and was re-elected for three years the following year. He was given an honorary doctorate from Edinburgh University in 1993.

Gwynneth Rigby is an independent consultant. Since 1992, she has been consultant to the National Commission on Education, on further and higher education. Other clients have included the CVCP, the National Audit Office and the Institute of Education. Her background is in university administration at the universities of Coventry, Newcastle upon Tyne and Warwick.

Jamil Salmi is a Moroccan education economist presently working in the Latin America Human Resources Division of the World Bank and the author of five books and several articles on education and development issues. He is responsible for education projects in Venezuela and Haiti. Previously, Dr Salmi worked in the Education and Social Policy Department of the World Bank and was responsible for the preparation of a recently published Policy Paper on Higher Education.

Hans Schuetze was educated at the universities of Bonn, Göttingen, Grenoble and California at Berkeley. He has a background in the Liberal Arts and in Law. After working as a lawyer and policy analyst in a number of positions, both in Germany and at the OECD in Paris, he is now a Research Fellow at Centre for Policy Studies in Education at the University of British Columbia at Vancouver, Canada.

Tom Schuller has been Director of the Centre for Continuing Education at the University of Edinburgh since 1990, where he holds a Personal Chair in Continuing Education. He worked previously at the universities of Warwick and Glasgow, and for four years at the OECD in Paris. His recent publications include *Life After Work* (Harper Collins 1991, with Michael Young), *The Future of Higher Education* (Open University Press 1991, Editor) and *Learning: Education, Training and Information for the Third Age* (1993, Report Paper 3 for the Carnegie Inquiry into the Third Age with Anne Marie Bostyn). He is the convenor of the Edinburgh City of Lifelong Learning initiative.

Jenny Shackleton was a mature student before entering further education as a lecturer in 1973. Following management experience in colleges and an LEA she became Principal of Wirral Metropolitan College in 1987. Throughout her career, Jenny Shackleton has worked in partnership with organizations seeking complementary ends. At present, she is a member of the National Commission on Education, the Independent Inquiry into the Role of the Police, and the Council for Industry and Higher Education, and a Director of a local Community Health Trust.

Leslie Wagner is the Principal and Chief Executive of Leeds Metropolitan University, having previously been Vice-Chancellor and Chief Executive of the University of North London from 1987 to 1993. Professor Wagner is Chairman of the Society for research into Higher Education and a member of the Board of the Open Learning Foundation, the Board of the Higher Education Quality Council and the Council of the Committee of Vice-Chancellors and Principals. He has written or edited four books on economics and the planning of education.

1

Introduction: The Changing University? A Sketchmap with Coda

Tom Schuller

Is the university changing? The question mark in the title of this book is not just a quirk. As the precedings of a conference, this book's initial intention is to challenge participants to provide answers to the oblique question; the same intention extends to the wider group who subsequently read the book. The theme set for the conference itself was non-interrogative, inviting participants to describe, analyse or evaluate presumed change. The book takes a step back and invites both participants and readers to think directly about the extent to which change is actually occurring, if at all, as well as what forms it takes. Change can be too easily assumed to be happening; we need to keep it in perspective. So this introduction sets out to provide a summary sketchmap to investigating university change. Figure 1.1 provides a simple pictorial representation; the text elaborates on it, drawing on the contributions which make up this volume and posing questions rather than answers. As a counterbalance to all these interrogatives, the chapter concludes with a brief but highly prescriptive coda, arguing against a linear expansion of university provision.

The sketchmap did not exist in this form as a predefined framework for the volume. It is the product of editorial induction, derived from a reading of the contributors' chapters, and of reflection on other analyses and evidence. There was, of course, a prior structure to the book, with each contributor invited to write on a given topic and to provide at the end a scenario, or scenarios, for the future. But this structure took a linear form, inevitably conceived of as a contents page; the idea of a map allowing the visualization of multiple cross-relationships emerged only later.

To this amateur cartographer, then, there are four main dimensions to the map: scale, boundaries, orientation and contours. Summarily, I interpret them as follows:

Scale refers to size or volume: numbers of students, range of institutions, amounts of funding, and so on. Mapping may be of changes in absolute size over time, or of size relative to comparable units, for example other national systems. Where is growth, and where decline?

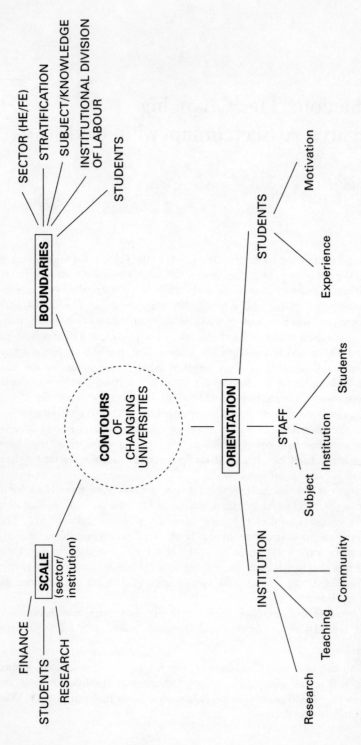

Figure 1.1 University change.

Boundaries are the lines which divide bodies of all kinds, at whatever level: institutions, people, activities or subjects. The lines may be formal or informal; they may have a legal, social or pragmatic status; they may be watertight or in varying degrees porous. Are they being redrawn, eroding of their own accord, or hardening?

Orientation deals with questions about where institutions or people are facing and going. This is the most ambiguous of the dimensions, covering values as well as trends. Functionally, how far are universities committed to their students and how far to the generation of scholarship and knowledge? Do the staff identify primarily with their immediate colleagues, or with others spread through the country or the world? To what extent might the same university be oriented in different directions, comfortably or otherwise?

Contours are a function of the other three dimensions, and define the shape of the system, institution or other unit. Thus the contours of the university sector change as individual institutions and groups of institutions within the sector grow or shrink, their boundaries shifting also but not necessarily to the same degree; or the contours of a university change as subject areas flourish or decline, and new institutional functions are assumed.

The map is undeniably sketchy. As editor I chose to cast the net geographically wide, which undermined any chance of tidy thematic analysis. The mapping metaphor may seem inappropriate, since maps generally refer to more or less stable terrains, whilst the purpose here is to provide a framework for gauging change. But metaphors work if they help others to think creatively, in conference or outside; so let that be the test.

The contours of change: scale, boundaries and orientation

We can begin by asking what is included in the university sector, and therefore what is excluded. With a stroke of the pen accomplishing the abolition of the binary line, the sector has more or less doubled. However, this has not solved the problem of where boundaries should be drawn – except maybe for those who now fall on the 'right' side. Ever-growing concern about the best way of handling further expansion of post-compulsory education brings into focus the relationship between universities and colleges of higher and further education (CFEs). CFEs are not universities, and most do not aspire to be, but 76 colleges in England already receive direct grants from the Higher Education Funding Council, and it is fair to ask whether the identification of higher education with universities and the exclusion of further education institutions from this sector make for sensible or equitable policies. This is a major theme of Jenny Shackleton in Chapter 3; hers is a plea not for university status, but for a proper articulation between the two sectors, which could mean bringing them into a single policy framework. What further changes, in funding, staffing and policy development, would that entail?

Whatever provisional conclusions are reached on where the boundaries of the sector should lie and how porous these might be, the issue of differentiation within the university sector remains. First, there is differentiation of function, an issue whose familiarity has coincided with the recognition of 'mission drift' as a black mark against university records. What scope is there for diversity within the sector in respect of the major functions of teaching and research? Are we moving towards the emergence of essentially graduate institutions, or teaching-only universities? Whose responsibility is it to ensure that there is a measure of coherence within the sector, with appropriate complementarity between the activities of universities? Funding councils can give policy steers, or at least supply financial incentives in one direction or another: are these likely to increase in specificity, or will it be left up to some notion of the 'market'? Leslie Wagner in Chapter 2 argues that the arrival of new institutions in a sense sheltered the older universities – in other words, that sectoral change may wash over individual institutions, with the reality of change in one part of the sector bestowing the fictitious appearance of change on the rest.

Diversity of function is not the same as difference in esteem or ranking. Ranking is very much in evidence in education at all levels, but arguably in the higher education sector it has always existed, only implicitly so. There are two aspects here. First, what has happened, and will happen, in respect of formal ranking systems and the financial and other implications which they bring in their train? However critical universities have been of the introduction of research assessments and judgements of teaching quality, few have abstained from making heavy use of them for internal management and external relations purposes. Secondly, neither formal nor informal ranking systems are fixed. If some universities can improve, then under current logic others will fall back, even though the game is not straightforwardly zero-sum. Institutional mobility may become far more apparent than it has done in the past, as we move into second and third rounds of the various assessments, with benchmarks of various kinds more easily available and clearly visible. This is a key observation in Craig McInnis' account (Chapter 4) of the experience from Australia and New Zealand. Other aspects of sectoral change range from the internal stratification of vice-chancellorial pomp, so mercilessly lampooned by Laurie Taylor in his column in *The Higher* to more substantive and positive features such as the growth of 2 + 2 degrees as examples of higher education/further education (HE/FE) collaboration and the partnerships to which Shackleton refers.

Coming back to the issue of definition of what counts as a university, we could look at changes in the philosophical conception of a university and relate these to changes in the epistemological landscape and the socio-political context. Which disciplines have more or less run their course, with little more to be mined in the way of knowledge and little demand for it anyway, and which have forced their way in as newcomers to the university curriculum? What is the process which determines change in the relative weight of different disciplines? Is such change knowledge-induced or materially propelled – in other words, does it come because of an opening up of new areas of intellectual discovery, or because of economic or occupational changes which affect the demand for research or teaching?

Comparing the trajectories of, for example, Theology, English Literature and Marketing as university subjects might yield some solid insights here; it could also generate some speculative but fruitful analysis of what 'disciplines' are likely to have emerged, or submerged, ten years hence. The same exercise applied elsewhere – in China, for example – would yield rather different results.

It is not only the paths and places of individual subjects which count. What is the spread, or range? The term 'university' suggests that the institution should be in some sense all-embracing, as Radim Palous suggests in Chapter 15. Since it very obviously does not embrace all the population, or even all of the population that wish to study, perhaps we should look to subject spread for the implied universality. Is it breadth that distinguishes the university from the liberal arts college on the one hand and the technical institute on the other (cf. the use of *Schmalspur-Unis* – 'narrow-gauge universities' – to refer to Fachhochschulen in Germany; Gilbertson 1995)? It is hard to say, but it is clear that many universities are grappling with the sheer impossibility of maintaining a full range of subject provision. What university could aspire to the title without offering Philosophy or Biological Sciences? Yet simply listing subject areas which must be taught (and researched? – see later) for an institution to qualify does little to resolve the issue, only sending us back to investigate what lies behind the prospectus title: how many strands of philosophy or branches of Biological Sciences must be present to make up the subject?

So much for the changing contours of knowledge, the curricular character of the institution. Let us turn to the people who inhabit it. Some of the changes already referred to point to a significant redivision of academic or, more broadly, institutional labour. The question is how far this redivision is already under way. I have used the traditional binary categorization of teaching and research, but how adequately do these characterize what staff do in universities – and what students are exposed to? Alistair MacFarlane in Chapter 5 summarizes the challenges which remain to be faced in respect of teaching and poses a question about the balance between past and anticipated change. His itemized projections – notably the shift from 'synchronous single location learning support to asynchronous networked learning support' – are specific enough to make anyone sit up and take stock of the future. What forms will 'teaching' take, and what changes in the composition of teaching activities can we expect? Judged by their recruitment policies, how seriously are universities taking the learning revolution? What is the relative status of information technicians and librarians compared with 'lecturers', and for how long will lecturing continue as the formal designation of the core academic activity? We should also not forget that the boundary between staff and student is weakening as more graduate students take on teaching roles – or work for the university in other capacities.

It is ironic that staff defined as 'researchers' are for the most part marginal in status, yet for many universities research is the defining activity; certainly it is the area where mission drift and functional differentiation are most closely scrutinized, formally and informally. Just as teaching/lecturing can mean very different things, so too can research. This is most commonly discussed in relation to the indissolubility or otherwise of teaching and research, with 'scholarship' now sometimes introduced as the bridging middle term. However, there are two aspects of the research process where change is strongly in evidence and can be expected to continue. The first is quantity, in the light of what Craig McInnis (Chapter 4) calls the 'commodification of knowledge'. The stress (and I use the term advisedly) on research means a knowledge explosion which has to be handled somehow. Institutional expansion plus teaching/research indissolubility equals exponential increase in research output and, probably, a backward-sloping quality curve. Secondly, the competence and motivation of researchers seen in a lifetime perspective demands reflection. Can we expect anything other than increased specialization, with successful researchers clustering in particular institutes or managing to buy themselves out of teaching in order to investigate smaller and smaller fragments of the knowledge map? Here we can see the interrelation between changes in epistemology and professional function.

As with teaching and research, the notion of what constitutes the third part of the traditional triad, 'administration', is open to change and multiple interpretation even as a concept. In the public sector generally, a combination of broad economic trends and particular government ideologies has driven along a shift from administration as keeping things ticking over to management as active, proactive and even pre-empting professional practice. The notion of academic management has a serious and challenging sense to it, as well as much unnecessary market rhetoric. Just as administration is not the same as management, so management is not the same as leadership, at least not institutional leadership. The theme of Robin Middlehurst in Chapter 7 would hardly have been intelligible not so many years ago. What is the nature of leadership in universities, and how far does this reflect the changes which have occurred in institutional and sectoral practice? The historical legacy of the binary divide is still making itself felt here, with different management and leadership styles clustering recognizably, though not neatly, within the old university and former polytechnic sectors. What is happening at other levels in the hierarchy? Here, another term currently (but I hope not transiently) fashionable in management vocabularies emerges: the 'learning organization'. How do universities measure up on this score? The fact that Stephen Brookfield in Chapter 11 may strike some readers as verging on the fantastic is a powerful reminder of how far there is to go before staff development is given due priority – and he is referring only to academic staff. If people are an organization's most valued resource, universities have a lot of it, and therefore much to do before they claim this valued organizational status. Brookfield focuses on teaching, but his vision of employee learning could readily be broadened to encompass the institution and all the individuals within it. However we divide their functions, people working within universities are just that – people, who have affective as well as cognitive sides which require nurturing. Brookfield's concern with personal growth strikes me as the modern, micro-level version of the historical humanist sweep exhibited by Palous in Chapter 15.

Institutions outlive their staff, but many of them share its biography for an extended period. Historical academic immobility – in the late 1960s, about 60 per cent of academic staff in the UK had only ever worked in one university (Williams *et al.* 1974) – has disappeared, with the growth in short-term contracts and increased career change, noted by Craig McInnis (Chapter 4). Does the withering of this life-long relationship signal the end of the university as a community of scholars, the 'collegium' which forms one of Ian McNay's (Chapter 9) four institutional types (Schuller 1990)? Changes in internal university relationships can be looked at from a number of angles, most of which throw severe doubts on the idealized notion of community. Exactly what is the community which university staff are expected to feel part of? There is a complex matrix made up of personal, disciplinary and institutional loyalties, which reach beyond the physical boundaries of the places where people work. The nature of these relationships is greatly complicated, or rather the permutations are greatly increased, by new technologies which have radically changed the nature of academic communication. Moreover, Leslie Wagner (Chapter 2) points out that collegiality could be redefined, for instance in terms of commitment to student access and opportunity rather than of peer relations.

Gender and age intersect with industrial relations issues, and the combination has a far wider application than to the academic staff alone. The exclusive maleness of the original institutions has been tempered, with female and male students enrolling now in almost equal numbers. However as the gender breakdown of senior positions shows, academic hierarchies have been slow to shift (Lie *et al.* 1994). This is linked to the ageing of the academic profession, with the proportion of core academic staff aged 55 years or over rising to 17 per cent by 1992–3. The average age of core staff was 45 years, compared to 33 years for those on temporary contracts (Halsey 1995: 304). Qualitatively, moreover, the organizational culture of most universities remains substantially male. The notion of academe as a community has generally been highly Athenian, to put it mildly, with myriad low-status employees who would not recognize themselves as participating in a collegial democracy. This goes well beyond discrimination or disadvantage within the academic hierarchy, and raises questions about the nature of the university as an employing organization.

Universities, relatedly, are now very significant players in the local economy. Especially where there is more than one university in a city, higher education is likely to be one of the biggest businesses, with its responsibilities to the local community covering a number of aspects (CVCP 1994). It is a deliverer of services to local citizens, as undergraduates, graduates or continuing education students, and to local employers. It is itself a major employer, with an army of typically low-paid staff on cleaning and janitorial duties. It can be a provider of leisure and other facilities for the local population. It generally holds a large property portfolio, and has in modern times often been a property developer with a singularly poor aesthetic record. Gwynneth Rigby in Chapter 12 points to the choices which have to be made in the extent to which there is a specifically local commitment, whilst sounding a sceptical note in the light of the conformity of institutional aspiration. What changes have occurred in the overall conception of the university in all these roles?

Finance is the issue specifically addressed by Rigby. She focuses primarily on student funding rather than, for example, the arcana of institutional funding formulae, the diversification of funding sources or the spreading practice of internal financial devolution or cost-centring; a recent addition to this list is the entry of universities into the capital markets, as a consortium bids to raise £100 million (*The Higher*, 10 February 1995). Funding is probably the only issue to feature in every single chapter and is universally preoccupying, as the contributions by Hans Schuetze on Canada (Chapter 14) and by Thomas Owen Eisemon and Jamil Salmi (Chapter 6) covering most of the world so strongly demonstrate. Cartographically, finance is ubiquitous, more than ever before, or at least within living memory.

The feature which has evinced probably the most change is the student population, addressed directly by Christine King's contribution (Chapter 10). The change has been summed up, rather ominously, in the following way (Williams and Fry 1994: 8): 'The expansion of the past ten years amounts to the advent of mass higher education in quantitative terms. The prime concern of the next ten will be coming to terms with the qualitative consequences.' Between 1986 and 1993 the age participation index of young school leavers rose from 14 to 31 per cent. The rate of increase is just as impressive if we go back further, to the peri-Robbins period of planning, birth and growth, when a figure of 5–6 per cent of the age cohort was regarded as extraordinary and adults as undergraduates barely figured. How do we extrapolate from here? Do we go with the CBI calls for 40 per cent of the cohort to graduate by the year 2000? Proponents of life-long learning have tended to make semi-triumphalist claims about the changing student population, pointing dramatically to thresholds crossed as more than 50 per cent of new entrants into UK higher education were aged 25 years or over in 1993, and part-time numbers close up on the full-timers (Slowey 1994). All true, and almost all welcome enough; but where are these 'non-traditional' students distributed? King's chapter chronicles what this might mean, but we need to look more closely at the profile of the population and the shape expansion has taken. The social composition of the student population has always provoked debate, especially when related to supposedly antithetical ideologies of merito-cracy and egalitarianism.

Massive expansion has taken place. In the élite institutions, this has mainly meant admitting a significant but still restricted number of students from a similar class background to their previous population, but with a more equal sex com-position, plus a huge expansion of graduate work. Meanwhile the polytechnics have brought with them into the university sector a great dowry of students from more diverse backgrounds, socially, ethnically and chronologically (see Ainley 1994 for a well-grounded account of intra-sectoral differences). The great influx of mature students entering initial higher education has been into part-time sub-degree programmes in non-élite universities. Women now make up over 48 per cent of the total home-student population and girls' performance in schools continues to improve faster than that of boys. How much further will this shift go? The effects of greater gender equality are still only just emerging, with the relationship to social class a highly contentious issue (Benn and Burton 1994). Quantitative change does not necessarily entail change in gendering by subject. Likewise, ethnic minorities generally are not numerically underrepresented, but their members cluster in certain subject areas and in former polytechnics. How do we concep-tualize equality of access? Is it a permanently receding chimera?

The dynamics of change within the student population inevitably affect the nature of the student experience (Haselgrove 1994). There are at least two phases here: the period of studying itself, and its subsequent effects. Finance immediately enters as a major factor, as Rigby shows in Chapter 12. Seen from one angle, the UK has managed to achieve the worst of both worlds: a system of student support which has always been highly regressive, and which now fails adequately to support even those who benefit from it. This is too negative, given the system's comparatively very high success rate in terms of student completion. However, the change from élite to mass higher education has not been accompanied by a parallel, and supportive, change in the financial system, and the consequence is unparalleled hardship and stress for many students.

The great divide, peculiar to the UK, is between full-time and part-time students. In one sense, as Tight (1991) has observed, this is an administrative division which has little to do with how much time is actually spent studying, but it coincides strongly with age and class. It is a boundary which is rapidly crumbling as more and more supposedly full-time students take part-time jobs. One consequence of this is a re-orientation of students to a more instrumental approach, meaning that they tend to look only to those courses, or within those course to those elements, which contribute directly to their gaining a qualification. The inter-relationships between financial trends and educational experiences are striking.

Plagiarists apart, once a graduate always a graduate. But we have to ask what is happening to that status. Contrary to most expressed opinion, by the end of the 1990s the UK will have the highest output of graduates in Europe, unless non-completion rates rise extraordinarily (Williams and Fry 1994: 3). Does 'saturation' have empirical meaning? If it does, what is happening to the marshier parts of the graduate labour market? We do not know, and will not until significant numbers start disappearing, believed drowned in debts and disappointment, but Rigby sounds a warning note when she says that the glittering prizes may look more than a little tarnished. In other words, changes in the output of universities must be affecting not just the structure of occupations, the content of jobs and the ranking of qualifications, but also the nature of rewards.

This is all the more true when we consider the fact that what Williams and Fry call extended education – all education and training beyond a first degree – has grown even more rapidly than undergraduate study, with a particularly massive expansion in Advanced Diploma courses. About 15 per cent of all the student population is now postgraduate. Many of these are participating as continuing education students, returning later in life. For many, however, it is a straightforward extension of their initial education, largely in order to attain the positional good which a first degree once represented. Is this extended education – or distended? What shape do we want our system to be? I state my position in the coda.

Spatial and temporal contexts

Change can be assessed over time in the context of a single institution or system, but also in relation to the wider spatial context. International comparisons are most commonly used as a stick to belabour either ourselves (meaning the population generally or educationalists) or those we consider to be responsible for the country's educational shortcomings. They can be a source of impetus for reflection and change, though their effectiveness in this regard is hard to measure. Their function in the map has three aspects which can be very briefly sketched out.

First, comparisons can provide bearings on the agenda for change. How far are the issues with which we are grappling the same as those in other contexts or countries? It is clear from the contributions by Alison Girdwood (Chapter 8) and all the overseas contributors that issues such as student finance, state funding and quality control have emerged as strongly as they have done in the UK, if not more so. Secondly, however, how far is this country proceeding along the same lines as others in responding to this agenda – in other words, what is the direction of change? Consideration of the role of private finance, with a shift in the distribution of costs from state to individual, is evidently one common trend; it would be interesting to identify issues where directly contrary trends occurred in different parts of the world. Chapter 6 by Eisemon and Salmi demonstrates that the problems of underfunded expansion have very different resonances around the world, even though many of the issues of principle – equity of access, and accountability – remain constant. Thirdly, what is the scale of change? Reductions in the unit of resource in the UK can be legitimately experienced as huge by the inhabitants of British universities, but as Girdwood shows, these would be welcomed as trivial by their African counterparts (or colleagues? – see the discussion of the notion of an academic community, p. 7). These latter two contributions give some indication of magnitudes of difficulty confronting policy-makers and academics; does this help readers in richer countries to 'get things in proportion'?

The primary focus of this book, and of this chapter, is the UK, but this may vary upwards or downwards. If we take the latter direction and look at the constituent elements of the UK higher education sector there are clear differences between Scotland, Northern Ireland, England and Wales. In part, this is a result of size and history (Paterson 1994), and institutional changes such as the introduction of separate funding councils, but it is also a function of the nature of relationships within the policymaking community.[1] Will the move towards more transparent funding formulae, now common throughout the UK, balance out the scope for greater diversity inherent in the creation of separate funding councils? John Field, in Chapter 13, on the European dimension, raises a similar set of issues at a different level; he also offers a judiciously restrained view on the pace of change, pointing out that, contrary to some of the rhetoric, pan-European policy development on higher education has in fact been quite limited.

Mapping is a quintessentially spatial activity, but as Einstein's century comes to an end, we should be getting used to the indissolubility of space and time. Quite literally, the measurement of change is impossible without an implied or stated timeframe. This book's question mark is intended to raise in readers' minds questions about when and in what temporal frame changes are taking place. Should we be reflecting primarily on those changes which have already happened?

If so, over what timescale? Chapters 2 and 15 by Leslie Wagner and Radim Palous, respectively, offer overviews with equally valid but very different temporal horizons, the one measured in decades, the other in centuries. Or should we be anticipating change, looking at the little eddies which maybe presage a greater turbulence? Alistair MacFarlane's contribution (Chapter 5) is one which gently suggests that we may be in for a period which will make the current one appear tranquillity itself.

Both the direction and the magnitude of change cannot be assessed without some common understanding of how broad the temporal focus is. This platitude seems often to be ignored. Awareness of duration in a policy context is particularly sharply reflected in the French use of *les trente glorieuses* to designate the postwar period of growth, full employment and rising welfare standards (e.g. Gaullier 1989), throwing into relief the exceptional character of the period. Whilst the barely concealed pessimism of the phrase may be open to challenge, it effectively undermines cosy assumptions about linear progression in education as in other policy areas. Wagner's perspective is of exactly the same duration. He is not so much pessimistic as selectively sceptical about the scale of change, looking as closely at where it has not occurred (teaching and learning) as where it has. He is also sensitive to the rhythms of change, reminding us that the frequency with which an issue or aspiration is mentioned bears only a partial relation to its resolution or realization. Most of all, however, he ventures to introduce reversibility, the idea that mass might be turned back into élite, at least in respect of full-time students. McInnis (Chapter 4) too uses thirty years as the period of the rush from élite to mass and higher education on the other side of the globe; and he too hints at reversibility, with the latest figures suggesting a drop in student demand. Girdwood's chapter (Chapter 8) is the most straightforwardly, and sadly, historical, with its contrast between the high hopes of early higher education in Africa and the modern reality of month-by-month funding. Palous' contribution (Chapter 15) has the longest of timeframes, and also an explicit sense of periodization as he reminds us of continuity as well as change in the university mission. It is, finally, more than poignant when he observes that the Czech people 'have a reason for a disposition to historical sensitivity'.

A.H. Halsey concluded the revised version of his classic survey of the academic profession (Halsey 1995: 302) thus:

> It is difficult to disagree with Martin Trow that in the last ten or twelve years British higher education has undergone a more profound reorientation than any other system in the industrialised world.

Halsey attacks the lack of trust and funding on the part of the current UK government. But I believe I also detect, in slightly coded form, a doubt in the mind of one of the long-standing exponents of educational expansion and equity as to whether the transition to mass higher education has turned out as hoped for – even leaving aside the twin enemies he mentions. It is my view, certainly, that the expansion has been too much 'the same as before but bigger' (and cheaper), and not in fact a real re-orientation. Hence the coda.

Coda: reshaping the contours

In late 1994, the Secretary of State posed three broad questions on the future of higher education. They referred to purpose, shape and size. Here is an itemized response, focusing primarily on the second, as befits the conclusion to a mapping exercise. I have avoided the philosophy of the first, and shirked putting numbers on the third.[2]

1. Higher education should continue to grow, but this should not mean pumping the same model up into ever larger sizes. Squeezing more students into the institutions currently defined as making up the higher education sector may yield statistical gratification to those who relish talking big numbers, or who have an eye to international comparisons. However, much of the expansion smacks more of machismo, on the part of institutional leaders and of politicians, than considered reflection. Fear of appearing to oppose expansion may have inhibited alternative proposals from within the system.

2. The bulk of the expansion of initial higher education should take place in what is currently designated the further education sector. This receives less than its due, financially and in other respects. The expansion over the last decade of non-degree provision is welcome, but needs proper underpinning and recognition. It is in everybody's interests – of students and staff in both sectors, as well as of that semi-mythical beast the nation – that further education should receive higher priority.

3. Articulation between further and higher education should be improved, probably up to the point where further education is recognized as part of the higher education sector. Lines have to be drawn, but is it really sensible to create a new binary line so sharply, just as we are starting to grapple with the implications of abandoning the old one?

4. There should not be pressure on all universities to expand undergraduate provision. However, those that choose to concentrate more on graduate work should be encouraged to diversify their graduate populations and provision. A differentiated system does not have to be a system hierarchically ordered according to a single set of academic criteria.

5. There should be more emphasis on shorter and broader provision as a foundation level of higher education. There is no case for expanding full-time specialized honours degrees as the norm for mass higher education.

6. Part-time provision will become more firmly the norm, especially beyond foundation level. It will need to be financed at least on a par with full-time provision. The distinction between the two is, anyway, likely to collapse.

7. The distinction between initial and continuing education will inevitably become more blurred. In spite of this, a balance shift in favour of continuing education could – and should – be made, through student and institutional financial support mechanisms.

8. Continuing education will take increasingly diverse forms. In particular, partnerships between universities and clients will involve new forms of delivery

and accreditation: fewer one-off short courses, liberal or vocational, and more long-term relationships, building on negotiated research priorities.

9. The relationship between teaching and research must continue to change, reflecting diverse patterns of both specialization and integration. The implications of this for staffing, staff development and management are great, especially in the light of the demographic profile of the academic labour force.

10. There is much to be learned from the Scottish tradition of breadth and flexibility, including the Ordinary/General degree as an initial qualification, with Honours as an optional development.

Acknowledgement

Thanks go to John Field, Unni Hagen and Ian McNay for comments on an earlier draft of this chapter.

Notes

1. 'Policymaking' here means both the political and civil service roles and those of institutional policymakers (McPherson and Raab 1988).
2. The original statement of these appeared in the *Times Educational Supplement* (Scotland), February 1995.

References

Ainley, P. (1994) *Degrees of Difference: Higher Education in the 1990s*. London, Lawrence & Wishart.

Benn, R. and Burton, R. (1994) 'Access to higher education: a class or gender issue?', *Adults Learning*, November.

CVCP (1994) *Universities and Communities*. A report by the Centre for Urban and Regional Development Studies for the Committee of Vice-Chancellors and Principals.

Gaullier, X. (1989) *La Deuxième Carrière: Ages, Emplois, Retraites*. Paris, Seuil.

Gilbertson, G. (1995) 'Germany's snobs left standing', *The Higher*, February 10.

Halsey, A.H. (1995) *Decline of Donnish Dominion: The British Academic Professions in the Twentieth Century*. Oxford, Oxford University Press.

Haselgrove, S. (ed.) (1994) *The Student Experience*. Buckingham, SRHE and Open University Press.

Lie, S., Malik, L. and Harris, D. (eds) (1994) *The Gender Gap in Higher Education. World Yearbook of Education* 1994. London, Kogan Page.

McPherson, A.F. and Raab, C.D. (1988) *Governing Education: A Sociology of Policy since 1945*. Edinburgh, Edinburgh University Press.

Paterson, L. (1994) 'How distinctive is Scottish higher education?', *Scottish Affairs*, 7, Spring.

Schuller, T. (1990) 'The exploding community? The university idea and the smashing of the academic atom.' *Oxford Review of Education*, 16(1), 3–14.

Slowey, M. (1994) *Changing Conceptions of Continuing Education – The Implications for Higher Education*. CVCP Research Seminar, October.

Tight, M. (1991) *Higher Education: A Part-time Perspective*. Buckingham, SRHE and Open University Press.

Williams, G. and Fry, H. (1994) *Longer Term Prospects for Higher Education: A Report to the CVCP*. London, Institute of Education.

Williams, G., Blackstone, T. and Metcalf, P.D. (1974) *The Academic Labour Market*. Amsterdam, Elsevier.

2

A Thirty-Year Perspective:
From the Sixties to the Nineties

Leslie Wagner

Introduction

Both the earlier and later periods of the last thirty years, from the 1960s to the 1990s, have been ones of rapid change for UK higher education. In both periods, however, the changes concerned mainly its external life, the issues of finance, governance and structure. The internal issues of values and purpose, of what is taught, and how it is taught, have been subject to far less change. As a result, the external and internal worlds are now out of balance. The external changes have produced a mass higher education system whilst the lack of internal change has resulted in the retention of the values of an élitist system. This imbalance is the cause of many of the tensions and dysfunctions which higher education presently experiences.

Robbins and Dearing

One of the difficulties in presenting a comparison of the 1960s and the 1990s in higher education is that the former period is readily associated with a single figure whilst the latter is not. The Robbins Report (1963) is a landmark for the changes of the 1960s and the eponym is still used and recognized as easy shorthand. With whom are the changes in the period 1989–94 to be associated? No dominating report or figure stands out. Politically, there is Kenneth Baker or Kenneth Clarke or even John Major. The most influential figure, however, is likely to have been Sir Ron Dearing, drafted into chairing the newly formed Polytechnic and Colleges Funding Council (PCFC) in 1989 and also the University Grants Committee in 1992, before becoming the first Chair of the integrated new body the Higher Education Funding Council for England. The greater need for his services to rescue the Secretary of State for Education from his follies on schools' curricula and examinations prematurely ended his formal association with higher education in 1993. However, the policies he developed at the PCFC in its early years and the perception of success it gave to the polytechnics in the early 1990s were important influences on the seminal 1991 White Paper. While Dearing does not have a report like Robbins to his name (at least in higher education) his influence in the 1990s may have been as profound as the latter's in the 1960s.

The five years following the publication of the Robbins report saw:

- an expansion of student numbers and funding which in percentage terms more than matches recent experience;
- the creation of new universities;
- the transformation of the colleges of advanced technology into universities;
- announcements establishing the polytechnics and the Open University;
- the establishment of the Council for National Academic Awards (CNAA) and of a new Department of Education and Science (DES); and
- a substantial increase in overseas student fees.

In addition, there was of course the experience of student unrest which influenced changes to university and academic governance. Of course, not all of these were foreseen in the Robbins Report or were a direct result of its recommendations. However, the report published under a Conservative government created the environment of optimism and growth within which the succeeding Labour government acted.

Any period of change creates the conditions for subsequent change and it is possible to trace the upheavals in higher education structure and finances in the early 1990s to that earlier period of post-Robbins transformation. The expansion of the late 1960s began higher education's initially slow march from élitist to mass participation. Indeed, according to Martin Trow's (1973) classic quantitative definition of mass higher education – enrolment of between 15 and 40 per cent of the age group – the UK was already moving into a mass system before the recent expansion. The creation of the Department of Education and Science and the transfer of responsibility from the Treasury in 1964 marked the end of the hands-off approach to university finance. The era of pushing a cheque through the letter-box and walking away was over. Governments and their funding agencies wanted increasingly first to knock on the door, then to open the door, then to peek inside, then to walk inside, then to observe what they saw, then to ask questions, then to expect answers, then to suggest changes and then to change the size of their cheques if the changes did not occur.

The establishment of the polytechnics as a group of institutions with a national identity was bound, if they were successful, to lead to a greater national and lesser local influence over their planning and governance. This was reflected in the work of the Oakes Committee in 1977, the establishment of the National Advisory Body in 1981 and eventually the removal of the local authorities in 1989, followed by the final transformation of the ending of the binary line in 1992. The CNAA's successful role in quality assurance and development for the public sector in the twenty-five years after Robbins led eventually to the translation of the principle to the whole of higher education, although the political price required was the abolition of the CNAA itself. The raising of overseas students' fees in the late 1960s began a process which continued through the 1970s and 1980s towards full costing of such fees and, more significantly, to the development of an entrepreneurial approach to all sources of income other than that provided by Funding Council grants.

The major difference between the 1960s and the 1990s is in funding. The earlier expansion was fully funded both for recurrent and capital expenditure. In contrast, the more recent expansion has been accompanied by severe reductions in unit funding, more intensive use of buildings and minimal contribution to capital development. This may be all that is needed to explain why the post-Robbins changes took place in a mood of optimism and confidence about the future whilst the more recent ones have been accompanied by pessimism and gloom.

External and internal worlds

The post-Robbins and more recent changes highlighted above are concerned essentially with the external world of higher education, the issues which are decided for higher education by others, particularly government and its agencies. It does not cover the internal issues of values and purposes, of curricula and of teaching and learning which higher education determines much more for itself. One hybrid of external and internal worlds is student number growth, the quantitative measures of the move from élite to mass higher education. From one perspective, this is an internal issue, for it is higher education itself which determines how many students it wishes to enrol. However, this internal decision is heavily influenced by external factors and the rapid growth of the early 1990s was in part a response to the financial squeeze and funding policies which government imposed. Institutions found it easier to manage the problems created by declining unit costs by taking advantage of the economies of scale which result from growth.

The contrast between the changes in the external and internal worlds of higher education over the past thirty years is stark. For, whilst the external changes in the early 1990s can be seen as developments of the post-Robbins changes, the focus in the internal issues is of continuing debate rather than change. Moreover, in some instances the debate seems hardly to have moved on in the past thirty years.

Credit accumulation and transfer is a good example. It is raised in the Robbins Report and its first major introduction came in 1970 with the credit-based operation of the Open University, which then began a search for agreements with traditional institutions on the transferability of its credits. In 1979, the DES funded a major feasibility study led by Peter Toyne. The Leverhulme Reports in the early 1980s advocated its widespread development but significantly recognized that the reform 'was one of the hardest to implement' (1981). The CNAA established its own national scheme in the early 1980s and some regional schemes and consortia were also developed. Yet, despite many projects and numerous reports, the Department for Education felt it necessary to set up yet another study in 1991 with the major term of reference, 'to investigate, propose and negotiate principles for the award and transfer of credit between different providers within higher education and beyond'.

A dozen years on from the Toyne Report we were still at the stage of needing to establish principles for credit accumulation and transfer. The study was led by David Robertson and resulted in 1994 in a major report published by the Higher Education Quality Council (Robertson 1994). The initial response does not give grounds for optimism that any rapid changes will occur. The HEQC itself has indicated that it can only take responsibility for the quality assurance elements of credit transfer and accumulation. The more general response has been that whilst there is a broad measure of support for many of the fundamental changes proposed in the report, they are more likely to be implemented in the early part of the next century.

This crab-like process of change is experienced in many other areas of higher education's internal life. Robbins advocated more degree courses covering a broader knowledge of a range of subjects rather than a deeper knowledge of one subject. There is also in Robbins' discussion of the aims of higher education a hint of the need to inculcate what has become known in the last decade as 'transferable personal skills'. Progress has been made in both these areas. The broadening of degree courses' curricula has been led by the polytechnics whilst, in recent years, the Enterprise in Higher Education programme has influenced perceptions of the personal skills higher education can provide for its graduates. The supremacy in the hierarchy of esteem of the single Honours discipline remains however.

Teaching and learning is another area of slow change. Robbins discusses the virtues and vices of lectures and tutorials and these are still the main form of teaching experienced by most students in higher education. There have been numerous reports, the latest being by MacFarlane (1992), many pilot projects, regular programmes of support and some very exciting pockets of innovation in many institutions. Most of it, however, is marginal and is not systematized. The technology, both hardware and software, available to higher education to enable it to improve, enrich and make more efficient the learning experiences of students, has moved far beyond the interest and capacity of most staff in higher education to use it. Indeed, the greatest progress could be made in persuading academics to use the technology of a decade or more ago rather than the technology of the years ahead. Many academics are opposed to making any significant change to their approach to teaching, their view exemplified best perhaps by this splendid letter to *The Guardian* from a lecturer at Nottingham University, in 1991:

> I do not wish to be a teacher, I am employed as a lecturer and in my naiveté I thought my job was to 'know' my field, contribute to it by research and to lecture on my specialism! Students attend my lectures but the onus to learn is on them. It is not my job to teach them.

Perhaps the area of higher education's internal life which has seen most change is the modularization of courses and semesterization. A survey by the Committee of Vice-Chancellors and Principals in 1994 indicated that over half of the universities had moved or were about to move from a term to a semester structure linked, in most cases, to the modularization of their courses. This development has received widespread support from, amongst others, The Royal Society.

Whilst the change goes back at least twenty-five years, however, the move to modularization for many universities has only begun recently. The pioneers were the Open University and polytechnics such as Oxford, City of London, Hatfield and Middlesex in their early years. Gradually through the 1970s, more polytechnics, encouraged by the CNAA, introduced modularization to their courses and with that came a significant amount of serious study of the implications for curriculum design, teaching and learning and assessment. Some more recent modularization proposals particularly in the older universities give the impression of re-inventing the wheel, showing little evidence that the lessons of those studies are known let alone absorbed. The development of modularization is one of the more successful innovations in UK higher education and repays careful study.

New institutions

The end of the 1960s saw the establishment of new institutions of higher education, the Open University and the polytechnics outside the traditional framework of the university system. Even though the Open University had the university title and powers, it was separately funded by the Department for Education and Science and its vice-chancellor was not initially a member of the Committee of Vice-Chancellors and Principals. The polytechnics had neither university title nor powers and were subject to greater regulation and a completely separate funding system. This contrasted with the establishment of the new universities parallel with the Robbins enquiry and the implementation of the Robbins recommendation that the colleges of advanced technology should be designated technological universities integrated into the existing system.

The establishment of the Open University and the polytechnics was an admission that their missions were not being delivered and could not be delivered by the traditional universities. In the former case, the focus was adults seeking a second or, in some cases, a first opportunity. In the latter case, it was professional and vocational higher education more closely integrated with the world of employment.

Both these innovations have undoubtedly been successful in their own terms. They have delivered what they were set up to do. In fact, virtually all the innovations which have occurred in the internal life of higher education have been led by the Open University and the polytechnics. Both, in their different ways, have shown that access need not lead to lower standards and that a far greater proportion of the population than was previously imagined can benefit from and succeed in higher education. Both have pioneered modularization and credit transfer. The Open University has shown the benefits to be gained in quality and student satisfaction from a systematic approach to teaching and learning which uses modern media intelligently and effectively. The polytechnics have broadened the curriculum base and shown how professional and vocational higher education can maintain rigour and reflection. Yet there is little evidence that their experience has had much impact on the traditional universities. This is not surprising. For the establishment of different institutions structurally distinct to carry out different functions legitimizes the traditional role of the traditional institutions. Thus, if it is the role of the Open University to cater for unqualified adults and the polytechnics to be more vocationally oriented, it can be argued that there is little point in others competing in the same market. Similar arguments can be applied to the Open University's teaching approach which may be appropriate to the needs of distance learning but which may not be suited to traditional campus life, and also to credit accumulation which may be appropriate to the inevitably fragmented nature of Open University study but which cannot be applied to the more intensive experience of traditional higher education with its more specialized degrees. And while, of course, it is understandable for the polytechnics, with their need for students, to create new markets with new combinations of subjects and new areas of study, the traditional universities have no need for such gimmicks.

The point about these arguments is not that they exist for that is inevitable, but that they are given additional force and legitimacy by being applied to institutions which were deliberately established outside the traditional system. Establishing separate institutions may be the most effective way of introducing change but that very separateness prevents that change permeating the traditional institutions. Indeed, the establishment of separate institutions and systems legitimizes the traditional universities, protects them from reform and simultaneously devalues those reforms. The changes of the early 1990s, therefore, are very significant for they can be interpreted as an attempt to create change through integration not separation. In particular, the development of the polytechnics was judged to have run its course. By the early 1990s, there was little further innovation which could be applied to the polytechnic sector alone. So the Education Act 1992 recreated a single system of universities (the colleges remain as a much smaller sector) all with degree-awarding powers, financed by a single agency. The increasingly artificial distinctions of the binary line were removed and instead differentiation was to be delivered not through structure but through mission and purpose. At the same time, the Open University was brought within the same system. It is a bold move. The changes of the late 1960s delivered innovation through separate institutions but left the traditional universities relatively unchanged in their internal life.

The integrative changes of the early 1990s seek to create change from within. Most observers are pessimistic, believing that the 'aristocratic embrace' of the traditional universities will smother the innovative 'jabs and prods' of the former polytechnics and the Open University. The structural changes are one leg of the attempt to create change in traditional universities. The rapid expansion of the system is the other. The sharp increases in the early 1990s confirmed the system's transition to mass higher education and made a reversal to an élite system impossible. Indeed, the changes of the early 1990s are the latest manifestation of government's long-standing attempts to stimulate internal change by creating external change. The internal life of higher education remains largely under its own control. For nearly thirty years, going back to Shirley Williams' 13 principles in 1968, it has been a source of frustration to outsiders. Unable to enter the inner sanctum, outsiders are limited to creating the external changes of structure, funding or growth which it is hoped will stimulate internal change. Post-Robbins changes were through new institutions and were delivered while maintaining the traditional system largely intact. The 1990 reforms seek change through integration.

Élite and mass higher education

The problems faced by higher education in the mid-1990s arise from a system which has become mass in its size but which remains élite in its values. The recent external changes of numbers, structures, finance and governance have not been matched by appropriate internal changes of values, purpose and activity. Peter Scott had characterized these élite values as a desire for intimacy. Scott argues that it is the 'loss of intimacy' experienced with mass higher education which creates an ambivalence in the recent changes (Scott 1994).

Peter Scott is correct in identifying this central psychological cause of the unease with recent change. But academics are not alone in their ambivalence. It is reflected in government through ministers who now

- almost alone defend 'A' levels as the major route into higher education and set their face against any reform;
- who insist on a gold standard both for entry and exit qualifications against which all must be measured;
- who rhetorically support broader access and greater diversity in the student population yet condemn any sign of increase in non-completion rates;
- who cut funding yet expect personal service to students similar to that in decades gone by; and
- who in general wish their own experiences of higher education in the pre- and post-Robbins élite period to be replicated in the mass era of the 1990s.

The ambivalence is shared by most universities who understand the mass nature of the current experience they offer students (and staff) but who continue to affirm the romantic intimacy experienced by previous generations. Nowhere is this better expressed than in the information provided in prospectuses. Ernest Boyer, President of the Carnegie Foundation, reflecting on his perusal of prospectuses in the USA (but whose observations could equally apply to the UK) commented as follows (Boyer 1993):

> I was impressed with the way 'family' and 'community' found their way into the language. Indeed, I then studied all the pictures and I was impressed that they too conveyed this close connection between faculty and students. From the pictures alone I concluded that about 60 per cent of all classes in America are held outside, underneath a tree by a gently flowing stream.

The post-Robbins changes were safer and more limited. Different functions it was assumed required different types of institutions which, in any event, were expected to accept the values and mores of the traditional institutions. The CNAA, for example, was expected to ensure that its awards were 'comparable in standards to awards granted and conferred by universities'. The system as a whole might be opening up but there was little challenge to élite values and the structure itself created a differentiated hierarchy of esteem, power and funding.

The changes of the 1990s are much more risky, seeking integration not separation. They have occurred at a time when the move to a mass higher education system has gone beyond the political point of no return. The clash between élite values and that mass system is a daily feature of academic life. What does the future hold?

Future scenarios

It has been argued that the transition to mass higher education has made the reversal to an élite system impossible. It might be appropriate to begin this final section by challenging that argument.

Higher education has remained élite in its internal world. Can it match this by a reversal to élitism in its external world? At first sight, it would seem difficult to reduce the numbers admitted to higher education substantially, seek a much more homogeneous student body, increase the resources spent per student, and re-divide the sector on binary or even ternary lines. However, there is a mechanism whereby all this might be achieved which is attracting increasing support and that is private funding.

At present, full-time students are not charged for their tuition. Increasingly, such students or their families are expected to contribute to their maintenance costs either directly or through borrowing from the student loan scheme or through other arrangements. The pressure to increase the student contribution is intense, with most commentators observing that it is only the exigencies of the 1996–7 election which is preventing more immediate action. Some of those who advocate a greater student contribution either to their maintenance or their tuition costs see it as a way of reducing the £6 billion or so spent on higher education each year. Others, particularly those in the universities, see a student contribution to tuition costs as a way of increasing the resources available to universities rather than primarily a way of reducing public expenditure. The more ideological see it as a mechanism for introducing a more direct market mechanism into student choice through price rather than as at present through 'A' level points.

It is possible to imagine a scenario which offers both these options. The more benign option would provide, through public expenditure at the existing level (uprated over the years for inflation), for the minimum resource per student but would encourage universities to charge top-up fees to achieve extra resources and provide extra services – a little like private rooms in NHS hospitals. The other option would reduce the public expenditure contribution and expect universities to make up the shortfall through top-up fees, more akin to charging fees to all patients in NHS hospitals. Some universities might levy fees which increased their resources per student beyond the level previously achieved through public expenditure alone. The vast majority would struggle to charge fees which enabled them to generate income sufficiently to make up the shortfall.

Either of these options could have profound effects on the move to mass higher education. Charging students tuition fees, on top presumably of contributing to their maintenance costs, is likely at worst to reduce significantly the demand for full-time higher education and at best see a switch in the pattern to part-time higher education. In any event, élitism would emerge in the following forms:

1. Full-time enrolments would drop. It is interesting to surmise whether they would drop to the 15 per cent of the age-group figure of the mid-1980s, which would breach Trow's technical definition of mass higher education.
2. Some universities would be able to change significant top-up fees generating income which would enable them to offer a higher level of resources and quality of service.
3. These universities could use some of this income to offer scholarships to those · they wished to attract but who were unable to pay the fees. In this way they would attract both the wealthiest and most able students.
4. Except for this small number obtaining scholarships, opportunities for full-time higher education (particularly away from home) would be restricted to those with parents in the upper income group.
5. Opportunities for full-time higher education, even in their home town for those in their twenties (a growing and sizeable group), would be restricted.
6. The élite institutions, whose values would dominate the system, would be those able to charge high top-up fees in a declining market, attracting full-time students nationally to a luxurious experience with little innovation in course structures, curricula content and teaching and learning strategies. The majority of universities, particularly if public expenditure fell, would find themselves in a downward spiral of resources, a narrower student clientele (increasingly part-time) desperately seeking to maintain quality, lacking the capacity or resources to innovate and at the same time being compared unfavourably with the performance of the élite universities. Some would close.

This is a depressing but not impossible scenario. It is possible because the internal life of higher education remains élite and because the external life could be radically altered through changes to the funding system. However, an alternative scenario is also available, and that builds on the developments both of the changes thirty years ago and those of the more recent past.

The key to achieving this more desirable scenario is to match the diversity created by the changes in the external life of higher education by diversity in its inner life also. This diversity does not, however, mean that anything goes, for there are some values, sometimes classified as élite, which are at the core of the higher education experience, namely the commitment to intellectual rigour, scholarship and the exchange of ideas. These are fundamental principles for all universities, however diverse their missions. Beyond these core values, however, the élitism expressed by Scott as a desire for intimacy seems more like a desire for inertia.

One key distinction is whether academics are more interested in their subject or their students. It is those who are more interested in their subjects who, to quote Scott, affirm 'narrowness of curricula structures, standardisation of student profile, conformity to the traditional pattern and styles of teaching and the attraction of individual and small group research'. Moreover, collegiality is just as likely to be fostered among academics who subscribe to institutional values expressed in terms of accessibility and opportunity as in those who subscribe to the paradigms of a particular discipline. Indeed, the latter often produces internecine intellectual warfare in which collegiality is about the last value which is being affirmed!

So it is possible to postulate a scenario in which the external changes of the past five years continue to allow a genuinely diverse higher education system to evolve, diverse in its student and other clientele, in the structure of the courses and awards offered to them, in the range of curricula available, in the modes of attendance allowed, in the pedagogic styles and techniques used and in the range of assessments devised. It is clear from that list that genuine diversity requires recent external changes to be matched by changes to the internal life of universities. These changes require the notion of excellence in higher education to be widened from the single-dimensional concept of intellectual achievement to include other forms of excellence such as access, curriculum innovations, pedagogic change, student support and commitment and employer relations. The most effective way in which the external world can change the internal values of higher education is by giving its applause and rewards to those who seek to make higher education diverse rather than narrow.

Two scenarios are therefore available. One is driven by greater private finance, narrowing the dimension of higher education and removing many of the benefits achieved in the past five years. The other is driven by a genuine belief in diversity and fuelled by the reward and status system offered by the external world impacting on higher education's internal worlds. Readers are invited to consider which they prefer and which they think will prevail.

References

Boyer, E. (1993) *Scholarship Reconsidered: Priorities for a New Century in Universities in the Twenty-First Century*. London, National Commission on Education and The Council for Industry and Higher Education.

MacFarlane, A. (1992) *Teaching and Learning in an Expanding Higher Education System*. Edinburgh, Committee of Scottish University Principals.

Robertson, D. (1994) *Choosing to Change*. London, Higher Education Quality Council.

Robbins, Lord (1963) *Higher Education*, Cmnd. 2154. London, HMSO.

Scott, P. (1994) The Meanings of Mass Higher Education. Inaugural Lecture, University of Leeds.

Trow, M. (1973) *Problems in the Transition from Élite to Mass Higher Education*, Berkeley, California, Carnegie Commission on Higher Education.

3

The View from Further Education

Jenny Shackleton

Introduction

The college I joined as Principal in 1987 contained both further and higher education, in addition to community education, adult basic education and much else. Its higher education was wholly part-time and vocational for home students, and comprised around 5 per cent of the total volume of provision. In effecting the rapid and radical re-organization and development of the college over the following three years, considerations of higher education were absent or marginal. However, in 1995 higher education is an integral part of the college's thinking, and has an equal, but not special, claim on the college's human and physical resources, alongside all other claimants. A number of universities and bodies representative of higher education (HE) are respected friends and partners, and the college receives funding on its own account from the Higher Education Funding Council for England (HEFCE).

I begin this chapter by exploring the reasons why a college with a serious commitment to mass recurrent learning for all local people has decided to allow higher education an integral role in its future. I then reflect on the nature of the provision, and the ways in which it has developed in this college. Finally, I consider what the future shape of HE may be, and argue that it should be seen and developed within an overall framework for post-compulsory education and training.

For concreteness, I am using my first-hand experience of my own college in order to offer a view from further education (FE) of the changing university. However, I have excluded unique local factors, and attempted to broaden my perceptions to make them more generally applicable to FE and HE in the UK. That said, this account is fairly impressionistic and managerial. Since I refer both to higher education in my own college, and HE more widely, in this chapter, I have distinguished between these by using 'higher education' for the former and 'HE' for the latter.

Integrating further and higher education: learning from others

In 1987, Wirral Metropolitan College (henceforth referred to as 'Wirral Met' or 'the College' for brevity) was an adequately resourced but seriously under-developed college of further education. It was self-absorbed, largely oblivious to external factors, and also resentful of change. Power, privilege and resources were heavily slanted towards the areas in which higher education provision resided (mainly Business Studies and Science); those areas which best expressed the College as a service to the local community were impoverished and exploited. This state of affairs had accumulated over many years, compounded by national agreements over pay and conditions. It had also been worsened by the formation of the College five years earlier, since two of the institutions then brought together had previously been well resourced in order to compete with each other across old LEA boundaries for higher education students.

It would be unfair to suggest that the presence of higher education in the College had been the cause of the neglect of other provision; however, it had certainly contributed to this, since all levels of management were dominated by those most attached to higher level provision, and least aware and committed to the mainstream mission of further and continuing education. This skewed com-mitment had also substantially excluded women in most respects: as managers or lecturers; as adequately remunerated support staff; as members of the com-munity meriting access to the full range of education and training opportunities. It had also encouraged the College to be lazy and hold double standards, such as taking the resources provided to generate income and consuming them with-out result, and building up privileged and protected working conditions, utterly different to those of their colleagues or students. This was all most unfortunate, given that despite these deficiencies there was both a need for, and a talent to deliver, vocational education and training for those in technological, specialist and supervisory roles within the large corporations situated along the Mersey Estuary. However, since the fundamental requirement was to create an organi-zation which took its identity from the full range of local needs, and which generated and responded to demand accordingly, the existing higher education programmes in the College were for the time being simply rationalized, and resources, reward and authority redistributed.

Looking back to 1987, whilst it is clear that higher education now has a rightful place in Wirral Met, one cannot discount the genuineness of the fears expressed over 'academic drift' in colleges. There is in FE a deep bias towards HE; many of its academic staff feel most at home and most fulfilled when associated with it. This can also show itself in protective behaviour towards HE by staff not otherwise associated with it. For example, GCE 'A' level staff may act as gate-keepers to HE by resisting the introduction of Access to HE courses, or wishing to retain inappropriate assessment methods out of a traditional view of who is, or what constitutes, an HE student. These strains across the boundaries of FE and HE are bound to be most marked at a time when the recent dramatic growth in participation in HE has meant that the student in front of the lecturer is no longer necessarily either the same sort of person as that lecturer, or in some way easily recognizable to him or her as a potential HE student.

Between 1987 and 1990, then, higher education programmes received no specific attention by Wirral Met; they were adequately resourced, but disallowed as a specific strategic objective. The College's only partners connected with HE were the Business and Technician Education Council (BTEC), the relevant professional bodies, and a number of employer associations. The College mission was emerging from a major review and re-organization, and in a different climate it might have been read as an endorsement of higher, as well as further, education. However, in the absence of any signal that this was so, the key headings of the mission statement – comprehensiveness, entitlement, access, progression, working with the community, supporting the economy, internationalization – were interpreted as applying to further and continuing education only.

The College mission statement, which is relatively long, specific and detailed, has at its core, the following:

- Personal achievement is everyone's right, and the College will organise itself behind this right.
- Identifying personal capability, potential, pathways and goals is a powerful aid to learning and organisational growth. The College will assist all of its clients, partners and staff to do this, within a framework of standards.
- The physical, mental and psychological involvement of learners with their own development, and that of their peers, will be adopted as an organisational principle for the College.
- To encourage the College to examine its ability and preparedness to support personal growth and achievement, positive quality assurance and control measures will be linked to learning, teaching and learner support.

Whilst the deficiencies of Wirral Met had to be addressed on their own account anyway, the improvement programme needed to be linked to an attainable and exciting future. In the search for adequate inspiration we had turned to the USA, from which we drew an idealized and transportable picture of a community college. This picture was encapsulated in our mission, our ten-year critical success factors, and our long-term plans for shifting from a course-driven to a student-driven organization.

Whilst it took some time for us to realize it, in adopting an idealized, transferable model of an American community college we were accepting the place of higher education within the College at the appropriate time in its development. However, this was not higher education of the monolithic kind that appeared to dominate the thinking in the UK: the three-year full-time programmes nationally offered and leading to Honours degrees.

First, we realized that a community college of the size of Wirral Met (over 30 000 enrolments each year, amounting to 8000 full-time equivalent students) could not impose a ceiling on student attainment at around the equivalent of GCE 'A' level. With 80 per cent of its students adult, and 89 per cent part-time, the starting and finishing points of conventional programmes often constituted a very poor match indeed with students' needs. Our students were both struggling with elements of programmes, and also finding their attainments underrecognized by their qualifications. Whilst they required full and respected national qualifications, they also needed less rigid ways of accumulating those qualifications, and elements of them.

From this we took away the conviction that a college established as the main provider of post-compulsory education and training for a local community and labour market, could not fulfil its mission of mass recurrent learning by drawing a line below higher education as defined in the UK. We also became committed to all-through credit accumulation linked to the modularization of teaching, learning and assessment. This commitment gave rise to a continuing action research programme part-funded over five years by the Department of Employment (Wirral Metropolitan College 1991 and 1994).

The second set of reasons was concerned with the need to internalize quality control as a condition of mass student achievement. Our US research included the Bronx Community College, a very large community college which was in effect a university college of the State University of New York. The scale and equality of attention given to the adoption, monitoring and evaluation of all programmes, irrespective of their level and type, was striking, as appeared to be the benefits of this approach for all aspects of management. In transferring the lessons of this to the UK, the College committed itself to the processes of validation as a preferred vehicle for development and quality, all the way from the unit of credit to the institution. However, although this led to our seeking to adopt the kinds of validation processes used by universities in the UK, being mindful of the power structures and cultures of HE here, and the unwelcome aspects of bureaucracy noted in the USA, the College rejected the arguments in favour of a close association with any one university.

The third set of reasons for accepting higher education programmes as part of the College's overall identity were social, economic and cultural. From the USA we noted that mass participation in HE depended upon a local, even extremely local, offering. The reasons for this were financial and organizational for the student, and also concerned many students' desire for some continuity in teaching and learning and broader relationships. All these factors were important for Wirral Met's FE students, and there was no reason to believe that they were less important or desirable at later stages of learning.

In evolving the College's mission, the writing of Alexander Astin (1987) had been crucial. In considering the relationship of the College to the local Merseyside economy, the work of Michael Porter (1990) was helpful in indicating the educational factors needed to underpin a strong and developing economy.

- an open and recurrent access to education and training;
- a system for vocational, technical and specialist training;
- high, explicit and rising standards which are adhered to;
- mobility among trained and specialist personnel;
- respected and high-quality HE offered outside the universities;
- a high percentage of citizens moving into Science and Technology;

- learning comprises vocational education and training;
- close connections exist between education and employers;
- firms invest heavily in on-going training.

By 1991 the multiple deprivation of Merseyside had begun to be better monitored and described than hitherto. Women were about to form the majority of employed people in the area, albeit that this trend was associated with part-time jobs, low wages and a disempowered workforce. Whilst government policy continued to stress the importance of craft skills and occupational training, employers were discernibly beginning to appoint adults, especially women, with higher levels of education and less focused skills. The last thing that a college in this environment ought to be doing, therefore, was restricting its programmes and qualifications to those which barely enabled people to secure jobs, ignoring the need to keep up with rising employer demands. To engage properly with the local labour market and economy, the College clearly needed to retain its capacity to serve all lower and intermediate roles in the local workforce for the indefinite future, whatever the employment position of the individual at the time.

Its strong links with employing organizations also provided one of the main means available to the College of refreshing itself, keeping in touch with the sharp changes from which it was partially protected, and maintaining its perceived value and purpose within the local area. It is essential that the local FE college changes constantly to reflect and influence the local economy, changing patterns and types of employment, and people's lives more generally. The shallow and narrow interpretations of demand-led education and training forced on FE colleges in the 1980s have made this needlessly difficult, however, by polarizing attitudes to vocationalism and relevance.

Seen from a closed institution in 1987, the shape and openness of the American community college had been striking physically, and also in the services given to students, and the contributions students were able to make to the life of the college. To realize its potential, Wirral Met had to develop its own powers of thought and action, and this gave rise over time to an informed view of its relationship with other social partners beyond employers, locally and nationally. The result was an enhanced view of education and training as a positive response to a range of besetting issues in an area of acute multiple deprivation. This response had to engender wide support and take a shape which as far as possible set aside old patterns of relationships. Strategies for childcare and early years education, health care, the new technologies, volunteer support, and the like, all required support structures which involved learning, assessment and certification both for the clients and for the partners. Thus joint learning began to be built into the fabric of partnership, which then depended for its effectiveness upon the techniques of project management.

In summary, then, having halted for several years the expansion of its vocational higher education, and suppressed all conventional expectations in that direction, Wirral Met came to recognize that it could not help local people achieve beyond their own and other people's expectations without having a provision in place beyond the threshold to HE. Subject to the local college having the capacity

to offer higher-level provision, local HE appeared to be an inevitable consequence of deciding to aim for mass recurrent education and training. The purposes and character of that HE had to be drawn from the needs of the locality;
however, the standards to which it was tied needed to be universally recognized
ones for that type of provision.

Naturally, beyond these reasons for participating in HE lay some appreciation
of the wider benefits. Where there is a fragmented and élitist structure for schools,
vocational education and training can be quite strikingly associated with failure.
Under LEA management, local educational policymaking consistently favoured
schools and penalized Wirral Met, despite the quite desperate need for supply-
led vocational education and training measures to help encourage inward investment on Merseyside. It was therefore recognized that the incorporation of
higher-level provision within the College would make the latter more difficult to
classify in negative terms, so that in time the College, the curricula, and its learners
might be afforded equal status to that of the selective schools, sixth-form colleges
and the independent sector.

Processes and phases

The re-emergence and development of higher education in the College was not
a matter of relaxing the restrictions on existing provision. It was a matter of
designing a specification for its higher education which built upon and extended
the design features applied to the other provision. By 1991, Wirral Met had in
place a number of these:

- a commitment to core studies which incorporated some of the lessons from
  the Enterprise in Higher Education programme;
- a learning framework which encouraged aspects of modular delivery couched
  within a framework for credit accumulation and transfer;
- a widely available computer network carrying high-quality information and
  learning materials;
- well-developed services for student information, advice and guidance.

The aim was to ensure that students might eventually study by any mode of
attendance with the College up to the level of CATS 2, NCVQ 5, BTEC Higher
National Diplomas or Diplomas of Higher Education. Further, where there was
a strong rationale and capacity to do so, the College would also offer Honours
degrees and postgraduate study programmes. It was assumed that it would take
ten years to put in place a full range of higher education provision of this nature,
and that the College would initially at least have limited external support for this
endeavour.

Over the next three years, some 15 universities or other HE institutions were
contacted to see whether they were prepared to validate one or more programmes
to be offered at Wirral Met. Some were within the Polytechnics and Colleges
Funding Council (PCFC) sector, while others were already universities. The reasons for contacting so many were threefold. First, it became clear very quickly

that there was no simple way of assessing the willingness or ability of an organization to act as a validator. Secondly, it was essential to maintain a wide range of partnerships while the relative roles and relationships of colleges and universities were evolving. Thirdly, each institution had different strengths and weaknesses relative to Wirral Met's needs. Four years on the College has stable and positive relations with eight universities, and no immediate wish to reduce this number further. Each relationship serves a particular need: some relationships are for the simpler course-based validations, whilst others have a clear systemic intent.

The search for partners within the university sector has been fascinating and illuminating. We now know that it is better to choose a university with a clear sense of identity, however traditional that may be, than to take at face value a go-ahead image. To achieve validation within reasonable timescales, it is important to select a university with its structure for external validation well established. For large-scale validations of programmes of an unconventional kind, though, there appears to be no quick fix of any value or dependability. The generation of mutual knowledge and trust is crucial, and takes time and effort.

Throughout this period, many other FE colleges were getting into franchises and associate college arrangements in ways which Wirral Met had decided against, since they appeared to us to establish such unequal relationships. Wirral Met was spared many of the later difficulties which other colleges faced because in 1990 it had taken the decision to seek financial support from PCFC in its own right on the basis of its own strategic plan for further and higher education. The geographical location of the College and the nature of its catchment area supported its long-term goals, and so from 1991 the College became a recipient of PCFC, and later HEFCE, funds. Without doubt, this enormously aided the establishment of effective relationships with our various university partners, since the invitation to them was clear-cut: to validate one or more College programmes in return for a reasonable fee. The College's financial independence has enabled the partnerships, so far at least, to withstand the strains which have appeared between many other colleges and universities since HE student numbers have been capped.

In broad terms, the College now offers the following types of higher education programme. There are those which lead to Honours degrees alongside professional qualifications, which are mainly studied part-time by those in full-time employment. There are then Honours degree programmes on which students largely study full-time because there is no tradition of release from employment in that sector, which may be represented locally mainly by small companies and self-employment. There are part-time or full-time programmes up to CATS 1 or 2, for which there is guaranteed progression to a neighbouring university. There is a large modular Combined Studies Honours degree programme which offers broad continuing educational opportunities by any mode of study. There is a generic Professional Studies Honours degree programme to which more specific modules of study may be attached. This programme is a particularly attractive element of our local people-led regeneration strategy. Alongside and associated with these are many BTEC programmes. There is then a wide range of postgraduate professional qualifying courses offered part-time, and many versions of teacher and trainer training programmes. This amounts to 500 full-time designated higher education students (which is our current agreed maximum intake), and around 1500 designated or undesignated part-time higher education students.

In growing its higher education provision, the College has recruited internally and locally, not nationally, and looks for the mature student rather than 18–21-year olds. It has specialists within its support services able to deal with specific HE issues where these differ from FE. This is particularly important since many local students are confused and sometimes disadvantaged by the distinctions which are made between FE and HE when it comes to regulations and financial support. Since these distinctions are often historical, or pragmatic on government's part, rather than rational, they are often neither appreciated nor accepted by academic staff either. These difficulties are an inevitable consequence of treating further and higher education as equals within one institution.

Wirral Met's first experience of funding councils occurred through PCFC, and it was extremely helpful to learn lessons about the need for accurate and timely returns in this way. The College had become used to the arbitrary variations in practice to be found among course teams and faculties covering all provision. It was therefore essential to opt for a high level of monitoring and control in order to achieve consistency within our higher education from the outset. This was initially strongly resisted internally, and for the foreseeable future we shall need to retain a very proactive style of corporate management for our higher level programmes. This is no longer an exceptional style of management to adopt, however, since the management of further education within the rules of the Further Education Funding Council (FEFC) requires a similar level of standardization and consistency across the remainder of the College's provision.

To bring this section to a conclusion, I should note some of the lessons and issues which continue to preoccupy Wirral Met. The first and foremost concerns teaching and learning. The higher education programmes in Wirral Met generally recruit year groups of 40 or fewer students, and the programme teams are assigned a standard allocation of approximately 1.3 lecturers per 20 students. The allocation is accompanied by the request for as much variety and diversity as possible in teaching and learning methods. In most cases, the response is fairly traditional, with a preponderance of classroom teaching for groups of around 20 students, and limited use of larger and smaller groups, project work, tutorials, resource-based learning and the like. Since FE lecturers are generally both skilled and qualified teachers, they usually apply their chosen teaching methods more than satisfactorily. However, this does not answer the problem of uniformity and overdependency upon one type of teaching and learning: whole-class tuition, which is the most common method still in FE. There is a particularly strong need beyond CATS 2 to use the available resources to support students' learning in other ways than teaching them for 20 hours each week, in order to foster the kind of scholar one would expect an Honours graduate to be.

Closely linked to the last point is the need to develop the overall learning environment as quickly and fully as possible. Wirral Met has invested substantially in resource-based learning linked to its computer network of over 800 personal computers. Access to the facilities for all students and staff is as full and easy as we can make it. Given the scope and value of the facilities, programme teams are encouraged to guide their students' access to essential materials through the use of customized learning menus. Considerable resources also go to programme teams willing to convert their materials to multimedia form. However, there is much further to go in developing our educational technology and our library and learning environment overall. Although increased investment in our existing libraries alongside our information technology network will sustain us for a while, the longer-term answer must be electronic links with and beyond the university sector, together with the inter-institutional development and sharing of materials.

The third key issue is the development of a scholastic environment in support of both staff and students. When Wirral Met was first undergoing validation, it became clear that the scholastic activity which was underpinning some (but not all) of our vocational programmes needed to be developed and universalized, and also acknowledged as valid in the assessment of the College's adequacy to offer higher level programmes. We had been mortified to find that several of our nationally respected fine artists, for example, had had their qualities overlooked because they had not 'published'; exhibitions had not counted.

The College is therefore working on 'the scholarship of application', as Patrick Coldstream (1994) has recently termed it, in order to engender a vibrant setting for teaching and learning. In so doing, it has a number of distinct and previously unconnected starting points, such as its action research in teaching, learning and assessment, social and educational policy development, organizational development and change management, consultancies to local companies, and new technologies. Unlike much university research, the stimulus for this scholarship comes from internally felt needs, or the needs of the local area, and is intended for local consumption. However, the standards set for the activity are national, and there is always a broader relevance to what is attempted, albeit not always a universal one. This is generally ensured through the partners, structures and funding sources involved.

The fourth issue is quality assurance and control. Until very recently, FE colleges have been under considerable, or very little, or mixed, pressure to internalize responsibility for standards and quality assurance and control, on the basis of their direct experience with their awarding bodies. In all cases, their main qualifications have been externally awarded; there have been lower levels of institutional autonomy and accountability, and different traditions of institutional management. These factors have impeded the internalization of a concern for quality. The growth of higher education and the evolution of the College's learning framework for modular provision and credit accumulation and transfer have been the twin stimuli for Wirral Met's quality assurance framework, which has been advised upon by the Open University, one of the College's key partners for its more systemic thoughts and actions (Open University QSC 1994). The principles upon which the framework is being built are threefold: (1) that the primary responsibility for quality lies with the College; (2) that self-evaluation lies at the heart of the framework; and (3) that a measure of externality is essential. This framework is intended to cover all of the College's provision without exception, thus raising long-term questions about the appropriateness of a plethora of examining and validating bodies.

What of the future?

Although the detailed work to visualize mass recurrent learning in terms of its inputs, processes and outputs has yet to be done, some thought as to its outputs is evident in the recent consultations around the National Targets for Education and Training (NACETT 1994). In responding to the call of National Advisory Council for Education and Training Targets (NACETT) for advice, the National Commission on Education has suggested the following target for higher education.

[By the year 2000], by 24 years of age 45 per cent of young people will achieve a first degree, a higher education diploma, or an award of equivalent level.

In doing so the Commission (1994) notes, 'it does not seem necessary to set higher level targets for adults. All the evidence is that people with the best education also receive most training and work-related education'. However, there is clearly a present need for those already over 24 years of age to maintain or gain a foothold in the labour market by also becoming more highly qualified.

The nature of the future National Education and Training Targets are as important as their size, since a widely expressed target can encompass and value those aspects of HE which may well be neglected because no one organization or sector asserts responsibility for them. Responsibility for the full range of higher level education and training is at present split most uncomfortably between two government departments and three funding agencies or mechanisms. The prime user representative, the Confederation of British Industries (CBI), continues to be long on demands and short on practical assistance. Soundly based and expressed Targets can help to create collaboration among these bodies, in place of the fragmentation which we have at present.

Whatever the organization or superstructure, mass participation in HE will be diverse, and available to many on the basis of their ability to benefit, however modestly, over an indefinite period of time, rather than their ability to succeed three or four years on. Linked to this, expectations of the advantages which HE will bestow must diminish, and this may already be evident (Coldstream 1994). However, limited and even negative incentives are a fact of life for certain forms of FE and certain FE students, and there is no reason to safeguard artificially the incentives to study in HE over and above those for FE, particularly given the greater economic and social vulnerability of the FE student.

The current costs of HE through universities are bound to be under continuing pressure, especially given that these costs are high relative to those of other nations, and the fact that mass HE cannot come about without mass learning at other levels, which also has to be funded. If one regards any one element of HE funding (student grants, for example) as sacrosanct, then the sense of growing impoverishment will continue. However, given its high global costs, there is a strong case for reconsidering the funding of HE as a whole, and I would endorse the proposals of the National Commission on Education as a useful contribution to this (NCE 1993: 315–319). From FE's point of view, it would also be crucial to remove the discontinuities and malfunctions which occur across further and higher education when it comes to student entitlements including the right to obtain financial support at the time of need (Wirral Metropolitan College 1993). The FE student cannot apply for a student loan, and is generally unable to obtain a discretionary award. Remission of fees may be available up to CATS 1, since this may be funded by FEFC, but not beyond.

The future scenario may then be of a very diverse HE provision and student body, with multiple sources of funding for the institutions and the students involved. In so relatively untidy a scenario (which is inevitable with mass provision), lifetime personal educational records, and objective information, assessment, advice and guidance would be essential, as would be some kind of personal learning account enabling the individual to be either in credit or debit according to his or her circumstances. Naturally, most people would study locally, and the boundaries between FE and HE would blur. With more diversity and choice there would also need to be stronger external regulation and control, and in this respect some rationalization and standardization of awards would be advocated. The time for a single framework for qualifications up to CATS 2 and higher technician awards, which brings together general and vocational qualifications is long overdue; the common design base for General National Vocational Awards (GNVQs) is a hopeful sign, but no more than that. Neither FE or the universities can play their proper parts within mass HE with confidence and quality without such a reform, which would require a National Qualifications Authority plus some intermediate tier of support to enable credit accumulation and transfer to operate on a large scale, with acceptable results. For degree-level study and beyond, since relatively few colleges would have the capacity to operate at this level, a regulatory body or mechanism for high-level awards, which surely must emerge given the evidently variable standards for awards operating within and among the universities, would presumably have a role across all providing institutions. A potential reward for universities in such circumstances might be the new role of educational and professional leader within a particular locality, executed through the validation of school and college provision and qualifications. It is evident though, that while some universities are thinking and moving in this direction, others would find it very difficult indeed to offer such leadership outside subject-based provision for the academically able pupil and student.

So how realistic is this scenario? The answer to this probably depends on where one is located institutionally, geographically, financially, and so on. It seems that the closer a college or university is able or wants to get to local people and changing social, cultural and economic needs, and the less available the alternatives to learning as the prime vehicle for regeneration and development, the more attainable appears the ideal of mass learning encompassing mass HE (Reich 1991 suggests that, in most places, the key to regeneration in the future will be the quality of people). The less close the institution to its potential users, especially geographically, the less desirable mass learning may appear to be, and the more evident the barriers and drawbacks associated with it.

In these early days of funding councils, lines of demarcation have been drawn and justified as though student need followed structure (Eggar 1994). This is clearly not so, and daily problems arise from the poor fit between funding council

boundaries and students' reasonable entitlements. The current line drawn between FE and HE is irrational, and cannot be sustained for much longer than
five years, because it essentially divorces FE from its mainstream function of
preparing people for technician-level roles in tomorrow's workplace. It is to the
HEFCE's credit that it has begun to accept some responsibility at least for thinking about these cross-binary issues (HEFCE 1994). In this scenario, the current
boundaries between funding councils will turn through ninety degrees, with a
sub-national funding mechanism for all post-compulsory education and training
replacing the current national two-tier structure. Hopefully, such a development
will also enable some element of democratic accountability to return to this area
of public funding.

Conclusion

In essence, I have argued that, inevitably but in an ad hoc and pragmatic way,
FE has gained significance for HE, and will increasingly do so. Its universal
significance for the UK is its bottom-up influence, which it is bound to exert on
HE in any healthy large-scale education and training system. In other words,
mass participation in further and continuing education and training will inevitably change the nature of HE. Schools may also have a part to play here. FE's
influence will also be felt through the 'mixed-economy' colleges which increasingly offer FE and HE to those with different backgrounds, talents, opportunities
and constraints, in circumstances where the HE is an integral part of large-scale
but local social and economic regeneration strategies, involving a rich variety of
partners. Theirs will be by no means either the only or the most important influence
in favour of diversification; however, the other influences may not be institutional
in the same way.

Whilst funding councils and other bodies will certainly have a positive or negative
impact on the nature and development of HE, and of the role of FE within HE,
I believe that much stronger factors, such as internationalization, new technologies, and socio-economic change, are driving and will continue to drive the colleges and universities towards a common operating environment, shared concerns,
and explicit and complementary roles and relationships. We all need quickly to
acquire the understandings, attitudes and skills essential for these new types of
collaboration.

References

Astin, A. (1987) *Achieving Educational Excellence*. London, Jossey Bass.
Coldstream, P. (1994) 'Life beyond the glittering prizes', *The Higher*, 2 September.
Eggar, T. (1994) Speech to the Annual Conference of FE Sector Colleges, Birmingham.
Higher Education Funding Council for England (1994) *Higher Education in Further Education
    Colleges. Funding the Relationship: A Discussion Paper* (draft). Bristol, HEFCE.
National Advisory Council for Education and Training Targets (1994) *Review of the National
    Targets for Education and Training*. London, NACETT.

National Commission on Education (1993) *Learning to Succeed*. London, Heinemann.

National Commission on Education (1994) *National Targets for Education and Training*. London, NCE.

Open University Quality Support Centre (1994) *Report on the Quality Assurance Arrangements for the Learning Framework at Wirral Metropolitan College*. London, OUQSC.

Porter, M. (1990) *The Competitive Advantage of Nations*. London, Macmillan.

Reich, R. (1991) *Works of Nations: Preparing Ourselves for 21st Century Capitalism*. London, Simon & Schuster.

Wirral Metropolitan College (1991) *Learning Gain in Further Education and Achievement Based Resourcing; Final Report*. Birkenhead, WMC.

Wirral Metropolitan College (1993) *Financial Barriers to Further & Higher Education for Adult Students*. Birkenhead, WMC.

Wirral Metropolitan College (1994) *Project to Implement a Model of a CAT System for Further Education; Final Report*. Birkenhead, WMC.

4

Less Control and More Vocationalism: The Australian and New Zealand Experience

Craig McInnis

Since the mid-1980s, governments in Australia and New Zealand, as elsewhere, have insisted that universities play a key role in the ongoing restructuring of their economies. Increasing student participation levels, declining government funds, and the rise of corporate management styles are common to both countries. The system-wide goals have been focused on turning the universities towards serving the national interest, specifically, to compete in global markets where advanced technologies and changing work practices require a better educated workforce. The main lever has been the creation of managed competition between universities to encourage institutional flexibility, responsiveness and openness. Although the universities had already been moving in these directions, they had little choice but to change more rapidly under government pressure.

There are some key differences between these countries that should be noted. Australia ended the binary divide in 1987 and now has a Unified National System. Competition between Australian universities is intense and some universities are still suffering from deep discord and ambiguity of purpose in the backwash of post-1987 amalgamations. The binary divide remains in New Zealand, leaving the universities with less obvious sources of competition or pressure for internal restructuring. Size is also a factor, particularly with respect to the nature and extent of central control. Australia now has 36 universities (17 have been formed since 1987) and a student population of 576 000. New Zealand has seven universities and 97 000 students, with another 99 000 students in the 25 polytechnics and five colleges of education.

The policy of governments in both countries has been to increase participation as a priority, and the immediate challenge for universities is to manage growth and diversity within existing public funding. Over the last five years, the total number of students enrolled in New Zealand tertiary education has increased by 28 per cent. The universities have experienced a 57 per cent increase in equivalent full-time students (Ministry of Education 1994). The Australian system grew by 37 per cent from 1988 to 1993 (DEET 1994) peaking in 1992, with significant undergraduate overenrolments creating a major problem for class sizes and resources in most courses and institutions. Although both systems have grown, the pressure of unmet student demand that has driven so much of the expansion in Australia has not been as significant in New Zealand. While the Australian Government made school-leavers the priority when it funded an extra 40 000 places between 1990 and 1993, their numbers actually declined. The growth came from within the system as students extended their study into Honours years, combined or second degrees and postgraduate studies.

In the short term, the universities have been transformed by the sheer pace of change. Amalgamations, organizational restructures, entrepreneurial activities and quality assurance mechanisms, have been introduced in rapid succession. Universities are extremely busy places as they strive to establish their identity and credibility in the face of government, employer and student scrutiny. Much of this almost frenetic activity is a natural consequence of putting new structures in place. However, this disguises some basic shifts in the patterns of relationships between the major participants in the everyday life of the universities where the impact of change is ultimately tested.

The universities have certainly become far more open, flexible and resourceful than they were only five years ago, but they have probably moved too slowly for governments. The openness is evident on all fronts, from the breakdown of disciplinary boundaries to the articulation of courses, from diverse points of student entry to the blurring of the demarcation lines between the academic and administrative staff. Flexibility in structures and processes has been an essential prerequisite for universities responding effectively to opportunities for innovation, growth, and indeed, survival. Resourcefulness in generating private income has led to a substantial rethinking of most aspects of the university operation.

Two themes of particular significance to the changing character of the university are examined in this chapter: firstly, changes in patterns of authority and control, from governments and other stakeholders through to the internal processes of governance; and secondly, shifts in the relationships and activities that have distinguished the university as a learning community from other educational institutions. Most of the public debate in both Australia and New Zealand about the changing university has centred on these two areas, particularly in terms of the loss of autonomy for universities and academics, and the decline of the liberal university experience in favour of the vocationally driven focus on the transmission of knowledge.

On the distinctly negative side, as the universities have been swept up in the competitive and entrepreneurial environment, marketing has become a self-legitimizing force, and fidelity to the fundamental purposes of universities is constantly at risk. The commodification of knowledge, the lure of the short-term research project, and the absurd flood of rarely read but citable publications, are by-products of the competition for money and status. Being seen to be responsive and innovative has become its own reward regardless of the impact on the identity and integrity of the university. In these respects, many universities have unfortunately become more tractable, opportunistic and short-sighted. For example, the use of technology in delivering mass higher education is appealing – Australians seem to embrace it with particular enthusiasm – but little thought has been given to its impact on the social nature of learning in the university, or indeed the relationship between knowledge and the university. The market imperatives driving leadership styles and approaches to learning have exposed the universities to competition from other agencies, and as a consequence they risk losing their distinctiveness as providers of higher order education.

The perhaps unfashionably optimistic view taken here is that despite the concerted attacks on the universities, their resilience should not be underestimated, especially the strength of the core values of academics. Further, it is likely that the universities in both Australia and New Zealand will emerge from the current period of turbulence stronger, and more influential, than they were in the early stages of the thirty-year transition from élite to mass higher education. Loosening boundaries and competitive structures have opened new prospects for universities that might otherwise have ossified under the weight of ageing staff profiles and the dominance of a small group of resource-rich institutions. Innovative institutions and imaginative academics can now seriously assert their identity, based on specialist skills or regional locations and in the process create viable and lively universities.

While it is not unreasonable for observers to be pessimistic about the outcomes of change, there is plenty of evidence to suggest that universities and academics are actively adapting their practices to support rather than dispense with their core values. On the whole, the universities in Australia and New Zealand have not failed, nor have they lost sight of their key purposes. Most are doing what they did prior to the reforms of the 1980s, but perhaps in the transition with too much of an eye on image rather than substance. There is the opportunity – post-transition – to maintain the momentum of change from inside the universities. Indeed, with the experience of less dependence on government funds, universities have the potential for developing styles of leadership, organizational forms and learning communities more appropriate to their knowledge-based activities than the current structures and processes allow.

Patterns of authority and control

The Australian and New Zealand governments have asserted control over the universities through the dismantling of coordinating authorities, the strategic application of direct and indirect financial steering mechanisms, and the implementation of accountability and quality assurance processes. One of the most significant consequences of these changes in the short term has been the deep cynicism of academics with respect to government intervention and the administration of universities. A national survey of Australian academics revealed that about one-third felt their level of influence on university policy had deteriorated since 1988 (McInnis *et al.* 1994). Only 9 per cent of the academics surveyed actually agreed that the reforms of the 1980s would lead to a more efficient and effective system, while two-thirds were clearly negative.

Academics were already disillusioned, of course, with the long-term decline in both salaries and professional status. The imposition of performance indicators, annual appraisal processes and merit criteria for incremental progression simply added to the negative outlook. Indeed, the gap between administration and the academics has widened to such an extent that work satisfaction and sense of efficacy is increasingly connected to the department rather than to the university. Academics no longer feel they have much influence over the policy of the university, nor do they feel valued by the organization. The cynicism and disaffection of academics is a major challenge for university leadership, but the connection of academic morale and work satisfaction to the department has positive prospects if genuine autonomy is devolved to that level.

Financial steering mechanisms

Although the New Zealand universities ostensibly have control over the balance of general academic and specialized professional courses, in reality they are constrained by the funding attached to enrolments. Funding is based on the number of students attracted. The student-driven funding assumes that competition will encourage efficiencies in the universities. The intended effect has been to shift detailed decision-making from government to the universities.

Marginal funding has been used as a very effective device to direct activity across and within Australian universities. Universities compete for tagged grants tied to specific projects. The steering mechanisms at the margins have been used to push academic activities towards the national interest and to improve the efficiency and effectiveness of the universities. Closer links with industry, innovations in teaching, cross-institutional research programmes and the shifting of curriculum focus to Asian Studies are indicative of the breadth and depth of change generated directly by government policy and supported by special grants programmes. There are few areas of university teaching and research that have not had change accelerated, or initiated, by the finance steering mechanisms.

Accountability and quality assurance

Accountability and quality assurance processes have taken centre stage in the drive to change practices in the universities and to make them more transparent. The New Zealand and Australia governments have taken different approaches, and although the evidence as to effectiveness will take some time to accumulate, so far the level of activity is extraordinarily high. In New Zealand, the accountability processes required by government include a charter of goals and purposes, a statement of objectives (including a set of performance indicators) and an annual report to Parliament. An Academic Audit Unit was established in 1994. The Unit has no authority to impose sanctions, and relies on the universities to volunteer to be involved – which they have all done. The Unit will rely heavily on public reporting for its impact on the universities.

The hastily constructed 'learn as you go' and rather blunt national quality assurance process established in Australia, has already had some lasting effects.

Universities have been rewarded for the sophistication of their quality assurance mechanisms as demonstrated to a visiting panel from the National Quality Audit Committee. The first attempt at rating quality assurance mechanisms in 1993 placed the universities into six groups of about six universities each, and allocated $76.2 million (about 2 per cent of the total government operating grant for universities) accordingly. In 1994, the audit teams focused on a range of matters affecting the quality of teaching and learning as the criteria for the distribution of money, to be followed in 1995 by an emphasis on research. The process is now more transparent than in the first round, and the judgements by the audit teams made public.

The impact of the national quality process so far has been to establish the first serious league table of Australian universities with the major established universities in the top groups. It has also encouraged the less successful universities to follow the model of the established universities and thus, ironically, has worked against government's goal of encouraging diversity in the system. The unintended consequence of this though, is that the values and activities of the pre-1988 universities have been, on the whole, verified as benchmarks. The limits of change have to some extent been set.

Cynics might argue that most of these changes have so far been confined to constructing paper empires, and that the masses of quality documentation are not necessarily matched by genuine shifts in values or practices. Australian academics are certainly less than impressed: irrespective of institutional type, gender, discipline or age, 49 per cent rejected the statement that 'quality assurance mechanisms will ensure improvement to the higher education system', and only 19 per cent agreed (McInnis *et al.* 1994). Despite this, there has been a widespread acceptance of the need for more systematic and reflective approaches to teaching in particular. This is especially evident in professional courses and postgraduate programmes where the numbers are small and reputation is vital to success in attracting students.

Leadership, management and academic roles

Enormous faith has been placed in the ability of individuals to lead universities since the reforms of the 1980s. Australian and New Zealand vice-chancellors have taken the roles and status of chief executives and, on the whole, have adopted hierarchical styles of leadership to engage in this intensely competitive environment. In the initial stages of university reforms, tough and strategic leadership was seen as the key to successful restructuring. The strong interpersonal controls that characterize hierarchies have been strengthened in most universities by the formation of an executive class of administrators. This preference for executive hierarchy has largely meant the end of collegial decision-making – only 20 per cent of Australian academics now regard their universities as collegial (McInnis *et al.* 1994). As a direct consequence, the implementation of line-management practices has made leadership training for academic heads inevitable but there remains considerable ambivalence about what form it should take.

The growth in specialist support staff and administrators from outside the universities – experts in such areas as marketing, personnel management and strategic planning – has amounted to a significant redistribution of power. The roles of the organizational professionals are not entirely new, but there are now many more non-academic jobs to be done in the market-driven university. The urgency attached to such tasks as marketing or quality reports, tends to give them more opportunity for control in the corporate environment that demands rapid response. In this context academics have little choice but to get used to sharing power with the non-academics.

In Australia especially, executive managers are increasingly being appointed to take over the business affairs of schools and departments. These managers have extensive budgetary control, are responsible for such matters as the distribution and collation of student evaluations of staff and coordinating curriculum reviews. In practical terms, this means a reduction in administrative work for senior academics with heavy administrative commitments, allowing them to focus on their core activities of teaching and research. For most academics, though, there is no likelihood of the administrative load reducing. It will continue to distract from their research and teaching activities, and add to the seriously counter-productive consequences of fragmentation in their work patterns (McInnis 1992).

Loss of control over the management of the university is only part of the change for academics. They are increasingly treated as employees with regulated and codified work practices, most obviously achieved through accountability processes. About two-thirds of Australian academics now undergo formal ap-praisal processes, and with almost universal acceptance of student evaluation of teaching, research progress reports and formal appointment confirmation proce-dures, they are now faced with constant monitoring in one form or another. In addition, the importance attached to the competitive ethos, combined with the presence and influence of non-academic professionals, is putting the traditional work practices of academics under pressure. Similarly, increased contact with the professions, business and industry is reshaping academic approaches to their roles and styles of work.

At the same time, the transformation of Australian and New Zealand univer-sities into market cultures, and the extent to which academics have embraced the associated values should not be overstated. A key feature of an organization comprised primarily of professionals, like academics, is that it is a 'value-rational' organization, i.e. 'the members have absolute belief in the values of the organ-isation for their own sake, independent of the values' prospects for success' (Dill 1982: 308). There is clear evidence that academics still value things that are not necessarily to the immediate advantage of their universities. Some 80 per cent of Australian academics say they are motivated almost solely by intrinsic interest in their work, and more than two-thirds still believe that they are free to focus their research on topics that interest them (McInnis *et al.* 1994). Similarly, al-though the gap between the academics and the administration has become a gulf in terms of political efficacy, this does not necessarily mean that academics feel their professional autonomy has suffered, and for many it has actually improved. For these academics, the competitive environment has either passed them by, or enabled them to use money from teaching, research and consultancy to enhance their control over their work.

Institutional status and identity

Control is being maintained indirectly – perhaps all the more powerfully – by the management of institutional status and identity both externally and internally, and again primarily through government-sponsored competition. In Australia, the assertion of identity is more at issue, especially in the major cities. For example, the six universities in the city of Melbourne compete for various corners of the student market, locally, internationally and perhaps even nationally in the future. Given the relatively small number of universities in New Zealand – one to each of the seven metropolitan centres – there is less direct competition with one another (Preddey 1993). Although the New Zealand universities have always had areas of specialization, there is a trend of late for the smaller universities to give themselves distinctive 'boutique' qualities.

Australia has rapidly and irreversibly gone down the track of publicly ranking institutions. In addition to the national quality exercise, league tables have been produced from different sources for different purposes in the last few years. The total research grants awarded to universities generates a round of debates and statistical manipulations about which institution is really the most productive. Other national institutional comparisons have come from a privately produced annual student guide to the universities (Ashenden and Milligan 1994) and a widely criticized attempt to produce performance indicators showing university differences in efficiency (Gallagher and Conn 1994).

While some universities are seeking distinctiveness through regional or specialist and disciplinary niches, others are directing their energies towards innovation in course structure, delivery and research. The formation of graduate schools in two Australian universities (Melbourne and the Australian National University) indicates a trend whereby the established universities are asserting their pre-eminence in research training. Despite some initial uncertainty about their roles, the graduate schools will succeed on the basis of their attractiveness to international fee-paying students as concentrations of excellence. The institutional identity issue will intensify as the graduate market grows in significance in terms of both the income generated and the status involved.

The learning community

The notion of the university as a higher education learning community is changing in number of ways. It is not simply that the 'higher' has become problematic as the range of universities, students, and courses broadens, more importantly, the working and educational relationships between the key members – students, academics and administrators – are being redefined. The government imperative of access and participation, combined with technological innovations in teaching and information management, has set a pattern for course delivery which is substantially changing the nature of the student experience, especially the social aspect of learning. Likewise, global networks are opening up relationships in teaching and research promoted by political pragmatism and new forms of course delivery across borderless student markets that no longer necessarily require contact in the cloisters.

The research–teaching–study nexus has been central to the identity of the university. Whether or not the nexus is supported by empirical evidence is irrelevant, the ideal form sustains the symbolic distinction between universities, vocational colleges and schools. In this form, the relationship between teacher and student is 'sealed by their common pursuit of knowledge . . . [they] engage in research in close cognitive and physical proximity' (Clark 1994: 11). The loss of distinctiveness of the university as a learning community is changing partly as the nexus weakens, but also as the significance of the social nature of learning is challenged.

Growth, diversity and course delivery

Even the most selective universities have had to respond to the latest increase in the diversity of student backgrounds that has accompanied expansion. Amongst other things, the universities now find themselves responding with bridging programmes, learning skills centres, remedial clinics and myriad support services aimed at maintaining student progression and completion rates. In Australia, the student mix varies considerably across the universities, but still basically mirrors the former binary pattern with the large established universities taking mostly full-time undergraduate students directly from school. The post-1988 universities have considerably higher proportions of part-time and mature-age students. The New Zealand universities are still primarily operating full-time, year-long courses. About one-third of university students are part-time, while in the polytechnics part-time students make up well over half the total (Ministry of Education 1994).

One of the clearest examples of the underlying belief by governments that university education can be delivered more cheaply to a large and diverse population has been the establishment of Open Learning Australia (OLA). The initiative has had as much a symbolic as practical significance in its early stages and its rapid rise can be gauged by its rating as one of the top 12 'universities' in the major buyers' guide to higher education in 1994 (Ashenden and Milligan 1994). In fact, the OLA is not a university at all. Rather, it is a private company based on a consortium of nine universities acting as an educational broker between over 18 universities offering subjects, other tertiary education providers, and the general public. It is 'open' in a number of respects, with an absence of traditional prerequisites for entry such as age or prior study.

With a doubling of student numbers over the first two years to some 7500 enrolments in 1994, the OLA has become the pacesetter for government programmes of participation and flexibility. In terms of technological innovation, the

OLA still relies primarily on the printed word but it has gained public profile with its use of the national television network. The most advanced attempts at interactive multimedia and computer-based education are still university-specific. OLA is a case study of practice driving policy across the system. Beyond the technological, it has given a boost to the legitimacy of the national credit-transfer arrangements, and it has had the unintended consequence, in some instances, of setting new standards for on-campus teaching materials. A key advantage for multicampus universities, or those with limited resources is the reduced pressure to maintain comprehensive course offerings.

Academics and students

Academics are finding their teaching and working relationships hindered most obviously by the growing number of students in classes, and also by a greater range of student abilities. Dissatisfaction with the quality of students more than doubled between 1978 (18 per cent) and 1993 (38 per cent) (McInnis *et al.* 1994). This concern for student performance has been complicated by the market rela-tionship with fee-paying students. New Zealand students currently pay around 15 per cent of the cost of their courses but this is likely to grow to anywhere between 25 and 50 per cent in the near future. Australian students have been committed to paying significant fees through the taxation system. The more direct and expensive fee-for-teaching relationship is currently a contentious issue at the postgraduate level. The dynamics of the learning community are changing as academics come to terms with the notion of student as fee-paying consumer. There is considerable ambivalence as to how far they should go in treating the student as a customer. They strongly believe that students have become more demanding of their time, and feel under considerable pressure to be readily available with detailed advice that some feel borders on personal tutoring and 'spoon-feeding'.

The learning community is also being changed by the increasing use of casual academic staff on sessional, short-term or part-time contracts. Courses are some-times built around the staff with expertise direct from the workplace or from other universities. The notion of the university as a learning community suffers, however, when casual teaching staff are employed to cover for academics in overloaded courses. While administrations argue that their universities need this flexibility to adapt to changing student demands, the casual connection of aca-demic staff makes the research–teaching–learning nexus fairly meaningless. In this environment, the core staff are obliged to carry the demands of course continuity and integrity. Not surprisingly, the casual staff are frequently excluded from the process of curriculum construction and future planning and find themselves teaching courses over which they have little control. The possibility of an interdependent – but nevertheless segmented – profession has been raised, that is, one made up of those who conceptualize the work and those who execute it (Smythe 1994: 23). From the student perspective, casual staff are less likely to be readily available for consultation, sometimes unfamiliar with department policies and lacking influence on their behalf.

New relationships in research and teaching

The direct involvement of business and government in the operation of universities has led to the weakening of institutional and sector boundaries, and it has also effectively reduced the influence of universities over teaching styles and curriculum formation in the trade-off for financial support. Working with business is by no means a new experience for the universities, but the relationship has changed with the acceleration of three interrelated trends in both Australia and New Zealand: (1) the persistent pressure for vocationalism on universities; (2) the formation of new research and teaching alliances between business and universities; and (3) the growth of advanced university education through postgraduate enrolments.

The general pressure for vocationalism on the universities has been perceived by the universities as a serious threat to higher-order educational goals. While only a few academics believe that undergraduate teaching should be primarily directed towards fitting students for the workplace, they are increasingly being asked to justify their liberal educational activities in terms of occupational relevance. In New Zealand there is a meeting of the ways with provincial polytechnics providing a recognized first year for university purposes. Government is working towards a 'seamless' system which it hopes will integrate vocational and academic goals within a national framework for qualifications across the education sectors. Although the universities have resisted the inclusion of their degrees in the framework, they have supported the need for related developments such as the recognition of prior learning.

The most significant move to break down the demarcation between vocational and university education in Australia has been the national credit-transfer scheme which has created a more flexible system adaptable to the changing vocational needs of the individual (Haydon 1994). The impact on the universities has been considerable with respect to the admission of students from the advanced technical sector, but more interestingly, the flow has turned the other way, with university graduates seeking specific vocational training on top of a generalist degree (Golding 1994). This trend is likely to add weight to the moves to develop more generalist first degrees while pushing specialized university study to the postgraduate level.

Although the pressure of vocationalism on undergraduate degrees is likely to ease off as the technical sector gains prestige, it will remain powerful at the postgraduate level where the professions and the students have the closest interest in the currency of credentials. The priority of funding vocational education as an alternative to university study has been accompanied by a public campaign to improve its image amongst school-leavers. By 1994, the popularity of university for school-leavers in Australia began to decline, and so too did school retention rates. Eligible applications for undergraduate places dropped by 4.4 per cent and a shift to more directly vocational courses is becoming evident. Even if the universities are able to maintain their distance from technical education, this does not mean that the generalist faculties can wind back the clock and operate without reference to the demands of the workplace. One lasting impact of the reforms of the 1980s is a clear expectation that generic skills relevant to employment – independence, initiative verbal skills etc. – will be self-consciously fostered in university courses. The extent to which these are promoted is regularly tested in student course feedback questionnaires.

The changing nature of postgraduate study especially illustrates the impact of vocationalism on the character of the university. The sudden expansion of post-graduate coursework programmes in New Zealand and Australia – in line with international developments – has been fuelled by deregulation, competition and strong student and employer demand for advanced specialist education. In New Zealand, postgraduate diplomas have slightly higher numbers than Master's degrees (Ministry of Education 1994), and although 14 000 may seem small in terms of the system total of 212 000 students, postgraduate programmes are already having a significant impact on the direction of the universities as they seek niche markets nationally and internationally.

In Australia, enrolments in postgraduate courses increased by 62 per cent from 1988 to 1993, and within this, the number of students enrolled in Master's course-work programmes grew by more than 120 per cent (DEET 1994). Higher degree students now comprise more than 10 per cent of the total students in Australia, but as in both countries, their financial commitment to the universities is giving them the potential for a disproportionately high level of influence. The Australian government has made it clear that it has no intention of subsidizing the regis-tration requirements of the professions (Beazley 1993). Since professional employ-ers frequently contribute directly to course costs, their relevant professional registration bodies are taking a more significant role in monitoring the university curriculum and the quality of courses.

The learning community is also broadening rapidly with new research links between universities and industry. Australian industry has long been a reluctant participant in the business of research and the universities have not been par-ticularly competent in their dealings with business. The shift of research from university or public research organizations to partnership arrangements with industry has been promoted through key centres of teaching and research funded by government. In addition to promoting the interdependence of teaching and research, and gathering expertise together, these centres aim to encourage financial support from, and partnership with, industry and user groups. The change for the uni-versities has been seen in the new attitudes and infrastructure required to deal with the management of projects, and the shift in the orientation of academic researchers away from the more conventional rounds of government research grants. The growth of industry-based research degrees has pushed universities towards more flexibility in procedures and expectations of performance in the supervision of research students (Powles 1994).

There has also been a rapid increase in complementary arrangements between universities in the form of joint specialist centres, and joint bids for major equip-ment shared for mutual benefit. All parties recognize that to be internationally competitive in research, Australian and New Zealand universities need to con-centrate their expertise. Attitudes of industry towards the value of university research are changing. With the creation of the Unified National System in Australia, the competition for government-funded research generated a debate about the impact of spreading grants across the entire system as the new universities got the strong message that to be credible – indeed viable – they would have to raise their research profiles. Issue of critical mass and productivity remain, and the established research universities will no doubt continue to argue that their contribution is being undermined by thinly allocated funds from what is effectively a low investment by government.

The established universities are to some extent recognizing the potential contribution of individuals and groups from specialist areas in the new universities. This, of course, has advantages for both types of institution: the established universities can argue that it avoids the need to create research infrastructures in all universities (and thus limit the available pool of money) and the new universities are able to connect promising academics with substantial projects. Smaller regional universities are making strong inroads into the research field by linking their expertise with the international prospects of local industry. There is a possibility of Australian universities following the US experience whereby selected academics in primarily teaching universities make an annual commitment to collaborative research for a substantial period. In the best of possible worlds the research–teaching–study nexus is likely to be enhanced for all parties under these arrangements.

Conclusions

What the policies of the 1980s set in train was the final dash in a thirty-year period of transition from élite to mass higher education. The transition continues, but as yet there is no sign of a coherent vision of what universities should look like in the next decade and beyond. Instead of vision, there is a political 'schedule of necessity' (Keating 1994). The legacy of the last decade of pragmatism can be viewed in pessimistic terms as heralding the end of 'real' universities. A more optimistic view is that universities are emerging out of the upheaval better placed to shape their futures.

There will be winners and losers, and more pain to come with further substantial reductions in government funding. Amongst the winners will be those that focus on becoming selectively independent from government finance. They will be characterized by their ability to respond imaginatively to opportunities without losing sight of their fundamental goals. Those ahead now in this pattern of change decided early that their futures were tied to their ability to raise money from diverse sources. The losers will be those institutions (and academics) still largely dependent on a shrinking public purse and stuck in an educational gridlock. Despite the early drift to uniformity amongst the universities, it is likely that genuine diversity across the system will emerge. Although differentiation will become more significant, there is no suggestion of a caste system developing amongst the institutions. Institutional mobility, upwards and downwards, is a likely scenario.

Competition stands out as the most pervasive factor changing the university. At its worst, it reveals itself in the unwillingness of academics to share information as freely as they once did. Competitions for grants and consultancies have had the unintended outcome of closing scholarly conversations. Academics find themselves enmeshed, however reluctantly, in the politics of envy as their universities strive for competitive advantage. The combination of competition, teaching technology and student markets has opened up the possibility of the social experience of learning being seriously devalued and eroded. The development of marketable and interchangeable course units has the potential for taking decisions about the shape of courses out of the hands of the educators.

The positive side of the market environment is that new fields are being explored and resources combined to overcome disadvantages of size or location. Competition has also given urgency and legitimacy to teaching initiatives that might once have been ignored, and it has also challenged the complacent and somewhat insular attitudes that prevailed in some universities. The boundaries between the universities, and between the organizational units within, are constantly shifting as academics are encouraged to form networks of entrepreneurs in their own and the organization's interest. The universities are forming alliances – often with close competitors – in pursuit of markets. Just as the growth of the global economy has been accompanied by a reduction in the size of operating units of international corporations, so too the mega-universities are likely to segment into relatively small sub-groups each with the potential for greater autonomy.

These moves place university leadership in a crucial position. Internal tension and ambiguity in the administration and governance of the universities has been created by the simultaneous rise of hierarchical and market cultures. In the current period of transition, universities are being managed by a mix of the two styles with inevitable tensions compounded by the demise of collegial governance. The centralized style of control now favoured within the universities may be justified on the basis of the scale and urgency of the changes required, but ought not be considered the most desirable or effective form of organization. Market competition needs to be managed creatively beyond the transition if universities are to reassert their roles as sources of imagination and innovation in the transmission and advancement of knowledge. The major question over the next decade is whether there is sufficient maturity in university leadership to genuinely devolve decision-making to smaller and more autonomous academic organizational units. This is where the learning community can be most effective in addressing long-term national interest as well as sustaining the core ideals underlying the increasingly diverse forms of the universities.

References

Ashenden, D. and Milligan, S. (1994) *Good Universities Guide to Australian Universities*. Port Melbourne, Mandarin.

Beazley, Hon. K. 'Labor's post-school agenda for the nineties', in J. Anwyl and E. Atkinson (eds) *1992 and 1993 Spring Lectures on Higher Education: Contemporary Issues*. Parkville, CSHE, University of Melbourne.

Clark, B.R. (1994) 'The research–teaching–study nexus in modern systems of higher education,' *Higher Education Policy*, 7(1), 11–17.

Department of Employment, Education and Training (1994) *Selected Higher Education Statistics*. Canberra, Australian Government Publishing Service.

Dill, D. (1982) 'The management of academic culture: notes on the management of meaning and social integration,' *Higher Education*, 11(3), 302–320.

Gallagher, M. and Conn, W. (1994) Diversity and performance of Australian universities, *DEET Higher Education Series*, Report 22. April. Canberra, Australian Government Publishing Service.

Golding, B. (1994) Intersectorial Articulation and Quality Assessment in Australian Higher Education. Paper presented to Sixth International Conference on Assessing Quality in Higher Education, Hong Kong.

Haydon, A.P. (1994) Credit transfer and recognition of prior learning in Australian universities, *DEET Higher Education Series*. Canberra, Australian Government Publishing Service.

Keating, Hon. P. (1994) Speech by the Prime Minister, New Educational Realities Conference, Melbourne.

Larkins, P. (1994) Australian Universities: Direction Setting for the Twenty-first Century. Address presented at the Australian National University Strategic Planning Meeting. Canberra, Australian National University.

McInnis, C. (1992) 'Changes in the nature of academic work', *The Australian Universities' Review*, 35(2), 9–12.

McInnis, C., Powles, M. and Anwyl, J. (1994) 'Australian academics' perspectives on quality and accountability', *CSHE Research Working Papers 94.1*. Parkville, CSHE, University of Melbourne.

Ministry of Education (1994) *Education Statistics of New Zealand 1994*. Wellington, Ministry of Education.

Powles, M. (1994) 'Graduate students at the interface between universities and industry,' *Higher Education Policy*, 7(1), 37–42.

Preddey, G. (1993) *Country paper: New Zealand*. Department of Employment, Education and Training/OECD Conference, The Transition from Élite To Mass Higher Education, Sydney, June.

Smythe, J. (ed.) (1994) *Academic Work: The Changing Labour Process in Higher Education*. Buckingham, Open University Press.

5

Future Patterns of Teaching and Learning

Alistair G.J. MacFarlane

Learning, teaching and technology

Learning is an interactive and dynamic process, in which imagination drives action in exploring and interacting with an environment. It requires a dialogue between imagination and experience. Teaching provides the relevant experience and mediates the ensuing dialogue. Our limited raw information-processing capability requires us to interact with only a severely restricted part of our environment at any specific time. Thus when we learn we can only learn about, and acquire a facility in dealing with, a highly limited version of part of the world. Knowledge comes in chunks. The severely limited, circumscribed and simplified situations which we can attend to, or learn about, at any specific time we will call a 'microworld'. This idea is central to the discussion of the ways in which technology could be used to support learning which is given here. As we learn by interacting with our various environments, day after day, year after year, we weave from our experiences an intricate web of beliefs, concepts, descriptions, prescriptions, rules and procedures, facts and dodges. We weave microworlds into our macroworld, constantly modifying, stitching, repairing and creating our abilities to understand, to explain and to cope. This process is active, constant and never-ending (Quine and Ullian 1978). The primary role of technology in teaching, and in the support of the learning process, is to create appropriate microworlds, and to facilitate and mediate a learner's interaction with them. The wider role of technology is to create networks of interconnections – between groups of learners and teachers, and between learners and a variety of shared environments. The primary role of teachers is to manage and facilitate the learning processes of their students. The wider role of teachers is to create and develop effective and efficient environments for the support of learning.

As we move into the next century, technology thus provides us with both a challenge and an opportunity. The challenge is to find out how to construct and deploy highly supportive environments which could be used to provide self-paced tutor-supported learning deliverable in a highly flexible way to individuals, or to collaborating groups, and in a variety of locations and over a distance as required.

The opportunity is to radically change the ways in which we aid the learning process in order to give students a much higher degree of individual support, and a much more flexible approach to the management of their learning experiences. Only by seizing this opportunity will we be able to expand participation in higher education while maintaining quality, and only by an imaginative use of technology will we be able to make the ideal of life-long learning for large numbers of people a reality. The ideas for the machine-aided support of learning which are developed here, and the ways in which they are described, are biased heavily towards scientific and technical subjects. It is believed, however, that the principles which underly them are general, and so could be adapted for use in a variety of fields of learning.

Learning and its phases

The development of thorough conceptual understanding involves a series of learning phases – preparing to tackle the relevant material, acquiring the necessary information, relating it to previous knowledge, transforming it through establishing organizational frameworks within which to interpret it, and so developing personal understanding (CSUP Report 1992). If this process is to work effectively, teaching – however it is delivered – must be designed to support these phases of learning. The required support can be described in terms of necessary teaching functions which to some extent parallel, but also overlap, the phases of learning. These functions include:

- Orientating: setting the scene and explaining what is required.
- Motivating: pointing up relevance, evoking and sustaining interest.
- Presenting: introducing new knowledge within a clear, supportive structure.
- Clarifying: explaining with examples and providing remedial support.
- Elaborating: introducing additional material to develop more detailed knowledge.
- Consolidating: providing opportunities to develop and test personal understanding.
- Confirming: ensuring the adequacy of the knowledge and understanding reached.

After the initial phases of preparing for learning, the conventional process of acquiring new knowledge begins with a teacher presenting appropriate course material. The new knowledge has to be carefully selected to ensure relevance and potential interest, and then presented in a way which helps the student both to relate it to prior knowledge and to see a clear logical structure within it, as a first step towards establishing a personal organizing framework. Then the process of clarifying begins. Through explanations and examples, students are encouraged to begin developing their own personal understanding of the topic. If the prior knowledge is inadequate, remedial support will be required at this stage, to allow a firm base on which to build explanations and further clarification. Once the initial grasp of the material is sufficiently firm, opportunities have to be provided for elaborating the knowledge by examining nuances of meaning, and by incorporating more detail and additional examples or evidence. Thereafter, the knowledge requires consolidating, by encouraging application to new contexts and periodic review of what has already been presented. Ultimately, there needs to be a final consolidation which allows the students to integrate the course as a whole and that is often linked, through assessment procedures to the final teaching function – confirming that knowledge and understanding have reached an appropriate level. Such confirmation is involved in certifying standards to the outside world, but is also part of quality control to ensure that teaching has been effective.

Within conventional teaching methodology, the initial stages of orientating, motivating, presenting, and explaining or clarifying, are carried out through lectures. Further clarification and remedial support is obtained from textbooks or through tutorials, which also involve elaborating and consolidating. Laboratory classes and fieldwork introduce additional knowledge and skills, together with opportunities for consolidation and elaboration in relation to the lecture course. The additional reading suggested by lecturers and tutors continues the process of elaboration, while much of the consolidation comes from worked examples (as in the sciences) and coursework essays. In all areas of study, assessment requirements are used to encourage consolidation through the periodic review of lecture notes and the more thorough revision process which precedes examinations. Student progress needs confirming through comments on coursework and the results of periodic tests, while degree examinations are used formally to confirm the levels of skill and understanding reached by students. Finally, course evaluations are required to confirm the quality of the teaching. The provision of teaching and the support of learning should be seen in terms of a complex, interacting system. Assessment is only one of the factors influencing learning. The outcomes of learning depend on the combined effects of the whole learning environment provided by an institution and its courses (teaching, discussion classes, resource materials and assessment procedures). The provision of an effective and economical system requires a careful analysis of requirements and functions both at institutional and course levels.

While the conventional teaching methods continue to fulfil these functions, it is now imperative to consider whether there should be widespread adoption of more efficient and cost-effective ways of encouraging and supporting student learning. There needs to be a re-examination of both the purposes and the techniques involved in conventional teaching methods, and a widespread adoption of new methods which support the additional transferable skills now being required. In particular, it is necessary to consider carefully how, and to what extent, we can make use of technology in improving the provision of teaching and the support of learning.

Learning support

Education is the design, creation and management of environments which support the learning process, and teaching is the management of the learning process within such an environment. It is argued here that technology has an indispensable role to play in creating future learning environments.

Effective action is achieved via schemata – the rules and procedures which are assembled to guide action. Learning results from the progressive development and refinement of concepts and schemata, and leads to the acquisition of coherent frameworks of reasonable beliefs together with the necessary skills to put them to effective use. In interacting with the world, we encounter and use information in two ways (Simon 1982). One way characterizes the world as sensed – it provides, for example, the information needed for identifying and characterizing objects, and for building models of them. The other way characterizes the world as acted upon – it provides the information needed for an action to have a desired effect. Thus information can be both descriptive and prescriptive – one use of information is associated with specifying perception, the other use with specifying action. Descriptions and prescriptions are the warp and woof of our web of understanding. In interacting with a microworld we need to both comprehend it and to be able to act effectively upon it. To comprehend it, we need a necessary set of concepts, and to act upon it we need a necessary set of schemata. Understanding of a microworld is manifested by an ability to:

- Use the concepts assimilated and the schemata created in the learning process to successfully interpret data, explain sets of related events, and solve problems posed in terms of the microworld.
- Cope with new situations described in the microworld.
- Explain new situations arising in the microworld.
- Act in these new situations with satisfactory consequences.

To deal with a specific microworld, one can conceive of creating an intensely supportive environment for learning using computer-based systems which support and aid the human reasoning process, and communication systems which augment this by providing flexible access to tutors and to fellow learners. Such an environment allows one to interact with structured objective knowledge in such a way as to absorb concepts and develop schemas, derive an understanding of their use, and to test that understanding by appropriate investigations and exercises. it could support learning on both an individual and on a group basis, allowing the users great flexibility in finding their way through the structured objective knowledge which is made available to them, yet also allowing an instructor to monitor and, if necessary, direct the progress of each individual student.

In such a supportive environment a learner should be able to perform with appropriate support a wide variety of tasks:

- analyse
- browse
- search
- build representations and models
- compare and evaluate
- reason and hypothesize
- synthesize
- manipulate and modify

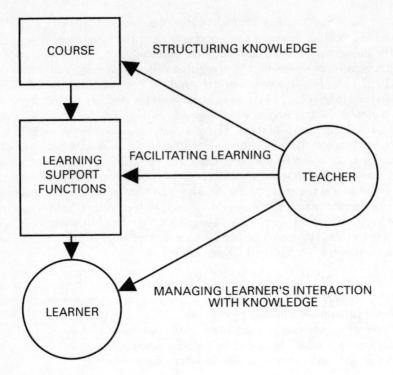

Figure 5.1 Roles of teacher and learner.

- experiment
- catalogue
- store and retrieve

Given such a system to use, the teacher's principal roles are:

- Structuring knowledge in such a way as to make it interactively accessible.
- Facilitating the learning process.
- Managing the learner's interaction with structured and interactively-accessible knowledge.

This approach to teaching, and to the support of the learning process, is illustrated in Figure 5.1. The teacher no longer acts primarily as a transmitter of information, allowing some learning-support functions to be supplied by a machine, as illustrated by Figure 5.2. An important implication of this form of learning-support system structure is that remote tutoring can be provided, as illustrated in Figure 5.3.

Figure 5.4 illustrates a learner's interaction with a microworld. The overall functional structure of a learning-support system can now be sketched out. The system must provide, among other things:

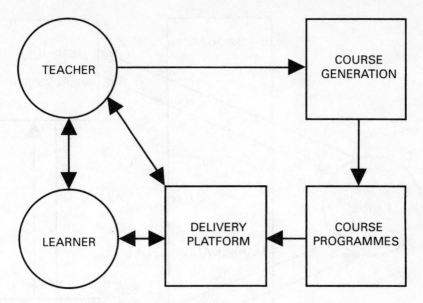

Figure 5.2 Machine-supported learning.

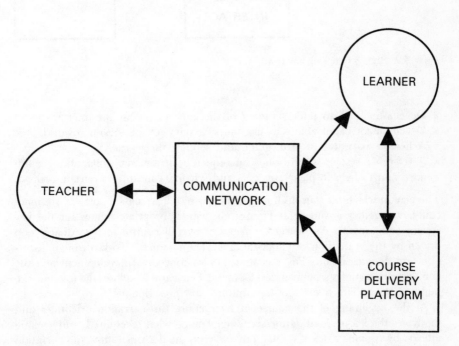

Figure 5.3 Remote tutoring.

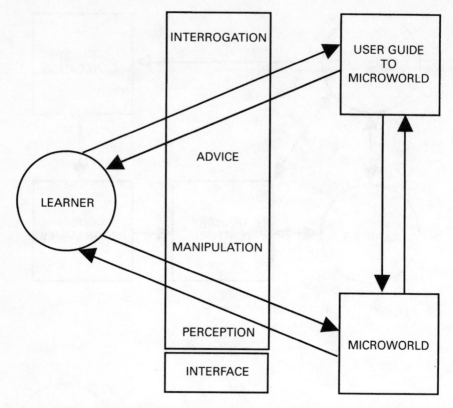

Figure 5.4   Interaction with microworld.

- Development of an understanding of the concept set for the microworld.
- Development of an ability to use the schemata set for the microworld.
- A flexible narrative to lead, guide and support the learner.
- A reference system to provide – on request – definitions, explanations, guidance and to help to place concepts and schemata in an appropriate context.

The way in which the various functional parts of a learning-support environment could fit together is shown in Figure 5.5, with appropriate names for the key system components. An instructor exercises overall control in a feedback loop driven by the evaluation of understanding. The instructor works through narration and demonstration. The narration guides conceptual development and the demonstration guides schemata development. The learner explores the microworld, building up an effective set of descriptions and prescriptions.

At the beginning of the course of instruction, the narration orientates and motivates the learner, setting the scene, explaining what is required, and evoking interest by running a set of scripts. Linking with the demonstration, the narration also introduces the way in which schemata are developed via user guides.

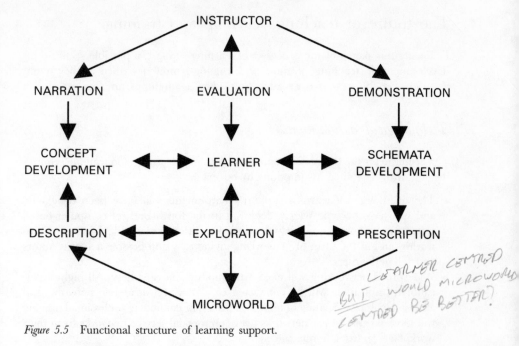

Figure 5.5 Functional structure of learning support.

The instructor, driven by the evaluation of understanding, controls the presentation, clarification, elaboration and consolidation of knowledge. This is done by providing interactive, feedback-controlled support of the development of the necessary conceptual understanding and schematic skills for the specific microworld for which the course is developed.

It must be emphasized that machine-based learning-support environments of this sort are seen as supplementing, and not as displacing, the essential role of the human teacher. Their use will free vital human skills for one-on-one and small-group tuition, of which so little is now available at so many levels of education. The use of technology for learning support could evolve in such a way that the group becomes the natural learning unit, where pupils and students reinforce increasingly each other's learning experiences, guided by both their peers and by their teachers.

There are wider implications to what is being proposed. Three of these are:

• Tutorial support delivered over a communications link into such supportive environments, based on portable computers in the home or workplace, could be the prime delivery mechanism for advanced professional training.
• The provision of powerful knowledgeable machines (which is one way of looking at a learning support system), with which one could interact easily, could go a long way towards overcoming the increasing fragmentation of knowledge into highly specialized domains.
• Powerful learning support environments coupled with remote tutoring could provide small and medium-sized enterprises with affordable training schemes.

The future of teaching, learning and training

Following this sketch of the processes of learning support, a possible scenario for developments in teaching, learning and training is now described as they might develop over the next two decades. Some key assumptions are first set out.

Technological assumptions

This scenario for the future development of teaching, learning and training requires the following technical assumptions to be made:

- The technology of learning-support environments will have been developed and will have become widely deployed in the forms both of computer-based systems providing interactively developed knowledge of a wide range of micro-worlds, and in the form of networking giving easy and flexible access to tutors and fellow learners.
- Widespread networking will exist, with multimedia capability. All higher educational institutions will be connected to a powerful academic network, and all individuals participating in higher education or continuing professional training will have access to such networks over commercial service networks from their workplace or from home.
- All higher educational institutions will have powerful local distributed computing systems connected to a national academic network. All teaching staff will have access to workstations and personal computers with multimedia capability. The local academic networks will have powerful knowledge servers providing a wide range of teaching and learning-support material.
- Powerful multimedia authoring systems will be widely available, which will have a high degree of standardization or reciprocal compatibility and transference, and these will be in widespread, routine use.
- All participants in higher education – staff, students, and those pursuing off-campus continuing professional training – will routinely use desktop and portable computers with multimedia and networking capability.

Organizational assumptions

In developing the scenario, the following organizational assumptions have been made:

- A national organization has been created which runs a national academic network linking all higher educational institutions, and providing a national service for the development, maintenance and sharing of learning support software and systems. Specific sites will exist which provide support for particular disciplines and topics, and coordinate their development. Easy and flexible access to the national academic network will be provided from all over the country via appropriate links.

- Higher education institutions will retain their autonomy, but will operate within a framework of local, regional and national coordination under the aegis of some national coordinating authority.
- A fully articulated national system of credit accumulation and transfer will be in operation.

Specific areas of teaching and learning support in which a highly cost-effective development of traditional systems will have then been achieved are as follows:

1. Access: Intake and recruitment arrangements for a variety of subjects will have been greatly improved by creating self-paced machine-supported access courses giving a satisfactory preparation for a range of subjects which require specific skills as prerequisites, such as Mathematics for Science and Engineering, or which require specific preparatory knowledge such as Chemistry or Biology for certain courses in Science and Technology. A very large leverage will have been applied to development and testing by preparing and supporting these (and the following areas) on a national scale, using a mixture of distance-learning and computer-based learning methods. Such systems will have been designed for the efficient achievement of high volume and high effectiveness.
2. Reduction of failure rates: As the volume being handled by teaching systems expands, an increasing degree of management of an individual student's learning will have become necessary in order to reduce and contain failure rates. Computer-based remedial learning support systems will have provided a cost-effective way of alleviating this problem.
3. Flexibility of movement between courses: An increasing range of course provision will have required the management of large numbers of possible pathways through combinations of course material. This will have resulted in a flexible provision of access material for courses which will allow easy transition to new subject areas, and the management of individually-tailored courses, based on a combination of distance-learning and computer-based learning methods.
4. Service teaching: This will have been seen as one of the most obviously cost-effective areas for the widespread introduction of new techniques. The media and methods used will be subject-related, and both distance-learning and computer-based learning methods will be in widespread use.
5. Tutorials: Managed support of tutorials will have provided a highly cost-effective way of underpinning the clarification, elaboration and consolidation components of the learning process. Self-paced working through tutorial materials with a high degree of individual support will be seen as an ideal use of computer-based learning-support methodology.
6. Virtual laboratories and design support systems: Many physical phenomena pose severe learning difficulties because of their intrinsic complexity. The quality and effectiveness of teaching such topics will have been greatly enhanced by an imaginative use of computer-based methods. The use of virtual experiments will have greatly reduced laboratory costs, and also increased teaching effectiveness by a careful coordination with real laboratory experiments. The widespread use of professional tools, such as computer-aided design packages

in engineering, will have made the use of computer-based systems mandatory for design courses with a high professional training content.

Generic changes in terms of shifts along a teaching/ learning spectrum

The benefits which will have arisen from the use of innovative methods, and from the use of technology in a learning-support process, can be considered in terms of a number of types of generic change which we will call shifts. The term shift is used to emphasize that each form of change can be thought of as associated with a progression along a spectrum of teaching/learning support, which ranges from simply imparting information at one end of the spectrum of possibilities to comprehensively managing the complete learning-support process at the other end.

These forms of generic change, their role in developing teaching methods, and the associated benefits which will have been obtained, are as follows:

1. A shift from synchronous single-location learning support to asynchronous networked learning support: The severe space and time constraints of traditional presentation methods using lectures and laboratories will have been removed by a shift to self-paced supported learning using a variety of possible support and delivery mechanisms. Distance-learning methods and computer-based learning-support methods are the two major forms of system which will have been developed for asynchronous location-independent teaching, but a wide range of other possibilities will be being explored, limited only by the ingenuity of system designers in their use of the huge range of media which will have become available for use.

2. A shift from passive learning to active learning: Learning will be seen as an active process in which concepts are acquired, incorporated into appropriate schemas, and tested in action. Computer-based learning-support systems will have provided great scope for the development of active learning environments, and thus for an increase in the quality and effectiveness of students' learning experience.

3. A shift from static presentation to dynamic presentation: Cheap methods of producing, transmitting and storing acceptable quality video and animation will have greatly improved the presentation of a wide range of material.

4. A shift from the use of real objects to the use of virtual objects: The use of virtual objects – that is, objects whose behaviour is simulated by computer, and which are interactively accessible – offers huge scope for linking theory and experiment in teaching Science and Technology. The careful use of virtual objects and system simulations will have had a dramatic effect on the quality, effectiveness and relevance of teaching in these areas, and will have resulted in a much more cost-effective use of expensive laboratory facilities.

5. A shift from impassive delivery to supportive delivery: Well-designed computer-based learning-support systems will have been made highly supportive in dealing with a learner's difficulties. This will provide great scope for remedial teaching.

6. A shift to multimedia: The imaginative and skilful use of a wide range of media will provide huge scope for imaginative teaching. Video, animation and audio will be of great value in improving presentation quality and learning effectiveness in every subject area, but will have particular value in Science and Technology where the spatial visualization of complex phenomena plays a key role in learning.
7. A shift from unidirectional presentation to interactive presentation: Interactivity offers great scope for benefits in clarification, elaboration and consolidation, and is the key to the production of highly supportive learning environments. Great benefits in quality and effectiveness will be obtained, provided by well-designed support systems.
8. A shift from broadcast delivery to personal delivery: The possibility, given skilful design, of developing learning-support systems which tailor their response to an individual's needs and performance will have been shown to be of great value in combining volume benefits with quality benefits. Properly developed, it will have greatly increased the scope for self-paced learning, and for access and remedial teaching, driven by an individual's motivation.

Changes at institutional level

As they respond to the pressures on them to increase their output while maintaining quality, and as they draw on an ever-widening spread of abilities and backgrounds in their intake, institutions will generate a much greater degree of flexibility in their teaching arrangements. Such arrangements will become ever more adaptive, and institutions will have been forced into significant changes in the way in which their teaching is organized. These changes will have been accelerated by a decoupling of research and teaching funding streams which will have forced commensurate reorganization in institutions.

A fully developed learning-support methodology which will allow a very high degree of self-paced exploratory learning will have been created and studied in order to identify those features of the environment which best support learning. In institutional terms, material will have been highly modularized, and new mechanisms devised for supervision and assessment. A whole spectrum of working methods will have been investigated and appraised – from individual working with a remote supervisor or tutor, through small group working, to the use of asynchronously accessed lecture material in video form. Management systems will have been devised and tested to track an individual student's progress and to provide straightforward yet intensively-supported access to remedial teaching.

In organizational terms the technical complexity of the support systems will have changed the roles of computing services and other support systems at institutional level. At regional and national level, organizational arrangements will have been created to ensure that standards are generated and adhered to which will permit and facilitate an effective and efficient sharing of scarce resources both in manpower and materials.

Changes at teacher level

Teachers will be involved increasingly in the support, development and management of learning environments. The organizational implications of this shift will have been seen to be very great. Much training will have been required and teachers will have had to adapt to greatly changed working styles. Teachers will be involved in communities spanning many institutions and operating on a national basis. They will be encouraged to contribute to the development of shared resources and materials. New promotion and reward schemes will exist which will provide motivation and a career-development framework. They will have become adept at helping individual students to progress through a supportive learning environment, and in managing groups of students pursuing the same courses at varying speeds and levels. Staff development will have emerged as a major problem with the move towards student-managed learning. Institutions will draw on a consortial pool of expertise to provide the necessary range of courses and training materials.

Changes at student level

The changes at the individual student level will be profound. Students will have been taught how to manage their own learning processes to an unprecedented degree. They will have learned how to swim in a sea of information, to use the rich resources of a supportive learning environment, to self-pace and self-structure their own programmes of learning. They will be able to choose from a spectrum of learning styles ranging from self-instruction with tutor support to group working of various types. The effectiveness of each individual student's learning process will be efficiently monitored, and appropriate arrangements provided for each individual student to interact effectively with supervisors and tutors. The supportive environment will offer students a powerful and continuous means for self-assessment, and for planning the development of their learning processes and skills generation. There will be a continuing need for academic counsellors and tutors, and for collaborative inputs in areas like study skills.

   Although lectures and laboratory classes will continue to play a role in the teaching process, it will have become clear how all those activities which are currently carried out in groups could be more effectively and appropriately carried out in a supportive learning environment. The role of the lecture will have been radically re-assessed, and re-presented for many purposes in an appropriate free-access format enriched – as relevant – with film and simulation material. The use of flexible interactive simulators will have replaced much of the traditional laboratory material. There will be seen to be great advantages in devising ways of supporting small groups working closely together; such methods of working will have usefully developed and enhanced the social and communication skills which will be demanded increasingly by employers.

   Whatever use of technology is made in developing new systems for the support of learning it will be necessary to take account of:

- The relative strengths and weaknesses of human and machine.
- The optimum ways of characterizing and using machine capabilities to facilitate and support learning.
- The nature of the supportive environments which could be created using information technology.
- How such environments could be developed and introduced.
- The problems and stresses which their introduction, deployment and use will cause.
- The policy and organizational implications at individual, institutional, national and international levels.

Large-scale changes to anything as complicated and as important as the country's educational and training systems will be complicated, prolonged and disruptive. It will have to be carried through in the face of the ever-present realities imposed by costs, space, time, organizational and institutional constraints, and by individual attitudes. Nationally co-ordinated changes to our teaching systems on the scale which will be necessary to maintain or increase quality, while further increasing volume, will require an unlikely degree of collective political will. A more probable outcome will be a set of piecemeal, disjointed, ad hoc responses to increasing economic and political pressures, as institutions fight to compete effectively in a developing educational market, while generating their own internal arrangements for innovative teaching, and negotiating a series of collaborations with like-minded partners. Whatever actually happens over the next two decades, two things seem reasonably certain – technology will have a key role to play in the effective provision of high-quality learning environments, and finding out how to do this in an effective way which commands general support will be a complex and painful process.

Acknowledgement

The description of the phases of learning which has been used here has drawn heavily on the work of Professor Noel Entwistle of the University of Edinburgh (CSUP Report 1992).

References

MacFarlane, A. (1992) *Teaching and Learning in an Expanding Higher Education System*. Edinburgh, Committee of Scottish University Principals.
Quine, W.V. and Ullian, J.S. (1978) *The Web of Belief*. New York, Random House.
Simon, H.A. (1982) *The Sciences of the Artificial*. Cambridge, Massachusetts, MIT Press.

6

Increasing Equity in Higher Education: Strategies and Lessons from International Experience*

Thomas Owen Eisemon and Jamil Salmi

Introduction

The state's role in promoting equity and national integration in higher education is an extension of its responsibility for providing universal basic education and expanding secondary education opportunities. This is done in a variety of ways: through open admissions policies, prohibitions against discrimination in admissions, preferential admissions policies, subsidies provided to disadvantaged students to undertake higher studies, as well as through policies affecting the establishment, recognition and location of higher education institutions. Generally, governments tend to be directive in matters related to equity and national integration by adopting policies designed to produce geographic dispersion of higher education institutions or to ensure ethnic and linguistic cosmopolitanism in student and staff recruitment to national public institutions.

However, as most developing countries are facing tightening budgetary constraints, the traditional role of the state as principal – if not exclusive – financier and provider of higher education is increasingly being challenged. In many countries, government's relationship with higher education institutions is becoming more supervisory than interventionist, reflecting a move away from centralized management practices and a heavier reliance on incentives. This, in turn, may affect the ability of governments to sustain their commitment to equity concerns.

This chapter examines policies that developing-country governments have adopted to increase equity through manipulation of institutional characteristics of higher education systems as well as through changing patterns of recruitment. Experiences of successful and unsuccessful policy implementation are presented and lessons drawn that may have general applicability. The implications of the

* This chapter draws on studies carried out in connection with preparation of the World Bank's (1994) recent policy study, *Higher Education: The Lessons of Experience*. However, the views presented here are the responsibility of the authors. They should not be attributed in any manner to the World Bank, to members of its Board of Executive Directors, or the countries they represent.

changing role of the state are also considered. The chapter argues that developing countries have achieved impressive success in expanding access to higher education for formerly disadvantaged groups especially through the expansion of teacher training, technical institutions, open universities and other forms of distance education. Many countries manipulate admissions criteria to correct inequalities but such policies may involve important quality and efficiency trade-offs. Direct grants to meritorious but needy students is the most effective instrument for increasing their participation in higher education, public or private.

Strategies to improve equity

Most countries have addressed equity concerns through quantitative expansion of their higher education systems, placing particular importance on ensuring a fairer geographic distribution of institutions. This provides tangible evidence of a government's commitment to increasing educational opportunities. Teacher-training colleges, the most common higher education institution and the most localized in their recruitment and mission, are usually the most evenly distributed. Technical training institutions and especially universities are more costly to establish, have broader missions and are more cosmopolitan in composition. Their location is often a matter of considerable political contention with many implications for both cost and performance.

In Egypt, which has one of the largest higher education systems in the developing world, the government has relied on two-year technical institutes to continue providing access to higher education to all secondary graduates while protecting the already-bloated universities. The technical institutes have expanded rapidly during the last 15 years and now enroll about 40 per cent of all secondary-school graduates. However, due to the lack of adequate financial, human, and material resources, most of these institutes provide poor-quality education and are no more than 'academic parking lots' for surplus students.

Satisfying political demands for establishing a local public university or college often leads to the proliferation of many small institutions whose staffing and instructional infrastructure is insufficient to adequately support the range of programmes they offer. Rationalization may be required for academic and economic reasons but implementation is difficult as the experience of recent reforms in China (Weifang 1991), Nigeria (Bako 1990) and many other countries attests.

Distance education

Distance education is less costly than institutional dispersion and is often effective in increasing access for some groups that are usually poorly represented in university enrolments. Distance education has been most successfully developed in Asia. In Thailand, for example, the two open universities, Ramkhambaeng and Sukhotai Thammathirat, founded in 1970 and 1978 respectively, have been the government's principal instrument for expanding access to the country's geographically well-distributed but highly socially-selective public university system. Until very recently, there were few private colleges and universities. Both open universities were established as self-financing government institutions. About a quarter (22 per cent) of the students enrolled in these institutions come from rural areas, the poorest social strata accounting for two-thirds (66 per cent) of the country's population (Stepanich *et al.* 1991). This is still much higher than the representation of rural students in public (11 per cent) or in private universities and colleges (10 per cent), but it is well below their representation in low-status teacher-training institutions, most of which are located in the countryside (52 per cent). The open universities have been much more important in increasing opportunities for students from poor family circumstances in urban areas (21 per cent of enrolment, almost twice their representation in the general population, 12 per cent). However, the main beneficiaries of the open universities in Thailand have been students from urban commercial families (34 per cent of enrolment compared to 10 per cent of the population).

In India, somewhat less than half (41 per cent) of students enrolled in open universities or in distance-education programmes operated by regular universities are women, compared to an enrolment of 32 per cent in formal university programmes (Swamy 1992: 13–20). The participation of the disadvantaged scheduled caste and tribal students, and those from rural areas is well below their representation in the formal higher-education system or in the general population. A high proportion of these students register for commerce. In India, in contrast to Thailand, the opportunities conferred by open universities and distance-education programmes are captured mainly by unemployed university students!

Private higher education, student loans, direct grants

Many countries, especially in Asia and Latin America, have relied on private institutions to increase higher-education opportunities. However, the equity effects of expanding private higher education are less clear. In Chile, the government reforms in the 1980s, which transformed the university system into a mass system dominated by private institutions, strengthened the 'élitization' of higher education (Briones 1992). In many countries in Latin America (Winkler 1990), particularly in Salvador, Venezuela, Chile and Brazil (Wolff *et al.* 1992), expansion of private higher education produces 'a double injustice'. 'The most privileged move from top secondary schools into free public higher education, while less privileged students pay for the inferior education provided in the private sector' (Levy 1991: 4). The case for using private higher education to increase equity, he continues, 'rests on several ifs: if government expenditures on higher education diminishes its expenditures on other levels; if public universities implement tuition, if loans offset costs'.

The introduction of loans to students admitted to private or public institutions has been recommended as a device to facilitate cost-recovery with significant equity benefits (World Bank 1986, 1994). The loans may be targeted – on the basis of need – or made available to all students as has been done in Ghana and Kenya, irrespective of family circumstances. In most sub-Saharan African countries and perhaps in many other parts of the developing world, kin groups rather than families mobilize resources for education, making targeting of loans and student support very difficult and providing much scope for abuse. Similarly, most African countries lack comprehensive, progressive and efficient systems of public finance, presenting practical difficulties for loan recovery and exacerbating the adverse equity effects. In Kenya which has had a student loan scheme since 1973, for instance, the default rate in 1987 was 81 per cent! A high proportion of students repaying loans, presumably, are school teachers whose incomes can be easily attached. The international experience to date with student loan schemes has been quite negative. Because of heavily subsidized interest rates, high default rates, and high administrative costs, the financial performance of these schemes has been so disappointing that it would have been cheaper, in many cases, to substitute loans with outright grants (Albrecht and Ziderman 1991).

More important, at least in so far as equity implications are concerned, is the fact that loan schemes are being introduced in countries like Chile, or are being revitalized in countries like Ghana and Kenya, at a time when governments are increasing the direct costs of attending university. Thus, whatever might be the merits of introducing a loan scheme to encourage more students from needy families to avail themselves of opportunities for higher education, under circumstances of more cost-recovery, student loans cannot be regarded as a policy instrument that is likely to increase equity in participation in higher education.

An increase in direct grants (scholarships) to needy students of high academic potential is apt to be more effective. Indeed in Chile, it is the competitive national scholarships scheme that has increased the enrolment of students from the most educationally and economically disadvantaged backgrounds in the country's best public universities, while loans and expansion of private higher education have expanded opportunities for students from more advantaged families, generally.

The administration of grant schemes is best done at the institutional level. In many countries, ministries of education or higher education do not have the managerial capacity or the political independence to administer scholarships in the most efficient and equitable manner. Universities are in a better position to administer such schemes, as illustrated by the successful experience of some universities, both public and private, which have set up well-targeted financial-aid programmes. For example, when the University of the Philippines raised tuition fees in the late 1980s, it also provided a special fund to support qualified students from low-income families. The Catholic University of Venezuela designed and implemented a differential financial-aid scheme which has been used as a model by several other Latin American private universities.

However, differential subsidies targeted to meritorious students from under-represented groups, and not available to others, causes resentment. In Singapore, subsidies to the few Malay students admitted to the country's highly selective higher-education institutions have been criticized on the grounds that the subsidies are not available to students from educationally advantaged but poor Chinese families. The government will divest itself of the problem by setting up an educational trust for the Malay community and suspending the subsidy programme (Gopinathan 1992: 26, 27).

Preferential admissions

The most direct way to increase the representation in higher education of typically underrepresented groups is to manipulate admissions through relaxation of
admissions requirements, awarding bonus points on entry examinations, through
admissions quotas, or some combination of these devices. Developing country
experience with preferential admissions schemes is rich and varied. India's efforts
to increase the representation of scheduled caste, Muslim and tribal students has
had the most impact on the composition of higher-education enrolments and
since preferential admissions policies are linked to policies affecting public sector
employment, certainly the most controversial.

India's constitution mandates the national and state governments to alleviate
the condition of the most disadvantaged segments of the country's population
through positive discrimination. Centrally funded universities and institutions having
the status of universities are assigned quotas for scheduled caste, tribal and Muslim
students, and at least until the early 1970s were obliged to fill them. (This has
been relaxed for some élite national institutions such as the Indian Institutes of
Technology; Chanana 1992: 17). Most state governments have enacted similar
policies affecting locally funded institutions, often substantially broadening their
application to less disadvantaged but demographically and politically influential
groups especially in central and southern India. Policies of preferential discrimination in education and employment have contributed significantly to India's
political turmoil in recent years. More positively, they have greatly increased
educational opportunities for the most socially disadvantaged groups (Chanana
1992: 14).

Nevertheless, the objects of India's reserved seat scheme remain economically
and educationally disadvantaged (Majumdar 1992: 38–44). Galanter concludes
'in the delicate task of balancing the merit principle with other interests, a flat
percentage limitation on the extent of reservations is of less use than it might
appear'. Nor, he adds, can 'the real impact of a scheme on the chances of others
and on the merit principle be . . . known from the percentage of places reserved'
(Galanter 1984: 417).

In Malaysia, the government adopted twenty-five years ago admission policies
to tertiary education institutions which discriminated positively in favour of the
Malay population (Bumiputras) and against the Chinese and Indians. A recent
analysis of the income distribution impact of these policies has shown that, even
though the advantage of the Chinese population segment has been reduced, reverse
discrimination has penalized the poor within the Bumiputra population (Tzannatos
1991). The prime beneficiaries appear to have been those Malays who were
already better off before the introduction of positive discrimination. These findings suggest that following a narrow definition of ethnic equality and concentrat-
ing resources on expensive upper-secondary and higher-education institutions for
the Bumiputras can be counterproductive. More equalizing effects would have
been achieved by investing these resources in the provision of better basic education for the entire population.

Less ambitious schemes have been tried in other developing countries. In the early 1980s, the public University of the Philippines decided to relax the rigorous admission criteria for students from poor and rural families on the grounds that the university's entrance requirements, a composite of secondary-school grades and tests of academic ability, unfairly measured the potential of these students. Students admitted under the scheme were provided with financial support and also remedial instruction if this was necessary for their course of study. Students' performance was closely monitored. The results indicated that the application of the existing admissions criteria actually overestimated the future academic performance of 'culturally' disadvantaged students with borderline scores, i.e. relaxation of requirements increased student failure despite the additional assistance the students received. The experience has been reported to illustrate that 'a trade-off is usually involved in programs of preferential treatment' (Klitgaard 1991: 12). In Indonesia where quotas are employed to limit ethnic Chinese representation in élite universities, it is estimated that the inefficiency produced results in an increase of 12 per cent in the marginal cost per graduate due to poorer academic performance and greater likelihood of repetition and drop out (Klitgaard 1986).

In many developing countries, however, admission to public universities is very selective and based on student achievement in national examinations that minimize qualitative variations at the secondary level. Minor manipulations of admissions requirements are unlikely to seriously affect the quality of entrants. Requirements may be manipulated to alter patterns of participation at either the higher or secondary level, or at both levels as in Rwanda where regional and ethnic origin are taken into account in allocating the limited opportunities for post-primary education.

In Kenya, admission to teacher-training colleges is on the basis of a national examination with candidates ranked and selected by district to ensure 'national representation'. The intention is to raise the representation of students from rural and remote districts. A similar scheme is used to select students for entry into the élite provincial and extraprovincial public secondary schools that send a disproportionate share of their graduates to the public universities, which have so far successfully resisted manipulation of their entry requirements. Any negative impact of these measures on the quality of higher education is apt to be much less than the deleterious effects of the rapid expansion of enrolments since the introduction of the 8–4–4 system in 1985 (Eisemon 1988; Eisemon and Davis 1991).

In Uganda, bonus points have been introduced to increase the representation of women at Makerere University. Since 1990, 1.5 points have been added to the 'A' level examination scores of female applications to Makerere University. Admissions are determined by a complex weighting of students' examination scores. Minimum points are established for each degree programme. These ranged in 1990–1 from 9.8 points for admission to Education to study the teaching of Biology to 45 points for Pharmacy and 44.6 points for Law. The minimum for the general Arts degree was 13.6 points. The proportion of females admitted to the university increased from 23 per cent in 1989–90 to 30 per cent in 1990–1 when the bonus points scheme took effect. Yet prior to the introduction of this scheme, the proportion of female applications with qualifications to enter Makerere who were actually admitted reached the level for male applicants (World Bank 1992: 32). Females are less likely to enroll in faculties and professional programmes requiring passes in Science subjects at 'A' levels. Females accounted for 40 per cent of the total intake into arts programmes compared to 18 per cent into Science programmes in 1990–1. A higher proportion of applicants gain entry to Science programmes, but they take more difficult subjects at 'A' levels. The poor representation of females in Science-based programmes reflects the smaller proportion of females eligible for entry. Manipulation of the present bonus scheme to increase female representation in these programmes would probably have little effect in the light of the high proportion of qualified students already being admitted. The more serious problem is the low proportion of females who are taking advanced instruction in Science subjects at the secondary level.

Conclusion

Reforms responding to equity concerns address complex issues. Implementation of strategies to increase access to higher education through institutional proliferation, especially of teacher- and technical-training institutions, are the least politically controversial and in some countries, the most effective for increasing the participation of educationally and economically disadvantaged groups. However, they increase the costs to the state. The deteriorating financial situation experienced by many developing countries will make it increasingly difficult for governments to sustain such policies. In many countries, a choice will be made, de facto, between continuing to expand access or maintaining minimum standards in terms of quality of teaching and research. One manifestation of this evolution, particularly visible in the former French colonies of North and Sub-Saharan Africa, is the division of higher education into a dual system: on the one hand, resource-starved, mainstream universities and other institutions for 'the masses', and on the other hand a small network of good-quality programmes ('grandes écoles' and similar institutions, professional programmes with restricted access) for the better-qualified students.

The equity benefits of private higher education, fee-charging open universities and student loans are more difficult to assess. In many circumstances, they seem to increase higher-education participation for educationally and economically more advantaged groups which are not necessarily élite groups. The poor and most disadvantaged benefit more from selective state support allocated on the basis of merit.

Manipulation of meritocratic admissions criteria is fraught with difficulty. There may be important efficiency trade-offs where there are large qualitative variations in secondary education and/or where preferential treatment is deliberately designed more to penalize particular groups than to benefit others. In the final analysis, investment in the provision of good quality primary and lower secondary education for all children may be the best way to reduce inequalities at the higher-education level.

References

Albrecht, D. and Ziderman, A. (1991) 'Deferred Cost Recovery for Higher Education: Student Loan Programs in Developing Countries.' World Bank Discussion Papers, 137. Washington, DC, World Bank.

Bako, S. (1990) 'Education Adjustment in Africa: The Conditionality and Resistance Against the World Bank Loan for Nigerian Universities.' Paper presented to CODESRIA Symposium on Academic Freedom and the Social Responsibility of the Intellectual in Africa, 26–29 November, Kampala, Uganda.

Briones, G. (1992) 'La educación superior en el modelo de la economía neoliberal,' in *PIIE, Las Transformaciones Educacionales bajo el Regimen Militar.* Santiago, PIIE.

Chanana, K. (1992), 'Accessing higher education: The dilemma of schooling women, minorities, scheduled castes and scheduled tribes in contemporary India,' in P.G. Altbach and S. Chitnis (eds) *Higher Education Reform in India: Experience and Perspectives,* Chapter 4. Washington, DC, World Bank.

Eisemon, T.O. (1988). *Benefitting from Basic Education: School Quality and Functional Literacy in Kenya.* Oxford, Pergamon.

Eisemon, T.O. and Davis, C.H. (1991) 'Can the quality of scientific training and research in Africa be improved?', *Minerva,* 29, 1–26.

Galanter, M. (1984) *Competing Equalities: Law and the Backward Classes in India.* Berkeley, University of California Press.

Gopinathan, S. (1992) 'Higher Education in Singapore: A Study of Policy, Development, Financing and Governance, 1960–1990.' Paper presented to World Bank/EDI Regional Senior Policy Seminar on Higher Education, June 28–July 3, Singapore.

Klitgaard, R. (1986) *Élitism and Meritocracy in Developing Countries: Selection Policies for Higher Education.* Baltimore, Maryland, Johns Hopkins University.

Klitgaard, R. (1991) 'Access to Higher Education: Discussion.' Paper presented to the World Bank Worldwide Seminar on Innovation and Improvement of Higher Education in Developing Countries, June 30–July 4, Kuala Lumpur, Malaysia.

Levy, D.C. (1991) 'Problems of Privatization.' Paper prepared for the World Bank Worldwide Seminar on Innovation and Improvement of Higher Education in Developing Countries, June 30–July 4, Kuala Lumpur, Malaysia.

Majumdar, T. (1992) 'Higher Education in India, Development, Financing and Governance: 1960–90.' Paper prepared for the World Bank/EDI Regional Senior Policy Seminar on Higher Education, June 28–July 3, Singapore.

Stepanich, D., Kohenkul, N.S. and Chang-jai, K. (1991) 'Higher Education in Thailand.' Paper presented to the World Bank/EDI Regional Senior Policy Seminar on Higher Education, June 28–July 3, Singapore.

Swamy, V.C.K. (1992) 'The Open University', in P.G. Altbach and S. Chitnis (eds) *Higher Education Reform in India: Experience and Perspectives,* Chapter 11. Washington, DC, World Bank.

Tzannatos, Z. (1991) 'Reverse racial discrimination in higher education in Malaysia: has it reduced inequality and at what cost to the poor?', *International Journal of Educational Development,* 11(3), 177–192.

Weifang, M. (1991) 'A Comparative Study of Higher Education and Development in Selected Asian Countries 1960–1990: Country Case Analysis of China.' Paper presented to the World Bank/EDI Regional Senior Policy Seminar on Higher Education, June 28–July 3, Singapore.

Winkler, D.R. (1990) 'Higher Education in Latin America: Issues of Efficiency and Equity.' World Bank, Discussion Papers, 77. Washington, DC, World Bank.

Wolff, L., Albrecht, D. and Silba, A. (1992) 'Brazilian Higher Education in the Midst of Reform'. Washington, DC, World Bank.

World Bank (1986) *Financing Education in Developing Countries: An Exploration of the Policy Options.* Washington, DC, World Bank.

World Bank (1992) 'Strengthening the Policy Environment for Investment in University Development in Uganda': A draft report submitted to the Government and donors. Washington, DC, World Bank.

World Bank (1994) *Higher Education – The Lessons of Experience.* Washington DC, World Bank.

7

Changing Leadership in Universities

Robin Middlehurst

Introduction

> Wise and prudent people have long known that in a changing world worthy
> institutions can be conserved only by adjusting them to the changing time.
> (Adapted from Franklin D. Roosevelt 1936)

The title of this chapter is deliberately ambiguous. At first glance, it suggests both
that leadership in universities is changing and also that there is a need for university
leadership to change. A second glance may reveal further ambiguities, particularly associated with the idea of 'leadership'. Many will see leadership as the
domain of those in certain positions: vice-chancellors, deans, professors, heads of
department and heads of functional areas such as registry, catering or estates. Yet
leadership may also be understood as a function that is widely spread in an
institution, extending beyond the formal roles and responsibilities of senior post-
holders. Other commentators, focusing on democratic and collegial values and
traditions, may find the very notion of leadership a strange one in the context
of universities. It is the task of this chapter to address these ambiguities and to
pose four questions for further debate:

- Why discuss leadership in relation to universities and their future?
- How is the organizational and environmental context for leadership changing?
- What kind of leadership is appropriate for universities in the future?
- How can universities achieve the leadership needed?

Why leadership?

The concept and practice of leadership is intimately connected both to the interactions, ideas and beliefs of people and to the boundaries of time, place and
circumstance. The major disciplines in which the study of leadership is set –
psychology, sociology, politics, history, anthropology – reflect this dual influence

of people and context. So it is within these dimensions that some preliminary answers may be found to the question 'why discuss leadership?'

Any cursory examination of higher education in 1995 compared with 1975 will reveal a host of changes. Greater numbers and variety of institutions, greater numbers and variety of students, alterations in funding amounts and parameters, changes in institutional structures and in expectations of higher education have all occurred in this period. Nor is higher education unique in experiencing such large-scale changes. Many areas of the public sector have been or are being transformed (Pollitt 1990; Pettigrew *et al.* 1992); professionals and professional organizations are changing (Watkins *et al.* 1992; Middlehurst and Kennie 1994) and transformation in the private sector is widespread (Peters 1987; Beckhard and Pritchard 1992). A major theme of this period is 'change' and change of a 'discontinuous' kind (to quote Charles Handy 1989). If current predictions of future trends hold good, then this theme will continue and accelerate because of global technological, economic and political developments.

Several authors have noted the relationship between change and leadership. Adair (1983) suggests that a changing context creates instability, uncertainty and a need for adaptation in individual roles and attitudes as well as in organizational structures and cultures. The existence and the experience of a turbulent environment, he argues, creates both a psychological and a practical need for leadership. Adair also suggests, in common with Zaleznik (1977) and Bennis (1989), that those who are leaders will themselves initiate change, whether as a result of their own psycho-social make-up or as a result of the social and cultural expectations surrounding 'leadership'. The link between leadership and change can therefore be made from both a context-centred and a person-centred perspective: change creates the need for leadership and leaders are, or are perceived to be, initiators and drivers of change.

If we delve a little further into the nature of the changes that have been taking place in higher education, the connections between leadership and change can be amplified. Clearly, a significant change in recent times is that brought about by the Further and Higher Education Acts 1992 and the ending of the binary line. Beyond this change to the topography of higher education, lies another of similar significance: that is, the decline in resources available to institutions from the state purse, particularly in the light of increased numbers of students and increased demand for research activity. Adapting to financial stringency has caused changes in many areas of an institution: alternative sources of income have been sought, new markets for university services have been developed and efficiency drives have been mounted, including some major restructuring initiatives. The impact of financial shortfalls has been felt often in increased competition between institutions; in reduced academic salaries, relative to comparable occupations, and poorer working conditions; in the parlous state of many universities' physical plant and equipment; and in the extent and availability of support for students.

These economic changes have been accompanied by political shifts in the environment of universities. Changing ideologies, born out of the dominance of the New Right in national politics over the last fifteen years, have also had an impact. When combined with the effects of economic stringency, alternative values have emerged to challenge traditions of collegiality and collaboration, autonomy and individual freedom, committee and consensus decision-making. These alternative values include competition, accountability to stakeholders and 'managerialism'. The political and economic changes described here have set in train changes in the external relationships of universities, for example, with government, employers, industry or students, as well as changes in internal relationships within institutions. The interplay between people and context and between internal and external forces is clear.

If we return to leadership and its association with change, then further dimensions emerge. Political and economic pressures have encouraged a shift from 'administration' to 'management' in the day-to-day operations of universities, or a shift from coordination and implementation roles to greater directive control through a line-management structure. Competing resource priorities have meant that hard decisions and hard choices have had to be made, often very quickly. At the same time, the increasing size and scope of university business, as well as pressures for accountability, have encouraged a growth in the bureaucracy and complexity of day-to-day operations. These trends suggest that both management and leadership have become necessary. When choices are required, the vision and direction-setting tasks associated with leadership and the decision-taking and implementation systems associated with management are both needed.

A preliminary answer to our first question is revealed by the emphasis on the links between leadership and change. However, the ability to imagine, to create and to make choices is also important when balancing the dilemmas of conflicting priorities, alternative markets and missions, competing interests from diverse constituencies, or opposing traditions and values. Leadership is commonly associated with vision, ideas and ideals as well as the capacity to interpret and to stimulate positive perspectives about change. It can be argued that leadership is needed to cope both with the changes and the choices facing universities and that it is needed at many levels of an institution.

How is the context changing?

Judging by the number of influential reports that have been published recently about the future of higher education (fourteen between 1992 and 1994) there is considerable external interest in what that future should look like. The Department for Education, in November 1994, acknowledged these concerns by calling for a 'review of higher education' including a consideration of its purposes in the light of internal changes in higher education and the needs of a changing world. No doubt as 'end of century fever' increases, further reports will emerge. The content of these reports address both immediate requirements for change in higher education, caused by, for example, a changing student population (NIACE 1993) or a mass higher education system (CSUP 1992), and longer-term requirements arising out of economic and social imperatives (*Realising our Potential*, HMSO 1993; *Learning to Succeed*, NCE 1993). In this section, the issues that these reports deal with in relation to universities' external environment will be addressed briefly, before considering different perspectives on the internal organizational context for leadership. In reality it is difficult to separate the two because internal and external contexts continuously impact upon each other.

Environmental issues

Resources

Resource issues are likely to remain a dominant concern for universities. As Williams and Fry (1994) demonstrate, the question of resources includes the amount and sources of funds available to universities, the availability of appropriately qualified and skilled staff, and the adequacy of plant and equipment, including buildings, well-found laboratories and information technology systems. Competing for state funds (and shaping the methods of allocation), finding alternative sources of funding, investing in new developments and attracting and keeping good staff will continue to be a major focus of attention for those in leadership positions in universities.

Accountability

Accountability will also remain a central issue both for public and for private institutions. The meaning of the term has undergone some subtle shifts over time and may well take on new overtones in the future. In the early 1980s, accountability was principally associated with 'accounting for the use of public funds', that is, with being responsible for the allocation of these monies and able to demonstrate efficiency and value for money in the uses to which they were put. The principal focus of accountability was government as official sponsor of higher education and proxy for the tax payer.

In the 1990s, notions of accountability have broadened to include other aspects of accountability owed to a wider group of 'stakeholders'. First, there is accountability to students, subsumed under the broad banner of 'quality'. This emphasis is illustrated by the establishment in 1992 of the Higher Education Quality Council and the Funding Councils' Quality Assessment arrangements and by the publication of the *Higher Education Charters* in 1993. Students are to be seen as customers of higher education and universities are to be more explicitly accountable for the quality of the teaching and learning that they provide and clearer about the standards of the awards they offer. With a rise in the numbers of students (or their parents or employers) who are paying directly for their education, we can expect this trend to continue.

A second focus of accountability is to industry, or if interpreted more broadly, to the economy. This can have several aspects, for example: accountability for the quality of graduates produced and the relevance of their knowledge and skills in a variety of occupational settings; for the amount, accessibility and quality of continuing education and training in higher education; and for the value (both utilitarian and immediate, and long-term and strategic) of the research undertaken in universities. A third level of accountability and a more traditional one is to society at large. This kind of accountability extends from educating and developing 'good' citizens to protecting and extending our intellectual and cultural heritage in a rich variety of forms.

Many of these areas of 'accountability' are recognizable as key purposes of higher education (see Atkins *et al.* 1993, for example) linked to different social and economic interests and also to different market needs. What is changing is the sharpness of the focus on each and all of these purposes. Between 1960 and 1980, one could argue that the purposes of higher education were broadly understood and acceptable to all constituencies and that they existed more in soft than in sharp focus. In the 1990s and beyond, such a broad consensus appears to have broken down and in its place has emerged strong pressure on universities to clarify, make explicit, measure and bring into sharp focus their aims, intentions and claims on economy and society. Within institutions these pressures drive right to the heart of the curriculum and to academic professionalism. As with resource issues, the questions surrounding accountability in all its different guises will form a major leadership concern for the future.

Markets and competition

Thatcherite emphases on market values and competition as a means to improved performance have had an impact on universities and colleges. Maintaining a presence in the market (whether for consultancy or contract research) demands flexibility and responsiveness to new opportunities supported by a flexible infra-structure for decision-taking and delivery to time and cost. Similarly, the ability to penetrate new markets depends on a well-developed entrepreneurial infrastruc-ture and a culture of differentiation and 'customer care'. The tension between, on the one hand, traditional activities which receive state support but which are fettered by state regulations and a collective system based on consultation and consent, and on the other hand, new activities which are market-driven, less closely regulated, and which reflect individual opportunities will continue to exercise senior managers. These tensions are likely to increase as other specialist and private suppliers (of research, education, consultancy and awards) challenge higher education's key services and its home and overseas markets.

Williams and Fry (1994) point to potential conflicts for institutions between concentration on teaching or research (or both). The authors highlight 'the competing claims of institutional diversity, equivalence, equality and dispersion' (1994: 3), pointing out that the current rhetoric is about institutional differentia-tion of function, but much of the present reality is towards convergence. Intense competition between institutions, they argue, is a certain outcome of convergence, while specialization will provide more opportunities for collaboration. Very dif-ferent leadership approaches may be expected in each case.

Information technology

Many of those who write about the future argue that we are in the throes of a technological revolution even more far-reaching than earlier agricultural and industrial revolutions. However, several decades of work on technology's potential impact on organizations have produced more conflicting than common perspectives. Nonetheless, some general themes do emerge. These include, first, increased role complexity arising both out of 'new ways of doing things' and from increasing interdependence of tasks, roles and decision-making. Second, problem-focused teamwork is developing as a common way of working. Third, new measurement processes, based less on the individual and more on the group, are evolving to take account of cooperative work practices. Fourth, planning processes are changing as technology provides both the conduit for moving critical data to all relevant decision-makers and the capability to disseminate changes in direction to all parts of a business. And fifth, accessible and transparent information technology infrastructures are being put in place so that 'the management of interdependence' can be achieved effectively.

In higher education, several reports have discussed the ways in which technology may be harnessed in support of teaching and learning (CSUP 1992; Royal Society 1993), and van Ginkel (NCE 1994) speculates on the power of technology and the impact of it on the university as a whole. Many aspects of research, he notes, are no longer conceivable without high-tech apparatus, and the possibilities of artificial intelligence, virtual reality and interactive networks are limitless. Van Ginkel (1994: 77) poses the question, 'will the university of the future have no buildings at all, and simply consist of myriad international networks to which people are connected – a world-wide neurological system with a bulletin board at its heart?' If this kind of scenario were to evolve, then the nature of the leadership task in universities would be very different from present manifestations.

Organizational images

We have examined some major external influences on leadership in universities. Most of these influences are already causing changes in higher education; in the future, their impact is likely to be greater still. In this section, the spotlight will be turned on the internal cultural world of universities, a world that is made up of varied structures, systems, processes, histories, behaviours, attitudes and values. A medley of organizational images is presented with two intentions in mind. The first intention is to illustrate different aspects of university culture since each perspective will have different consequences for leadership. A second intention is to stimulate thought about a key task of strategic leadership, that is, organizational analysis and design. Developing the appropriate social architecture for an institution or organization is an important foundation for excellence (Sadler 1994). As Morgan (1986) and others suggest, each individual's cognitive paradigm will affect both their understanding of the world and their frameworks for action. By expanding the range of alternative perspectives of a university, among leaders and others, the potential for imagining and designing alternative ways of operating may be increased. To quote Gareth Morgan (1986: 343): 'Organisation is always shaped by underlying images and ideas; we organise as we imaginize [that is, by linking images to actions]; and it is always possible to imaginize in many different ways.'

Universities as communities of professionals

[Two common images are welded together here, the collegial and the university as a professional organization] While the former traditional image and its associated values is apparently under threat within UK higher education (Trow 1994), the latter image is gaining ground and may represent an important organizational 'phoenix' for the future.

Central to the vision of a community is a group of people (traditionally, individual scholars) working together to their mutual advantage in a democratic and cohesive self-governing enterprise. Collaboration combined with independence is valued highly. Organizational features linked to this image include: consensus decision-making; academic freedom; autonomy and self-governance; and limited hierarchy based on seniority and expertise. The professional image extends the value of 'independence' still further. Characteristics which are generally associated with professionals include: intellectual skills, usually demonstrated through higher education qualifications and professional training; a licence to practise on the basis of specialist knowledge and skills; services offered to clients; apprenticeship and socialization into the norms and procedures of the professional group; adherence to the standards and codes of practice established by a professional association; and autonomy and discretion in directing one's own work. A number of points of contact between the collegial and the professional perspectives are evident, for example, seniority and expertise as a source of authority and influence; individualism, self-management and discretion over work; some collective interests, shared for purposes of self-protection, self-regulation, political lobbying and development of the profession or discipline; and a strong belief in and need for autonomy.

Universities as political bureaucracies

Once again, two well-known images are linked here (Weber 1947; Baldridge 1971). Within the political perspective, features of difference and competition within the institution are highlighted in contrast to the collegial/professional features of shared interests and cooperation described above. Differences arise out of competing values and territories (see Becher 1989, in relation to disciplinary differences); varied tasks, strategies and clients; and resource, power and status differentials between individuals and groups within the institution. All these features create a potential for conflict. Within the political perspective, the goals of the organization are assumed to be unstable, often ambiguous and contested, and decisions are seen to emerge after 'complex processes of bargaining, negotiation and jockeying for position among individuals and groups' (Bolman and Deal 1984: 109).

While a political image concentrates on conflict and competition and the often messy reality of achieving compromise, a bureaucratic perspective focuses upon order, coordination, regulation and control through systematic and rational processes. Central features of a bureaucracy include: a hierarchical structure of formal chains of command; carefully defined roles and responsibilities; circumscribed functional groupings (departments, units); and systematic rules and procedures based on clear policies and agreed goals. Bureaucratic structures and processes are associated with organizational complexity (that is, they offer a means of reducing chaos and ambiguity) and with formality (that is, the expectation that the organization exists to pursue official purposes and is accountable to sponsors for the achievement of those purposes).

Both of these perspectives operate in universities today, bureaucratic features having gained ground with the increasing intrusion of the state into university affairs (Tapper and Salter 1992) and with the rise of managerialism in universities (Pollitt 1990; Trow 1994). The political perspective appears also to have become stronger, particularly as a means of dealing with the external environment (of sponsors, clients and stakeholders) but also as a means of coping with the pluralist internal environment of universities and colleges.

Systems perspectives of universities: entrepreneurial; cybernetic; electronic

Underlying more recent perspectives on universities is the image of the institution as a system of interacting elements. Each element or component has boundaries which are more or less open and permeable and each will exhibit different levels of dependency and integration between itself and other elements (Moran 1972; Weick 1976). 'The university' may be thought of as a concentrated system linked to a variety of other systems (for example, the wider economy, local communities, funding councils, schools and employers, international research teams) in a network of relationships and interactions. The precise boundary between one system and another (for example, between further and higher education, or between various aspects of collaborative provision) is not always clear and a central leadership task is likely to involve 'boundary management', both practically and symbolically.

The entrepreneurial and the cybernetic images use the metaphor of the institution as a dynamic system. The entrepreneurial image extends in two directions: towards the notion of markets in which the institution operates through a series of trading and exchange relationships (Schmidtlein 1991) and towards the notion of the institution as a living organism, existing in a largely symbiotic relationship with its host society and engaging in a series of adaptive strategies to maintain this relationship (Davies 1987). The cybernetic image focuses upon the organization as a brain, capable of being flexible, resilient and inventive when faced with new situations (Morgan 1986), while also being able to operate as a self-correcting system controlled in part by negative feedback loops (Bensimon *et al.* 1989). An electronic (or perhaps neurological) image continues the metaphor, taking the logic of technological developments forward towards the creation of an electronic centre linked to myriad interconnecting networks and outstations which now represent the operations and structures of the university. Individuals (whether students, teachers, consultants or researchers – the roles are likely to merge) may be widely spread in locations around the globe, linked organizationally and intellectually through an internet system.

These different images of organization are likely to produce different kinds of leadership. The style that is appropriate and the function that leadership performs within and on behalf of the organization is also likely to vary. These issues are explored next.

What kind of leadership?

Expectations of leadership

Those who search for a single brand of leadership in universities or elsewhere are likely to be disappointed. Thinkers and researchers over centuries have considered and investigated individual personality and gender characteristics, behavioural traits, group interactions, organizational features, environmental pressures and cultural factors as determinants of leadership and leader style. While all of these have an acknowledged impact on leadership, no single view has emerged of which variables are most significant or whether it is possible to isolate an approach to leadership which transcends context and circumstance (Middlehurst 1993). In recent interviews with a small group of Chairs of Council/Boards of Governors in universities, the great variety of forms and styles of institutional leadership were a focus of comment; this variety is likely to be magnified still further if one considers all types of academic leaders (from philosophers to computer scientists, zoologists to fine artists) in addition to leadership within other staff and student groups in the university.

The question of 'what leadership?' is further complicated by two important issues. The first is the ambiguity contained in interpretations of the term 'leadership'. The term is commonly used both to denote the attributes and role of an individual 'leader' and to describe the attributes associated with a particular organizational or group function called 'leadership'. A second issue arises from different perspectives on the nature of organizational reality and from different understandings of causal relationships in organizations. Are leaders those who actually cause organizations to be successful or is the descriptor of 'successful leader/leadership' merely attributed following organizational successes which may in reality have been brought about by many other factors? Does leadership lie in the expectations of followers and observers or in the actions of leaders?

These two issues add up to more than semantics since they are likely to affect the way in which leadership is 'imaginized' (see Morgan 1986, *vide supra*) by those in leadership positions, by followers and constituents, and by key stakeholders. Where leadership is only associated with an individual and his/her actions and style, great pressure and responsibility is placed on key individuals (vice-chancellors or heads of department, for example) or groups (for example, senior management teams) to do leader-like things such as produce visions, motivate others and manage change. Indeed, most of those entering leadership positions are likely to construe their roles in these terms (Birnbaum 1989).

Contrastingly, where leadership is interpreted as a function or key task at different points in the organization, responsibility can be widely shared and can be performed by many individuals or groups within the institution. In both cases, the role that expectations play in shaping the concept and the practice of leadership must not be underestimated. What is regarded as appropriate leadership by a group and what will work in practice are often closely connected. Research on women and leadership highlights this point (Eagly and Johnson 1990). Although researchers have found it difficult to isolate particular 'female styles' of leadership independent of personality differences, stereotypes of both gender styles and leader styles have created conflicts which researchers have noted. Where male 'macho' styles have been regarded as appropriate for leadership but not for women, female leaders have faced the choice of acting out the stereotypes and being seen as effective, but 'non-feminine', or rejecting them and being regarded, potentially, as weak or ineffective leaders (Eagly *et al.* 1992). Expectations or 'mind-sets' about leadership appear to have a strong influence on practice.

The above comments are preliminaries to our third question. More flesh can be put on these bones if we examine different leadership approaches associated with the organizational images above. The particular economic, social and psychological state of an institution (or group) at a particular time is likely to be of considerable importance for leadership. In effect, these create another set of expectations for leaders. For example, in the author's interviews with Chairs of Council and Governing Boards, it was interesting to hear how, in their judgement, the choice of vice-chancellor was shaped by the particular circumstances of each university, the immediate history of the institution and the perceptions of those involved in the search process as to what 'type' of university theirs was and the particular niche that they wished to occupy. Individual leaders were chosen on the basis of their practical and symbolic contribution to these visions, the future being seen very much through interpretations of the present. In other cases, the degree of change that is affecting an institution or whole sector often results in calls for visionary and transformational leadership in order to avert a crisis or to revolutionize an institution's way of operating (Fisher 1984). It is with these considerations in mind that we can examine links between organizational image and leadership style.

Leadership styles

Within a collegial/professional perspective, leaders are viewed either as servants of the group or as representatives of the group's aspirations and achievements. Leadership is based on consultation, persuasion, negotiation and the development of consent, if not consensus. Authority and influence, based on expertise and professional credibility, can be exercized because 'the group' has ceded some of its autonomy in exchange for certain 'goods', for example, protection, economic resources, and an organizational framework which allows professional freedom to be exercized. This kind of leadership is largely transactional in nature and is constrained by strong cultural expectations (Burns 1978; Hollander 1987). One might describe this as a 'provider' perspective on leadership since the needs and interests of the professionals are paramount.

The role of leader is at the same time emblematic, symbolizing the values of the group (through personal background as well as approach) and active in terms of advancing the interests of the group through lobbying, negotiation and articulation of the group's needs, interests and standards. There is an expectation that formal leaders will consult and communicate widely and that other professionals will participate in shaping the direction of the unit/institution. Other forms of leadership (informal or professional) may also be widely spread across the institution, as individuals exercise individual freedom in different areas.

Taking a political or bureaucratic perspective of the organization leads to different views of leadership. Bearing in mind that a political perspective implies conflict and competition between groups, one ('Theory X') view of leadership is likely to see the leadership task as one of controlling information and resources and making use of status and power differentials to divide, rule and gain advantage (McGregor 1960). An alternative perspective ('Theory Y') will recognize legitimate differences of values and interest and will see the leadership task as working towards acceptable goals through joint problem-solving, negotiation, mediation and compromise. Diplomacy, persuasion, the establishment of networks and a keen sense of timing are likely to be important skills.

The essence of bureaucratic leadership (often interpreted as 'managerialism' in universities) is depicted as making decisions and designing systems of control and coordination that direct the work of others so that compliance with policy and directives is assured. Leadership is ascribed to the individual (or small group) at the apex of a hierarchy, who is assumed to set the tone of the organization and to establish its official objectives. The leader may be seen in heroic terms as the fount of authority, ultimate arbiter, chief problem-solver and defender of the enterprise – or alternatively, as chief controller and dictator.

As with the juxtaposition of political and bureaucratic perspectives, combining systems images into a single perspective does not do justice to the richness of each one. However, certain features can be emphasized. Focusing first on an entrepreneurial image, the leadership task is concerned with assisting the institution to take account of, adapt to and interact creatively with the external environment. In practice, the role will include facilitating and regulating the delivery of services by the operating units; developing and enacting a vision for the institution (or unit); political lobbying; business and market planning; risk analysis; incentive building; effective processes of staff selection, appraisal and development; and regular evaluation of individual, group and institutional performance (Davies 1987).

The cybernetic image differs in important respects in that the organizational infrastructure and the cultural norms and operating patterns of the institution, 'structures and processes' (Becher and Kogan 1992), are assumed to be 'self-correcting' and capable of working independently of individual proactive leadership. Where the systems are operating smoothly, a leader's task will involve monitoring performance against priorities so that negative feedback is acted upon and potential imbalances are adjusted. The leadership role in the first instance will include the establishment of priorities, the design of appropriate early warning and communication systems, the coordination and balancing of the various sub-systems within the institution and the directing of attention, symbolically and actively, towards the priority areas (Birnbaum 1988).

Leadership is interpreted much more as steerage and guidance than as command and control within the cybernetic image. However, a steady-state environment is an important prerequisite. Where turbulence and crisis exist, a shift from 'single-loop' (action–feedback–response) to 'double-loop' learning (action–feedback–re-evaluation–change) may be required (Morgan 1986). Whereas in the former case, leadership will involve being able to detect and correct deviations from pre-set norms, the latter case will involve both the seeking of feedback about existing practices and a critical questioning of the relevance and effectiveness of current norms and practices. In consequence, radical changes may be put in train. The questions that underpin the current Quality Council Audit (HEQC 1993) process provide a stimulus for this kind of leadership action, for example:

- What are we trying to do (as an institution/unit/programme/individual)?
- Why are we trying to do this?
- How are we doing it (and how well)?
- Why are we doing it this way?
- Why do we think this is the best way?
- How do we know that this way works?
- How might we do things differently/better?

'Distance leadership' as one might call leadership via an electronic network, might take a number of forms. It may closely resemble the cybernetic image with the principal activities being steerage and regulation of a network or series of networks; it may mean that leadership is widely dispersed among different individuals within different networks; or it may make any current notions of leadership redundant. In order to obtain a sufficient degree of leverage over the knowledge that is created and transmitted or the transmission media (or both), institutions may need to collaborate more closely, to enter into new strategic alliances or to develop new learning technologies and means of interaction with learners. To achieve any of these will require political skills, initiative and imagination, as well as large-scale training programmes for staff. The transition from traditional forms of higher education to electronic forms may demand 'transformational' leadership of a kind not yet experienced in higher education.

The images of leadership and organizations described here rarely exist as pure models. Parts of each institution may come closer to a particular image and formal leaders (for example, in the office of vice-chancellor, dean of director of estates) may adopt a range of styles in different circumstances. Common to each style is the idea of leadership as 'a process of social influence whereby a leader (or group of leaders) steers members of a group towards a goal' (Bryman 1992: 2). Effective leadership can then be described in terms of goal achievement, although in higher education other factors are also included in definitions of effectiveness, for example, resource acquisition and constituent satisfaction (Bensimon *et al.* 1989). None of these elements is straightforward: multiple legitimate goals exist in universities; resource acquisition relies on tapping a range of sources for funds, physical plant and equipment or for human resources; and many constituencies with different needs must be satisfied. Effective leadership in practice is likely to involve constantly balancing dilemmas and conflicting priorities

Leadership as a function

In previous sections, leadership has been examined through the lens of differing expectations and of different styles. An alternative perspective is now offered, namely a view of leadership as an organizational rather than a unique and personal function. Within this perspective, the need for leadership within an organization or group is accepted, but this need does not have to be satisfied only by inspirational leaders. One example is provided from a Canadian study of Public Services (Auditor General 1990) which examined the impact of values on service and performance highlighted both the holistic nature of the leadership task and the need for initiative and engagement by individuals at many levels with the changes being developed in an organization. This perspective is consistent with the organizational form of many universities where leadership is often widely dispersed, particularly in devolved systems. For example, leadership can exist at course team or research team level and at professorial and institutional levels. Leadership may also take different forms, academic, professional, administrative/managerial or educational (in the widest sense of that term.) The nature of the leadership task at different levels of the institution or in different arenas is likely to include different elements, but each can contribute to the whole. These elements may be symbolic, they may include cultural dimensions, they often require the use of different forms of power and influence, different styles and behaviours or different individual attributes or characteristics.

Another variant is to view leadership as a function that can be performed through systems as well as people. The Total Quality 'gurus', including Deming, Juran and Crosby (Bendell 1991) have contributed to this notion with their emphases on improving systems and information in organizations and through focusing on the analysis, design and control of key processes. Where information for decisions is at the fingertips of many individuals, where detailed understanding of key processes and the 'quality chain' is widespread and where appropriate behaviour is conditioned by the operation of effective systems, the need for inspirational or exhortative leadership may be reduced. In combination, effective systems, timely and relevant information and common understanding of key processes may act as substitutes for certain kinds of leadership (Kerr and Jermier 1978).

Leadership characteristics and capacities

By far the most common view of leadership relates to the personal attributes of individuals. In a recent Australian report on 'Leadership for quality in higher education', six leadership constructs were identified among a survey of 142 senior staff (Australian Centre in Strategic Management 1994). Top of the list were personal attributes, followed by management style, people/interpersonal skills, cognitive skills (capacity/thinking/analysis), vision/mission/strategic elements and general management skills.

The Australian study is interesting in investigating perceptions of leadership from those at different levels of an institution. All leaders rated the following characteristics as of primary importance:

- being open and honest with staff
- communicating information freely to staff
- following through on decisions and plans

- expecting ethical practice from staff
- basing decisions on reasoning, appropriate data and information
- managing budgets

However, there was variety between strategic leaders, managers of general staff and heads of school in relation to other aspects of leadership. Senior managers gave priority to organizational and strategic issues; managers of general staff units emphasized service to internal customers, seeing themselves as resources supporting staff, while the heads of school placed most importance on academic leadership. This last included being active in research, providing a role model for academic staff, representing the profession and providing informal guidance to junior staff.

In discussions with chairs of council/governors, it was clear to the author that individual characteristics and capacities were regarded as important in the selection process for vice-chancellors; they are also recognized as important for other leadership positions in higher education as job and person specifications indicate. However, these characteristics may need to extend more widely than among formal leaders and the kind of capacities sought for leadership may also need to be broadened to include some of those identified within other organizational settings, as described above.

How can universities achieve the leadership needed?

For leadership to flourish in universities a number of conditions need to be met. The nature of the leadership task needs to be appreciated widely, the need for leadership must be recognized and effort needs to be expended on understanding and developing leadership appropriate to the pluralist world of higher education. In all of these areas, it can be argued, universities face an uphill task in achieving the leadership they will need to survive and prosper into the twenty-first century and beyond. The reasons for this are threefold.

First, understanding of the scale and, particularly, the longer-term consequences of the changes that are in train does not appear to be widespread among all staff in institutions. As a result, internal pressure for the kind of 'transformational' leadership that is likely to be needed to address fundamental questions about the goals and future directions for higher education is not evident. The impact of change is certainly felt among staff, for example in heavier workloads, in changing roles and in new working patterns, but most institutions are still focusing their response to a shifting environment on changes in management structures and procedures rather than on any serious review of values, purposes and future scenarios, particularly across the sector as a whole. Changes that are occurring in universities and colleges are still perceived by many staff as an irritating and unjustified intrusion by the external world into the autonomous world of higher education. The intrusion is seen as unjustified since academic work is often considered self-evidently worthwhile both for internal regenerative purposes and for the social, cultural and economic benefit of students and society at large. Unfortunately, the utilitarian demands of 'society' (as reflected in recent reports) appear to challenge the notion that higher education *is* self-evidently worthwhile, seeking instead a rationale and a focus that is more open to the interests of different stakeholders. At the same time, the technology of knowledge is developing at such a rate that traditional balances of power and authority, where universities reigned supreme, may well be upset. In short, the whole *raison d'être* of universities – including both 'their mystery and their mastery' – is being challenged from a number of directions. Academics as a group will need to view their work from the perspective of external interests in order to evaluate it and explain it while also seeking to educate (or re-educate) external groups about the unique contributions of higher education to a changing society. Visionary and sensitive leadership is needed to help such 'inside–out and outside–in' thinking to take place. Yet until the nature of the leadership task is fully recognized, it will be difficult to accept the need for leadership of this kind within and across institutions.

Secondly, the notion of leadership is either frowned upon as antipathetic to individual autonomy and collective democracy or is embraced with crusader-like zeal by those in positions of formal authority. Neither response is appropriate. Instead, forms of leadership which empower individuals and groups rather than seeking to dominate them, which encourage and reward creativity and which can flourish throughout the institution are required. A degree of individual freedom may need to be ceded in exchange for collective advantage. Achieving this kind of leadership, particularly from within higher education is likely to be made still harder by the necessity of challenging various aspects of the status quo, for example, internal demarcations between academic and non-academic, between learners and teachers, between high-status and low-status groups (researchers and teachers; men and women; contract or part-timers and full-timers) or the balance between education, scholarship and research within an institution or unit. While variety and difference is of value, traditional boundaries are often anachronistic and detrimental to necessary re-evaluations of purpose, role and contribution within individual institutions and across the whole enterprise of higher education.

The third reason for taking a pessimistic view about leadership in universities is that little or no serious and systematic attention is given to the development of leadership among staff in higher education. This is perhaps surprising since academics, at least, strive to be leaders in their discipline or specialist field and leaders within their programme or research teams. We can perhaps trace the roots of this lack of attention either to negative attitudes towards management (and by association to formal leadership) or to negative views of training and development, or to both. In research into leadership development in universities, the author noted that certain 'cults' seemed to operate in relation to leadership development (Middlehurst 1993: 178), particularly among senior staff, for example:

- The cult of the gifted amateur (any intelligent, educated individual can undertake the task – in this case, leadership – without training).
- The cult of heredity (those with natural talent will emerge since they are born to the task; and furthermore, leadership is an art and therefore unteachable).
- The cult of deficiency (training is essentially remedial or for those who are personally ineffective; 'training is for the second eleven' as one pro-vice-chancellor put it).

- The cult of inadequacy (once qualified, loss of face is involved by admitting gaps in one's knowledge or competence).
- The cult of the implicit (development takes place by gradual induction into the norms and operations of academe; learning by osmosis is the hallmark of success).
- The cult of selection (the selection of 'good' staff will ensure good performance and will obviate the need for – and the cost of – development).
- The cult of the intellectual (there is no scientific basis to 'management' or 'leadership', therefore it does not deserve to be taken seriously).

Given that higher education is an important training ground for many professions, the 'entrenched amateurism' (as one Australian colleague put it) displayed in relation to investigating and preparing for leadership and governance – if not also to other aspects of professional development for staff in higher education – should at least give pause for thought. By not investing in training and development for their own leaders, universities are vulnerable to imported models; and in promoting training, development and education for others but not for themselves they are potentially guilty of hypocrisy.

Conclusions

Higher education is in a state of flux, but as much (or more) in response to pressures from outside as from within. To regain the initiative, to establish pride and trust in higher education and to shape change within and outside institutions, requires educational and administrative leadership. To achieve the kind of leadership appropriate to the task and the need, leadership must be understood and valued widely within institutions. This requires analysis, experiment, reflection and development as well as a degree of integrity, initiative and imagination among managers and staff alike. Surely these qualities have traditionally been the hallmarks of our centres of learning – do we need to re-invent them?

References

Adair, J. (1983) *Effective Leadership*. London, Pan.

Atkins, M.J., Beattie, J. and Dockrell, W.B. (1993) *Assessment Issues in Higher Education*. Sheffield, Employment Department.

Australian Centre in Strategic Management and Management Information Systems (1994) *Leading for Quality in Higher Education: a report to the Australian Government Department of Employment, Education and Training*. Brisbane, Queensland University of Technology Publications.

Baldridge, J. (1971) *Power and Conflict in the University*. New York, John Wiley.

Becher, T. (1989) *Academic Tribes and Territories: Intellectual Enquiry and the Cultures of Disciplines*. Buckingham, SRHE and Open University Press.

Becher, T. and Kogan, M. (1992) *Process and Structure in Higher Education*, 2nd edn. London, Routledge.

Beckhard, R. and Pritchard, W. (1992) *Changing the Essence: The Art of Creating and Leading Fundamental Change in Organizations*. San Francisco, Jossey Bass.

Bendell, T. (1991) *The Quality Gurus*. London, Department of Trade and Industry.

Bennis, W. (1989) *On Becoming a Leader*. London, Hutchinson.

Bensimon, E., Neumann, A. and Birnbaum, R. (1989) *Making Sense of Administrative Leadership: The 'L' Word in Higher Education*, Higher Education Report no. 1. Washington, DC, ASHE/ERIC.

Birnbaum, R. (1988) *How Colleges Work: The Cybernetics of Academic Organization and Leadership*. San Francisco, Jossey Bass.

Birnbaum, R. (1989) 'The implicit leadership theories of college and university presidents', *Review of Higher Education*, 12, 125–36.

Bolman, L.G. and Deal, T.E. (1984) *Modern Approaches to Understanding and Managing Organizations*. San Francisco, Jossey Bass.

Bryman, A. (1992) *Charisma and Leadership in Organizations*. London, Sage.

Burns, J.M. (1978) *Leadership*. New York, Harper and Row.

Davies, J.L. (1987) 'The entrepreneurial and adaptive university: report of the second US study visit,' *International Journal of Institutional Management in Higher Education*, 11(1), 12–104.

Eagly, A.H. and Johnson, B.T. (1990) 'Gender and leadership style: a meta-analysis,' *Psychological Bulletin*, 108, 233–256.

Eagly, A.H., Makhijani, M.G. and Klonsky, B.G. (1992) 'Gender and the evaluation of leaders: A meta-analysis.' *Psychological Bulletin*, 111, 3–22.

Fisher, J.L. (1984) *The Power of the Presidency* New York, Macmillan.

Handy, C. (1989) *The Age of Unreason*. London, Business Books.

Higher Education Quality Council (1993) *Notes for the Guidance of Auditors*. Birmingham, HEQC.

HMSO (1993) *Realising Our Potential: A Strategy for Science, Engineering and Technology*. London, HMSO.

Hollander, E.P. (1987) *College and University Leadership from a Social Psychological Perspective: a Transactional View*. Columbia University, New York, National Centre for Post-Secondary Governance and Finance, Teachers College.

Kerr, S. and Jermier, J.M. (1978) Substitutes for leadership: their meaning and measurement, *Organizational Behaviour and Human Performance*, 22, 375–403.

MacFarlane, A. (1992) *Teaching and Learning in an Expanding Higher Education System*. Edinburgh, Committee of Scottish University Principals.

McGregor, D. (1960) *The Human Side of Enterprise*. New York, McGraw Hill.

Middlehurst, R. (1993) *Leading Academics*. Buckingham, SRHE and Open University Press.

Middlehurst, R. and Kennie, T. (1994) 'Leadership and Professionals: Comparative Frameworks.' Paper presented at the 17th Annual Conference of the European Association for Institutional Research, Amsterdam, 20–23 August 1994.

Moran, W.E. (1972) 'A systems view of university organization.' In Hamelman, P.W. (ed.) *Managing the University: A Systems Approach*. New York, Praeger.

Morgan, G. (1986) *Images of Organization*. London, Sage.

National Commission on Education (1993) *Learning to Succeed*. London, Heinemann.

National Commission on Education (1994) *Universities in the 21st Century* Lecture series at The Royal Society. London, NCE.

National Institute of Adult and Continuing Eduction (1993) 'An Adult Higher Education: A Vision.' Policy discussion paper. Leicester, NIACE.

Peters, T. (1987) *Thriving on Chaos*. London, Pan.

Pettigrew, A., Ferlie, E. and McKee, L. (1992) *Shaping Strategic Change: Making Change in Large Organizations – The Case of the NHS*. London, Sage.

Pollitt, C. (1990) *Managerialism and the Public Services: the Anglo-American Experience*. Oxford, Blackwell.

Report of Auditor General, Canada (1990) *Values, Service and Performance*, 7.1–7.92.

The Royal Society (1993) *Towards a Partnership, Higher Education Futures*. London, The Royal Society.

Sadler, P. (1994) *Designing Organizations*, 2nd edn. London, Kogan Page.

Tapper, T. and Salter, B. (1992) *Oxford, Cambridge and the Changing Idea of the University*. Buckingham, SRHE and Open University Press.

Trow, M. (1994) *Managerialism and the Academic Profession: Quality and Control*. Quality Support Centre, HE Report, no. 2. London, Open University.

Watkins, J., Drury, L. and Preddy, D. (1992) *From Evolution to Revolution: the Pressures on Professional Life in the 1990s*. Bristol, University of Bristol.

Weber, M. (1947) *The Theory of Economic and Social Organization* (transl. A.M. Henderson and T. Parsons). First published, 1921. New York, Free Press.

Weick, K.E. (1976) 'Educational organizations as loosely-coupled systems', *Administrative Science Quarterly*, 21(1), 1–19.

Williams, G. and Fry, H. (1994) *Longer Term Prospects for Higher Education: A Report to the CVCP*. London, Institute of Education.

Van Ginkel, H. (1994) 'University 2050: the organization of creativity and innovation', in *Universities in the 21st Century*, pp. 65–86. London, NCE.

Zaleznik, A. (1977) 'Managers and leaders: are they different?' *Harvard Business Review*, 55, 67–78.

8

Evolving Roles and Responsibilities: The University in Africa

Alison Girdwood

Introduction

This chapter looks at the way in which the university was established as an institution in Africa, and the roles it has been expected to fulfil during its short history. The chapter gives a brief overview of the conditions currently experienced by many African universities, linking these to the structures and expectations created by the commissions which set up the first major African universities. The legacy created by the establishment of a specific model of higher education has contributed in part to the difficulties experienced by African universities today. While such difficulties are by no means unique to Africa, the scale of their impact upon institutions has been considerably more severe than in many parts of the world. Deteriorating conditions brought about by under-resourcing and rapidly rising enrolments have been exacerbated both by the financial conditions in the African continent, and by the nature of the relationship between universities and the state in many African countries. Discussion in this chapter is limited largely to Anglophone Sub-Saharan Africa, and specifically excludes South Africa, where educational structures are very different and are bound up with that country's political character and history.

Background

There are approximately 97 universities in Africa today, most of them public institutions funded almost entirely by government. While they were established in different phases, many of the Anglophone universities were built on a model selected in the 1940s – basically a high-cost, residential institution, established out of town, and thus having a separate infrastructure of roads, housing, sanitation systems, etc. and a large number of staff employed in service roles. Traditionally, although this pattern is changing, students have not paid fees, and have been paid living allowances (sometimes equivalent to or even above an average wage). Universities were initially well equipped, and were intended to be research institutions which could participate in international fora. Many were established as small élite institutions, and are now catering for a mass education system with budgets which have declined in real terms and inadequate (or poorly maintained) facilities. Research output is low.

Despite the rapid growth in the number of institutions (from six in 1960 to the present number), and rising enrolments, the participation rate remains low: a recent study has shown that for the 36 African nations for which data were available over the period 1975–90, the average enrolment ratio for Sub-Saharan Africa was 178 per 100 000 inhabitants. Comparative figures were 845 for Asia, 1849 for Latin America and 3045 for the G-10 countries (the USA, Canada, UK, Germany, France, Italy, Japan, Sweden, the Netherlands and Belgium) (Negrao 1994: 13). Further, a 1988 World Bank study estimated that the proportion of tertiary graduates in African populations was 0.4 per cent, whereas in other developing countries the figure was closer to 6 per cent (World Bank 1988: 70). Despite these figures, expenditure upon higher education as a proportion of education budgets is high, largely because of the high-cost model of higher education, and the fact that cost-recovery (from students) is low.

To speak of 'the African University' is of course an oversimplification; there is no such thing. There are other types of universities, notably the Francophone model (also high cost), the land-grant model transported from the USA (e.g. Nsukka University in Nigeria), and there are a few private institutions (largely religious in origin). Nonetheless, there are certain broadly observable features in higher education across Sub-Saharan Africa, and there is a long tradition of attempts to define precisely what 'the African university' is, and how it should serve its nation. Critical and reflective works have been published from the 1960s to the present (Unesco 1963; Yesufu 1973; World Bank 1988; Brown Sherman 1990; Coombe 1991; Ajayi *et al.* 1994), and these overlap with a series of theoretical works on the role of the university in the development process (Thompson and Fogel 1976; Hetland 1984; Coleman, with Court 1993). However, despite these, and despite recent attempts to further this debate (the Association of African Universities commissioned a number of publications for discussion at a major colloquium on the issue in January 1995), many institutions are simply too busy merely coping with adverse circumstances to have much opportunity to reflect upon their contribution to the development process and their role within their societies.

How did this situation arise? Leaving aside the unexpectedly difficult economic situation in Sub-Saharan Africa, why was the model of a high-cost institution with residential accommodation introduced as a norm for the continent, when it must have been apparent that it would not be financially sustainable? For Anglophone universities, the answer lies in colonial history, during the period at which it was becoming apparent that independence would be granted to the (then) British colonies.

The emergence of the African university

It is perhaps worth pausing to look briefly at the history of the African university, and its peculiar position within the public consciousness of many countries. Its history is closely bound with the hopes and aspirations of the immediate post-independence period, when the university as an institution was assigned an important part in the twin processes of nation-building and development. Expectations of the university were unrealistically high, and the functions it was expected to fulfil grew as the needs of the emerging nations became apparent. Disillusion now reflects – to a certain extent – the frustration and disillusionment of Africa's post-independence history; or, as a recent study has (perhaps controversially) described it, the 'transition from colonialism to neo-colonialism, increasing dependence and under-development' (Ajayi *et al.* 1994: 48).

Some of the published commentaries appear to suggest that there has been a fall from a former 'golden age' of African university education. While this is debatable (King 1991), it is true that the African university became a cherished symbol, closely bound up as its emergence was with the independence of the continent from colonial domination in the 1960s. Examples of the aspirations which African universities, once established, were required to fulfil abound in the literature (Unesco 1963: 17):

> As [a world institution] it must assume the basic functions and responsibilities that attach to a university: to teach and impart knowledge as an end in itself and for the edification of society; to seek and discover Truth which for centuries has defied the genius of man; to disseminate its finding to all, so that mankind generally and the African in particular may shed the shackles of ignorance and want, and the world may be a better place in which to live . . . As the birth of the truly African university is coeval with national independence, so will African freedom be dependent upon the continued existence and vitality of the university.

As any student of education, particularly in developing countries, will know, education holds a strong significance in countries where educational attainment may represent the only means of escape from wretched economic circumstances (Assie-Lumumba 1993: 64). Beyond this, however, there was always a great longing for higher education in Africa, from well before the arrival of independence in the early 1960s, with the university as an institution acquiring deeply symbolic connotations. From the latter part of the nineteenth century, there had been a number of articulate and impassioned calls for the provision of higher education in Africa from well-educated professional Africans (almost exclusively in West Africa), and from missionaries, who had provided the first educational opportunities for Africans, at a time when this was not a priority for colonizing nations. There were some early achievements such as Liberia College at Monrovia, which formally opened in January 1862, and Cuttington College in Harper, Cape Palmas, which opened in 1889 (Brown Sherman 1990). Fourah Bay College, a theological seminary in Sierra Leone, was founded in 1827 and introduced courses in higher education in 1876, in response to heavy demand from students. It was affiliated to Durham University, was expected to be self-funding, charged fees and was almost always in financial difficulties (Ashby 1966).

Higher education for Africans was not, however, given serious consideration by the British governments until well into the twentieth century, when British policy towards the colonies had changed, and self-rule was seen as a likelihood. Only when financial provision was potentially available under the Colonial Development and Welfare Act 1940 was there any realistic prospect of a system of higher education.

After much consideration of which type of higher education to introduce, the model selected was that of the high-cost, internationally recognized élite institution. The Asquith Report, entitled *The Report of the Commission on Higher Education in the Colonies* (Cmnd. 6647, 1945), was thus to be of great significance for African universities, as it established a pattern of higher education which was to outlast the concepts on which it had itself been founded. The report was stated as a fundamental principle that 'An institution with the status of a university which does not command the respect of other universities brings no credit to the community which it serves' (Asquith 1945: 13), and the so-called 'Asquith Colleges' were therefore linked in a formal relationship with the University of London, to ensure that their standards were equivalent to those in British universities. The early African universities were designed to train the élite for leadership, and to provide breadth and depth of education, rather than narrow professional training. This system had a specific and finite task: that of preparing peoples for self-government (Asquith 1945: 14). However, once self-government had been achieved, it would follow that provision of education would have to broaden, and it was already known that demand was high. Long-term projections were not, however, included within the report's recommendations, nor were these issues given attention.

The 1960s saw large-scale expansion, and a change in the rationale for higher education. A major influence on the development of higher education was the report of the Ashby Commission on post-secondary education, which emphasized that higher education was a national investment, and established links between higher education and economic development. The report recommended substantial expansion of higher-education systems, and the specific introduction of manpower planning as the rationale behind African educational planning. This accorded well with the national aspirations of newly-independent nations, and the process of expansion was taken up on a wide scale. The model which was perpetuated was that of the high-cost 'gold standard' institution recommended by the Asquith Commission. Statistically minute numbers of individuals were therefore able to aspire to employment in the modern sector, at direct cost to the poor.

A major concern in the early days of the African universities was that of 'Africanization', in both curriculum development and research, as well as the task of training new academic staff to take over teaching positions from expatriate personnel. The question of 'relevance' and the role of the African university were therefore key issues, and gave rise in part to the notion of the 'Development University', in which universities were to undertake research or participate in development projects in the rural areas. Universities therefore found themselves required to fulfil an increasing number of disparate functions, including both an academic function and a significant diplomatic role. They were also supposed to be key actors in the development process. Inevitably, many institutions became stretched beyond their declining resources.

The African university in the 1990s

The adverse circumstances now faced by universities are severe, and it is widely acknowledged that many African universities are in a state of crisis. While the precise nature of this crisis is only partially documented, a growing number of testimonies exist, citing difficulties both in purely material terms, and the devastating impact that deteriorating conditions have had upon the morale of staff and the education they are able to provide to students. An often-cited quotation, for example, is that given by Trevor Coombe in his report on a *Consultation on Higher Education in Africa* (Coombe 1991: 2), prepared for the Ford and Rockefeller Foundations:

> One of the abiding impressions . . . is the sense of loss, amounting almost to grief, of some of the most senior professors in the older African universities as they compare the present state of their universities with the vigor, optimism and pride which the same institutions displayed twenty or thirty years ago. It is not just the universal regret of age at the passing of youth, nor the sad awareness that a generation of unique academic pioneers has almost run its course. It is also the grim knowledge that the nature of the university experience today is profoundly different for many teachers and students, so different and so inferior that some wonder whether it can rightly be called a university experience at all.

While Coombe's report and numerous other accounts suggest that there is in fact some room for optimism, it is also essential that there must be change if conditions are not to deteriorate further. The prospects are daunting. As institutions, universities are notoriously resistant to change, and the economic environment in which African universities operate is an extremely difficult one. With only a few exceptions, public universities in Africa are dependent on governments for approximately 90 per cent of their funding (Negrao 1994: 4), and the funding allocated has declined or fluctuated in real terms over recent years (Gaidzanwa 1994: 8). A recent study has shown that public expenditures for higher education over the period 1980–7, when adjusted for inflation, increased at less than half the rate of the increase in enrolment (Eisemon and Kourouma 1992). Further, in some institutions, long-term planning has proved virtually impossible as government funding will fluctuate on a *monthly* basis (Mwiria 1992: 14). In others, the mechanisms for determining the allocation of funding from governments have simply failed to operate for long periods (Eisemon *et al.* 1993: 16), and most institutions receive funding on at best an annual basis, making long-term planning difficult. Countries involved in or emerging from periods of serious internal conflict are in an even more difficult, and sometimes anomalous situation: for example, the Eduardo Mondlane University in Mozambique, for which the government is able to provide only 28 per cent of the university's operating budget. The remaining 72 per cent of its recurrent costs – largely provided through expatriate teaching staff – is provided by foreign donors (World Bank 1991: 42). Such conditions leave little flexibility for either institutional change or for autonomous decision-making.

While there is internal and external pressure to reduce the proportion of educational expenditure on higher education, the real value of grants to higher education has in fact declined steeply. At the same time, enrolments in many countries have increased sharply. The 1988 World Bank study *Education in Sub-Saharan Africa*, indicated that the cost of educating a student in higher education was 60 times greater than a primary school pupil; Eisemon and Salmi put that figure at 200 times for Makerere, for the 1990–1 session (Eisemon and Salmi 1993: 155). Real per-student expenditures for Makerere had however *declined* about 40 per cent between 1987 and 1990, largely because of inflation and currency devaluation. A Higher Education for Development Cooperation (HEDCO) study (also at Makerere) indicated that the 1988–9 education budget was only 21 per cent of the 1970–1 level, and that per capita expenditure had fallen to about 13 per cent of its original value, because of the large increase in the number of students (Eisemon and Salmi 1993: 155).

Mwiria (1992) notes that in the 1990–1 academic session, the universities of Zambia, Ghana (Legon) and Makerere received 79, 53 and 34 per cent, respectively, of their requested budgets. In a detailed study of the situation at Makerere, Eisemon *et al.* note that prior to the 1990–1 financial year, the Ministry of Finance did not give out guidance on the levels at which budgets might be likely to be met, and, as a result, the University regularly received only about one-third of the budgets it had prepared. Furthermore, the budget, once submitted, is extremely inflexible, and all disbursement must be reviewed and approved by government. Virement is possible only to a very limited extent and, as a result, a proportion of a budget which was in any case insufficient can go unspent (Eisemon *et al.* 1993: 17–18).

Student numbers have increased dramatically, without any consequent increase in facilities. In some cases, institutions may not have the autonomy to determine the level of student intake, but may be told to accept a certain number. In Kenya, for example, student numbers increased from 8000 in 1984 to 40 000 in 1990 (Woodhall 1992: 17). Mwiria argues that although the introduction of 'double intakes' in Kenya has reduced the cost of higher education *per capita*, this has been at the expense of the quality of the education provided (Mwiria and Nyukuri 1992: 66).

Graphic illustrations abound of the situation faced today by staff and students in the majority of African universities. All aspects of university life are affected, from basic living conditions to the difficulties associated with undertaking any form of advanced research. Library provision and the availability of books and journals is a basic indicator, and the evidence suggests that such provision has dropped very dramatically. In 1989, the University of Addis Ababa had to discontinue subscription to 1200 journals (Berhanu 1994), and there is a need throughout the continent for up-to-date texts and scholarly publications. At Makerere, a visitation report commented that a department might get ten books for 600 students, or a single book for 50 (Eisemon *et al.* 1993: 28). In another recent report, Carol Priestley quotes from a SWETS report which states that more than 10 000 subscriptions were supplied in the 1970s. In the 1980s, this had fallen to just over 1000, and the number in 1992 was less than 100. Most African university libraries have not had any funds for periodicals for the past two to ten years (Priestley 1992: 2). Beyond the provision of books, there is a question over the provision of space, as noted in a recent study (Gaidzanwa 1994: 9–10):

> At the University of Zimbabwe, severe book and journal shortages resulted from the increased enrolments. In 1980, the student numbers stood at 2240 while the library could seat only 500 (excluding lecturers). In 1983, the library was extended to seat 1200 users and yet 4000 staff and students needed to use it. Since 1983, there has been no extension to the library while the student numbers continued to rise, peaking at 9288 in 1989. By then, the number of staff and students had grown to over 10 000.

Salaries in African universities have dropped dramatically, and a study conducted by Eisemon *et al.* (1993) showed that the average salaries of support and maintenance staff and those of professors ranged from US$4.70 to US$22.70 a month, with the vice-chancellor receiving only $4 more. It is a commonplace that many staff have second jobs, and some even undertake 'dual employment' within the same institution. Living conditions are difficult, with numerous students living in rooms designed for one or two. A further example by Eisemon *et al.* (1993) may serve to illustrate:

> Most of the halls of residence are accommodating students far in excess of their capacities, so that hall libraries and common rooms have been turned into sleeping places, and the resultant crowding everywhere seriously militates against serious academic endeavour. This overcrowding is extended to the toilets and washrooms, most of which ceased to function a long time ago and the unsanitary condition arising . . . where open sewage is a common sight, students have been compelled to sponge themselves in their room and to relieve themselves in places other than the toilets. The prevailing situation certainly is a very serious health hazard throughout the campus
> (Makerere Visitation Campus 1991, quoted in Eisemon *et al.* 1993: 41)

The agenda for reform: The World Bank's analysis

There is widespread belief that this situation must change, and indeed reform is taking place in many countries (notably Ghana, which has introduced major reforms). However, any study of the university in Africa in the 1990s will take World Bank literature as a key reference point, and their 1988 analysis *Education in Sub-Saharan Africa: Policies for Adjustment, Revitalisation and Expansion* still dominates current debate.

A recent study for the Ford and Rockefeller Foundations (Coombe 1991) and a series of publications commissioned by the Association of African Universities

(Mohamedbhai 1994; Akin Aina 1994; Assie-Lumumba 1994; Berhanu 1994; Gaidzanwa 1994; Mwiria 1994; Negrao 1994; Sawadago 1994) have attempted to introduce new perspectives and to broaden the debate. However, in almost all cases, the discussion is underpinned by the analysis and prescriptions for reform presented in *Education in Sub-Saharan Africa*. This tightly-written study identified the following areas in which higher education in Africa was said to be underperforming significantly, and in which change was required.

Quality

The study conceded that hard evidence of a decline in quality was not available, and its analysis was therefore confined largely to that of non-salary inputs, in particular chemicals and laboratory equipment. It was said that instruction in universities had been reduced to 'little more than rote learning of theory from professorial lectures and chalked notes on blackboards' (World Bank 1988: 75). Following on from a series of graphic examples of inadequate facilities, the study mourns:

> Chemists who have not done a titration; biologists who have not done a dissection; physicists who have never measured an electric current; secondary science teachers who have never witnessed, let alone themselves conducted, the demonstrations central to the curriculum they teach; agronomists who have never conducted a field trial of any sort; engineers who have never assembled the machinery they are called upon to operate; social scientists of all types who have never collected, or conducted an analysis of, their own empirical data; specialists for whom the programming and use of computers is essential who have never sat before or tested a program on a functioning machine; lawyers who do not have access to recent judicial opinions; medical doctors whose only knowledge of laboratory procedures is from hearing them described in a lecture hall – qualitatively deprived graduates such as these are now appearing in countries that have been hardest hit by the scarcity of non-salary inputs.

The World Bank paper concludes firstly that it is now the shortage of non-salary inputs which is the 'governing constraint' upon the quality of higher education in Africa, rather than the number and level of training of academic staff – a situation which represents a reversal of that in the early 1970s (World Bank 1988: 74). Secondly, the paper states that '. . . in its stock of high level skills and in its ability to generate knowledge and innovation, Sub-Saharan Africa is falling further behind . . . Tertiary education discharges ever less effectively its principal responsibilities.' (World Bank 1988: 75.)

Costs

The 1988 study draws particular attention to the high-cost structures of African universities and the costs of the subsidies provided to students (internal and external efficiency).

Graduate mix

An inappropriate mix in the graduates produced was found. Despite general concern at the low participation rate in higher education in Africa, the study draws attention to the fact that levels of graduate unemployment have risen sharply in Sub-Saharan Africa, and concludes that there is a need to constrain output (both in circumstances of high graduate unemployment, and in particular the proportion of graduates with degrees in the Arts and Humanities).

Public funding

The burden carried by public sources of funding was also highlighted. Financing was said to be 'socially inequitable and economically inefficient' (World Bank 1988: 70). It emphasized, firstly, that the cost of keeping a student in higher education in Africa was on average between six and seven times greater in Sub-Saharan Africa than in Asia, and nine times greater than Latin America. Secondly, the cost of publicly-supporting a student in higher education was sixty times greater than in primary education (World Bank 1988: 75). The study suggested that the additional resources recovered might be increased and used more efficiently to improve the quality of higher education, 'despite limited economic prospects and the unremitting need for public austerity' (World Bank 1988: 77).

The means of reform

The World Bank study recommended measures to address these problems, and these now form the basis for much of the reform being undertaken in Africa. Measures suggested have included the increase of pedagogical inputs and establishment of centres of excellence, but have focused primarily upon financial and structural reform. Measures to achieve the reduction of unit costs include

- cost-sharing by the beneficiaries of higher education;
- measures to facilitate the introduction of private universities;
- income-generating schemes (viewed reasonably positively in recent reports by Blair 1992 and Woodhall 1992);
- use of national service and student loans;
- graduate taxes and an educational credit market.

Most controversially, it was suggested further that successful implementation of policies to improve higher education would release scarce funding for investment in primary and secondary education (World Bank 1988: 68).

Not surprisingly, the suggestion that there had been over-investment in higher education and the prescriptions put forward in *Education in Sub-Saharan Africa* generated fierce debate. While programmes of reform have been initiated in a number of countries, notably Ghana, Uganda, Zambia, Kenya, Nigeria and Botswana, many have sparked off student rioting and resulted in periods of closure of institutions. The Bank itself acknowledges that implementation has been difficult and the results not always encouraging (World Bank 1994). Nevertheless, alternative options seem few, other than a perpetuating cycle of decline.

Relationship with government

Recent works, particularly from the World Bank (Saint 1992; Neave and van Vught 1993; World Bank 1994), have begun to focus more closely upon the relationship between government and the state. In many cases this is problematic, both in political terms and in financial terms. It was recognized from an early stage in the development of African universities that this was likely to be difficult, as shown by Ajayi (1972):

> As the African governments in the 1970s define their objectives more clearly and as the universities seek greater relevance and take more seriously their role in the development process as allies and critics of government, the clearer becomes the inevitability of friction, if not confrontation.

Confrontation has been frequent, and has resulted at times in institutional closure, or, in some cases, human rights abuses or harassment. These difficulties are in part constitutional, as many universities have the head of state as the university chancellor, and many university governing bodies are composed largely of nominees of the head of state, leading to a lack of autonomy going well beyond financial dependency.

This relationship is emerging as a crucial issue in African higher education, as most institutions have been affected by long periods of closure, following student disturbances and other disagreements with government. It is suggested by some authors that, to undertake reform in a manner which is likely to be more successful than previous attempts (i.e. if the university is to undertake 'ownership' of proposed reform) then universities must have greater autonomy to take both financial and policy decisions. The 'state supervision' model is suggested (Neave and van Vught 1993; World Bank 1994) as a means to determine their own mission, and to plan for this in a more systematic way than is possible in many institutions at present. Whether this solution is in fact feasible is more open to question, as the university remains a visible symbol and a possible source of criticism.

The African university has had a short and turbulent history, and institutions now face complex and difficult choices. Accounts suggest that they are doing this with courage, and in the face of difficulties of a magnitude most employees of northern institutions would find difficult to estimate (Coombe 1991). A number of African institutions have begun to undertake in-depth and constructive self-reviews and these seem to be showing grounds for some optimism (Court 1991: 5–7). Combined with increased autonomy, and the possibility of retaining income generated by the institutions themselves, it is possible that there will be real change, and that this change will finally be towards the truly African university.

References

Akin Aina, T. (1994) *Quality and Relevance: African Universities in the 21st Century*. Ghana, Association of African Universities.

Ajayi, J.F. (1972) Cited by I.C.M. Maxwell, in *Changing Patterns of University Development Overseas: the Search for Local Relevance*, p. 245. Edinburgh, Centre of African Studies, Edinburgh University.

Ajayi, J.F., Goma, L.K.H. and Johnson, G.A. (1994) *The African Experience with Higher Education*. Ghana, Association of African Universities.

Ashby, E. (1966) *Universities: British, Indian and African*. Cambridge, Massachusetts, Harvard University Press.

Assie-Lumumba, N.T. (1993) *Higher Education in Francophone Africa: Assessment of the Potential of the Traditional Universities and Alternatives for Development*. Washington DC, World Bank.

Assie-Lumumba, N.T. (1994) *Demand, Access and Equity Issues in African Higher Education: Past Policies, Current Practices, and Readiness for the 21st Century*. Ghana, Association of African Universities.

Asquith, C. (1945) Report of the Commission on Higher Education in the Colonies. Cmnd. 6647. London, HMSO.

Berhanu, A.M. (1994) *Universities in Africa: Challenges and Opportunities of International Cooperation*. Ghana, Association of African Universities.

Blair, R.D.D. (1992) *Financial Diversification and Income Generation at African Universities*. Washington DC, World Bank.

Brown Sherman, M.A. (1990) 'The university in modern Africa: toward the twenty-first century', *Journal of Higher Education (Ohio State University)* 61(4).

Coleman, J.S. with Court, D. (1993) *University Development in the Third World: The Rockefeller Foundation Experience*. Oxford, Pergamon.

Coombe, T. (1991) A Consultation on Higher Education in Africa: A Report to the Ford Foundation and the Rockefeller Foundation. London, Institute of Education.

Court, D. (1991) 'Issues in higher education: a note from East Africa', *Norrag News*, 11. Edinburgh/Geneva, Norrag.

Eisemon, T.O. and Salmi, J. (1993) 'African universities and the state: Prospects for reform in Senegal and Uganda,' *Higher Education* 25. Dordrecht, Kluwer Academic Publishers.

Eisemon, T.O. and Kourouma, M. (1992) 'Foreign Assistance for University Development in Sub-Saharan Africa and Asia.' Paper prepared for Senior Policy Seminar on Improvement and Innovation in Higher Education in Developing Countries. Washington DC, World Bank.

Eisemon, T.O., Sheehan, J., Eyoku, G., Van Buer, F., Welsch, D., Masutti, L., Colletta, N. and Roberts, L. (1993) *Strengthening Uganda's Policy Environment for Investing in University Development*. Washington DC, World Bank.

Gaidzanwa, R.B. (1994) *Governance Issues in African Universities: Improving Management and Governance to make African Universities Viable in the Nineties and Beyond*. Ghana, Association of African Universities.

Hetland, A. (ed.) (1984) *Universities and National Development: A Report of the Nordic Association for the Study of Education in Developing Countries*. Stockholm, Amqvist & Wiksell.

King, K.J. (1991) *Aid and Education in the Developing World*. Harlow, Longman.

Mohamedbhai, G.T.G. (1994) *The Emerging Role of African Universities in the Development of Science and Technology*. Ghana, Association of African Universities.

Mwiria, K. (1992) *University Governance: Problems and Prospects in Anglophone Africa*. Washington DC, World Bank.

Mwiria, K. (1994) *Enhancing Linkages between African Universities, the Wider Society, the Business Community and Governments*. Ghana, Association of African Universities.

Mwiria, K. and Nyukuri, M.S. (1992) *The Management of Double Intakes: a case study of Kenyatta University*. Paris, Unesco (IIEP).

Neave, G. and van Vught, F.A. (1993) *The Winds of Change: Government and Higher Education Relationships Across Three Continents (A Report to the World Bank)*. Paris/Twente, IAU/CHEPS.

Negrao, J. (1994) *Adequate and Sustainable Funding of African Universities*. Ghana, Association of African Universities.

Priestley, C. (1992) *Study on a Commonwealth Journal Distribution Programme*. London, Commonwealth Secretariat.

Saint, W.S. (1992) *Universities in Africa: Strategies for Stabilization and Revitalization* (Technical Paper 194). Washington DC, World Bank.

Sawadago, G. (1994) *The Future Mission and Roles of the African University*. Ghana, Association of African Universities.

Thompson, K. and Fogel, B. (1976) *Higher Education and Social Change: Promising Experiments in Developing Countries*, Vol. I. New York, Praeger for International Council for Educational Development.

Unesco (1963) *The Development of Higher Education in Africa*. Paris, Unesco.

Woodhall, M. (1992) *Financial Diversification in African Higher Education*. Washington DC, World Bank.

World Bank (1988) *Education in Sub-Saharan Africa: Policies for Adjustment, Revitalization and Expansion*. Washington DC, World Bank.

World Bank (1991) *World Bank Capacity Building Study on Mozambique* (draft extracts). Washington DC, World Bank.

World Bank (1994) *Higher Education: The Lessons of Experience*. Washington DC, World Bank.

Yesufu, T.M. (1973) *Creating the African University: Emerging Issues of the 1970s*. Ibadan, Association of African Universities.

9

From the Collegial Academy to Corporate Enterprise: The Changing Cultures of Universities

Ian McNay

One leading US commentator on higher education believed the only factor that united academics on a campus was a common concern over car parking. If the extent of coverage of issues in internal university newsletters is one indication of priorities, that observation still has strength. One editor commented that he had occasional letters on issues such as modularization, the re-organization of the academic year or research assessment; on car parking charges he had over a hundred.

Karl Weick (1976) gives academic respectability and rigour to this concept with the term 'loosely coupled systems' in his study of education organizations. He suggests certain characteristics which the term implies. These include: a relative lack of coordination; a relative absence of regulations; little linkage between the concerns of senior staff as managers and those involved in the key processes of teaching and learning; a lack of congruence between structure and activity; differences in methods, aims and even missions among different departments; little lateral interdependence among departments; infrequent inspection; and the 'invisibility' of much that happens.

This is the classic collegial academy with significant academic autonomy, or professional self-determination. There was loose definition of policy for the organization as a whole and loose control over activity or the implementation of any policy. In this chapter I take those two axes to outline a model of four organizational types – simplified vignettes of approaches to organizational process. This is represented in Figure 9.1.

The four cultures

I use the four labels collegium, bureaucracy, corporation and enterprise. Some of these labels may carry pejorative connotations; that is not intended. My view is that all can be justified: what is crucial is the appropriateness of the 'fit' with

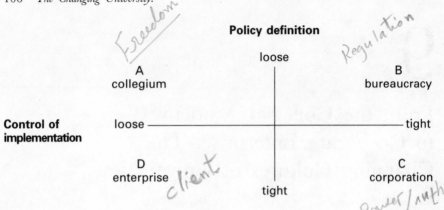

Figure 9.1 Models of universities as organizations.

circumstances. All four co-exist in most universities, but with different balances among them. These differences depend on a range of factors including traditions, mission, leadership style and external pressures. This chapter explores shifts in balances, particularly towards the emergent enterprise culture, and also examines the changing role of the administration in the four cultures – an important, but neglected, area of study. However, such staff have a key role in mitigating potential conflict between practices and procedures which differ by culture. Research preferences of staff in the collegial units may not fit with corporate priorities; decision processes and 'norms' of the bureaucracy may not be flexible enough for an enterprise in a competitive market.

The key word for the collegium is 'freedom'. Clark (1983) sees liberty as an objective of university provision, with echoes of Freire's emancipatory vision (Freire 1972). More importantly, it defines organizational expectations: institutional freedom from external controls, formerly by the church, now mainly by government; and academic autonomy, developed in the Humboldtian university as *Lehrfreiheit*. There was also *Lernfreiheit* in traditional universities in England but student freedom of choice has not been a major characteristic of them. The Scottish general degree allowed more and it is being recaptured in a different form in modular, credit-based courses, though I have reservations about how liberating these are (McNay 1994a). If the main tasks of the university are teaching and research, most developments will spring from these two activities and decisions will be based within the structures where they are organized – mainly discipline-based departments – within a frame of reference set by peer scholars in the international community. This is open to abuse through personal bias, it can be conservative and may not work except in small organizations.

In the bureaucracy, regulation becomes important. This can have many positive objectives: consistency of treatment in areas such as equal opportunities or financial allocations; quality of activities by due process of consideration; propriety of behaviour by regulatory oversight; efficiency through standard operating procedures. Committees become arenas for policy development or commentary and iteration with the executive. There are problems here, too: a concern for consistency of standards can lead to standardization for convenience; novel ideas cannot be judged through accumulated case law from established ideas; the rigidity can be compounded by the time involved in the cycle of decision-making. It may be a good model for maintenance in stability, but not for rapid change. It has an appearance of rationality, with, often, use of statistical bases to arguments and decisions, but can be contaminated by political manipulation.

In the corporation, the executive asserts authority, with the vice-chancellor as chief executive: indeed, my key word here is power, one of the four cultures used by Handy (1993) in his analysis of organizations. This culture is probably dominant, particularly in the treatment of people, with a consequent reaction of resentment, at times verging on anomie. Handy suggests it cannot be maintained for long periods without such consequences: it is a culture for crisis, not continuity. It is political also in its processes of bargaining and negotiation, with senior staff developing alliances and understandings outside formal decision arenas and disempowering committees. Working parties with members appointed, not elected, set agendas and condition outcomes. There are echoes in this model of the centralizing authoritarian state and its quangos in the UK during the 1980s, with an equal risk of the isolation of policymakers from reality, with a functional distinction drawn on the basis that 'teachers teach, managers manage'. The necessary iteration, and mutual information, between the two break down, thus subverting the aims of loyalty (Clark 1983) or domestication (Freire 1972).

In the enterprise, my choice of key word would be client. That carries with it connotations not only of the market, where *customers* would be more appropriate, but of professionalism where the knowledge and skills of experts, and the needs and wishes of those seeking their services, come together. In organization terms, it means that key decisions should be located close to the client, within a well-defined general policy framework, and that the good of the client should be the dominant criterion for decision-making. It is, in a world of resource constraint and accountability, also about costing, but in university terms it can also be about a curriculum committed to serve diverse communities or to develop enterprise skills and competences. One support pack to a BBC series, 'Winning', stressed that 'satisfaction is not enough', so perhaps Mick Jagger needs updating. Note the echoes of the culture of liberal adult education in the prescription (Gilliland 1993):

Customer 'delight' means doing that little bit extra to show customers how important they are. It is about understanding and anticipating their needs, constantly seeking out problems and quickly solving them for the customer. It is about building long term relationships, not quick fixes and is undoubtedly the route to competitive advantage.

Customer delight is essentially personal and spontaneous, aimed at raising the self-esteem of the person experiencing it. For that reason, it must be done in such a way that the recipient does not feel threatened, nor under any kind of obligation.

If, through the enterprise culture, we bring back delight to education that will be a major gain, and a sensitivity to markets will deflect criticism about lack of relevance. There are dangers: of curriculum distortion if it is conditioned by costs – sponsors of chairs are not evenly spread across subjects, for example; of compromise on standards if what paying clients want is a qualification and if payment systems depend on results; of loss of coherence and continuity if the fashions of the market become too dominant. Williams (1992) and McNay (1995) develop these points and Tasker and Packham (1993) are concerned about education being contaminated by commercial values.

In the next section, it is suggested that there has been movement among the four labels with different quadrants dominant over time.

Dynamic within the model

Weick was writing in the mid-1970s just as a senior Labour politician announced that 'the party is over' in the UK. The collegial academy has been under threat ever since. It still exists: one international group, studying 'the entrepreneurial and adaptive university' at Anglia Polytechnic University's Centre for Higher Education Management, visited Cambridge in 1994. They asked about the research committee – 'we haven't got one'; research policy? – 'it's a Good Thing'; control of quality? – 'we appoint top-class staff and let them get on with it'; allocation of funds? – there is little held centrally for regular distribution. As one Cambridge don summed up: 'Cambridge works in practice but not in theory.'

The challenge to this confident assurance by less ancient universities came in three waves. In the 1970s the polytechnics offered an alternative model – summarized as a bureaucratic hierarchy and linked with more vocational/professional programmes (Kogan 1984). James Callaghan, the Labour prime minister, speaking at Ruskin College in 1976, set in train the resurgence of an economic view of higher education, but based not on the act of faith of human capital theory and investment, but on output rather than input, on accountability not autonomy, on quality assurance processes, not trust. This was part of an international movement (Neave 1988).

In part, the polytechnics, as an alternative, more regulated system, in quadrant B (Figure 9.1), by being a sector where change *did* take place, offered protection to the (then) universities and allowed them to defer significant change. However, in the 1980s, in the second wave, budget deficits and evident poor controls at the universities of Cardiff, Bristol and Aberdeen, and elsewhere, pushed towards greater regulation (Shattock 1994); growth in numbers provided internal impetus to more formal mechanisms believed appropriate to larger organizations. In the third wave, in the 1990s, the requirements of Higher Education Funding Council for England (HEFCE) and Higher Education Quality Council (HEQC) for strategic plans, and visible formal mechanisms and protocols shifted the balance in most universities to give more weight to quadrant B.

The polytechnics, meanwhile, were moving to quadrant C (Figure 9.1). Their local authority inheritance meant that elements of the collegial academy were not widespread (see Table 9.1). In the light of the need for strategic planning and decisions on priorities, including elimination of certain activities, there was a planned

Table 9.1 Summary charcteristics of four university models.

Factor	Collegium	Bureaucracy	Corporation	Enterprise
Dominant value (Clark 1983)	freedom	equity	loyalty	competence
Role of central authorities	permissive	regulatory	directive	supportive
Handy's organization culture	person	role	power	task
Dominant unit	department/individual	faculty/committees	institution/Senior Management Team	sub-unit/project teams
Decision arenas	informal groups networks	committees and administrative briefings	working parties and Senior Management Team	project teams
Management style	consensual	formal/'rational'	political/tactical	devolved leadership
Timeframe	long	cyclic	short/mid-term	instant
Environmental 'fit'	evolution	stability	crisis	turbulence
Nature of change	organic innovation	reactive adaptation	proactive transformation	tactical flexibility
External referents	invisible college	regulatory bodies	policymakers as opinion leaders	clients/sponsors
Internal referents	the discipline	the rules	the plans	market strength/students
Basis for evaluation	peer assessment	audit of procedures, e.g. IS9001	performance indicators	repeat business
Student status	apprentice academic	statistic	unit of resource	customer
Administrator roles: Servant of . . .	the community	the committee	the chief executive	the client, internal and external

drift to the development of chief executive and senior management team concepts supported by more sophisticated *management* information systems (Toyne 1991). Note the shift from *student* records: the sophistication, whilst adding to the 'holy writ' status of statistics, did not always mean they had more validity than some biblical myths and numbers.

This development was legitimated, not within the public sector, but by a report on 'efficiency' commissioned by the CVCP (1985). The Jarratt Report was hawkish and much closer to McGregor's (1960) Theory X and Schein's (1980) coercive culture than the less-publicized parallel from the National Advisory Body (1987). Jarratt saw a much more directive and managerial role for senior staff and senior bodies acting by analogy with boards of directors in the commercial sector in the context of a strong corporate strategy. The older universities are following behind this trend, some with more reluctance than others. For some ex-CATS (Colleges of Advanced Technology) the justificatory crisis conditions came earlier, in 1981, with large cuts in funding allocations from the Universities Grants Committee (UGC). The University of Salford appeared to move through that to quadrant D (Figure 9.1) and Aston University still has strong elements of corporatism, developing within that an approach based on total quality management (Miller 1994).

The essential issue is over the location of power and decision-making. David Johns, Vice-chancellor at Bradford, uses the deadlines for response set by the HEFCE to claim that 'there is no time for democracy'. In one former polytechnic with which I have worked a (female) Pro Vice-Chancellor (PVC) described how a group of women set out to colonize the committee system believing the institution was in quadrant B; they found, when they succeeded, that like a mirage, power was still beyond them – in the senior management team in quadrant C. Decisions were effectively taken outside the formal arenas which simply endorsed them. One PVC (male) acknowledged this. He countered by claiming that the collegial democracy had been delegated to departmental level, but 'the heads of department couldn't manage democracy so there were two levels of corporate state, the greater and lesser'.

In quadrants A and B power is distributed, informally or formally, within the institution; in C and D it is concentrated at the centre and then delegated to the equivalent, in the wider community, of government agencies or contracted organisations. As Handy (1993) points out, the culture of centralized power is unstable. It may be accepted in a crisis but will be resented if sustained, leading to staff being in conflict or conspiracy to subvert, or conforming and developing a sterile, immature dependency on the centre, resisting any personal professional responsibility. Some vice-chancellors have sought to create a culture of constant crisis leading eventually to individual and collective stress and breakdown.

There were a number of strands leading to the enterprise culture in the 1990s. The first was the continuing squeeze on public funding of universities. There was a critical need for independent income generation – what in the emergent socialist market economy of China is euphemized as multichannel funding. Thus, universities entered the marketplace with their services. As Warner and Leonard (1992) point out, this means looking at costs as part of competitive pricing, and

Table 9.2 Organizational cultural shifts in one 'new' university.

Type	1989	1994	1999
Collegium	3.7	1.9	1.3
Bureaucracy	3.4	2.7	2.3
Corporation	2.2	3.9	4.0
Enterprise	0.7	1.6	2.5

Collated views of 25 senior staff. Ten points are distributed to reflect the perceived overall balance of culture

at services to students as the core business of the university to ensure they are satisfied and stay, given that government money follows student numbers. For a short period, policy on fee levels and retention of fee income drove institutions to expand the market from the supply side. This led universities to look at their structures with devolution of budgetary responsibilities, sometimes with disastrous consequences (Thomas 1995) and the development of cost-centres and activity-based budgeting. The freedom of the former polytechnics to retain earned income rather than have it offset against previous deficit funding released their energies and university companies exploited intellectual property rights.

On the other hand, the competitive market for students, the development of consumerism and of government charters, of students' awareness of their value to university budgets and the shift towards paying more of their own costs, led to demands for 'value for money' at several levels: government, students and corporate sponsors. In access and curriculum terms, marketing to overseas students, franchizing and compact schemes with feeder colleges, the development of the competence movement and an increased awareness of the importance of learning outcomes (Otter 1991) linked to the Department of Employment's funding for the Enterprise in Higher Education programme all pushed towards this quadrant.

How far have things changed? In my work with staff, on courses or in-house, the aim is to induce them to quantify their perceptions of shift. Table 9.2 gives the views of the 25 senior staff – Senior Management Team (SMT), deans, heads of service units – in a modern university, a former polytechnic. They were asked to 'score' three periods by distributing ten points among the four quadrants to show the balance within the institution. The findings reflect similar scores from elsewhere across both former sectors. All four cultures co-exist and will continue to do so, though some may have only 'trace element' status.

The model can be developed further. A summary of some key characteristics of the four cultures is given in Table 9.1.

In Figure 9.1, I have implied a clockwise movement as normal, with a basic movement in UK institutions from A to B to C to D as dominant. This is not universal: Cambridge, and to a lesser extent Imperial College, have gone from A to D in exploiting their intellectual capital. One private university in South America with which my Centre has worked started in C and remains there. The founding rector also chaired the board of trustees where the other members were his immediate subordinates. In the first twenty years, the main activity had been undergraduate training in professional areas. Now he wanted to develop research but would not give staff freedom; he wanted links to employers and market-oriented developments in continuing education but would not give staff devolved responsibility; he wanted a more efficient operation but would not divulge information to help develop regulatory norms. So, A, D and B were all ruled out.

The model can also be applied to national systems. In the UK, movement is mainly AB to CD; in Eastern Europe it is from BC to AD with, for example, Romania more in D with private institutions constantly springing up, and the Czech Republic more in A with problems of definition of responsibility and difficulties of decision-making. China, too, is moving from BC to D in a socialist market economy.

The evolving administration

In the golden age of the 1960s in the collegium, administrators 'had influence but not power' (Moodie and Eustace 1974). They were often long-serving and loyal to an elevated view of the university and its mission. As generalists, many were based at devolved level, maintaining a delicate balance of being responsive to local needs but responsible to a line manager at the centre. At times, they 'went native' and lost the balance which was essential to the role of liaison with, but at times protection of academics from, central demands. They were a trusted servant – 'subservient and often not directly involved in decision making' (Toyne 1991) – but sometimes with an influence in helping him avoid gaffes or discreetly solving problems. The emphasis was on low-key, informal, personal service.

With the information-based decisions and demands for data in the internal and external bureaucracies, Fielden (1975) charts 'the decline of the professor and the rise of the registrar' with cautionary words that control of information and its flow, and impatience at the decision processes of collegial consultation can lead to administrators having 'delusions of competence'. The 'servant of the committee' becomes more distant and impersonal and loses the trust of ordinary academics not involved in formal mechanisms. They develop loyalty to the 'system' justifying standardized procedures, insensitive to local exigencies, on the basis of egalitarianism; coordination to promote consistency can turn into prescription and the personal touch, except to chairs of committees, is replaced by paperwork procedures and precedents.

The Jarratt Report (CVCP 1985) recognized that 'senior administrative officers make an important contribution to policy formation'. It noted that 'over the past decade the nature of their role has changed somewhat and senior administrators now have an increasingly important task in supporting the vice-chancellor'. The shift, or drift, is to serving the chief executive, as he or she defines the interests of the university community. The loyalty is to the espoused ideology and to the small cabinet of senior staff – the 'government of the day' to echo the Clive Ponting trial. This echoes the legal view that the interests of the state are synonymous with the interests of the government of the day. The jury in the trial of Clive Ponting rejected this, supporting his claim to have served a higher ideal in making sensitive information public. Administrators may then have to mediate between strong chairs and committee members who refuse to be subservient. They increasingly have planning and control functions and risk appearing distant from operational reality with which policy and strategy must iterate. They work with temporary working parties, and 'tell' the university about decisions, which the senior academics may have to 'sell'. Specialist roles emerge and recruitment from outside to senior posts in finance, fund-raising, marketing may replace internal development and promotion as resource-based functions gain ascendancy over general policy input.

With the enterprise, services and support should be as close to the client as possible. Specialist advisors within large central units (e.g. finance, research, international offices) may have a 'portfolio' for a limited range of academic units and may then move closer to the collegium model. The difference is in the greater degree of proactivity rather than reactivity: 'customer-based, accountable businesses are what we are asked to be . . . administrators . . . become more significant, not subservient (Toyne 1991). Staff may work in an internal market with service delivery standards defined and monitored. There will be a strong corporate identity with possible fragmentation of the unitary administration and line management responsibility to one of a range of executive pro-vice-chancellors. What may happen is that, to match this, a 'multiskilled' (not generalist) administrator at faculty level may emerge within the flattened hierarchy of the entrepreneurial organization.

Where next?

As Table 9.2 shows, there is a belief that the enterprise culture will develop further. What form might it take? There are already embryonic models in university companies and science/business parks. As suggested by McNay (1994b), with the conflux of three factors – retirement of ageing academics, the grey bulge; the developments in communications technology; and the continuing squeeze on resources for universities and support to students – most undergraduates could follow a national curriculum in core subjects and be 'taught' off campus for most of their programme. They will pay more; so will the rising numbers of postgraduates who have always been mainly self-funded; compacts with companies will guarantee flows of favoured staff for continuing professional development. For such mature clients, the quality of the learning environment needs to improve in many places with refurbishment funded through disposal of assets, like student residences, less in demand with today's patterns of study. Library, computing, careers and counselling services could well be 'privatized' with supplementary fees giving access to specified levels of provision. If academic departments are market-led, or at least market-oriented they could resemble units in a business park, franchized outlets in a departmental store or independent businesses in an academic shopping complex, with the combined studies modular programme as a supermarket equivalent. Administrative services could also be privatized and contracts developed for services such as finance, legal, customer flow analysis, market research, organization development consultancy.

Is all this fantastic? We already have supermarket elements in prospectuses as catalogues, home delivery in distance learning and consumer guides, *Which Degree?* There are already many companies and service spin-offs in universities; science park arrangements have proved attractive for joint-venture investments; management centres can rival private-sector equivalents and are better than many conference facilities. So the pragmatic view is there. The vision also fits current thinking on organizations. Mintzberg (1989) sees the future in the 'fragmented' organization. Deal and Kennedy (1988), echoed by Tom Schuller (1992) in his vision of the academic community, call it 'atomized' with the following features:

- Small, task-focused work units (10–20 persons).
- Each unit with economic and managerial control over its own destiny.
- Interconnection with larger entities through benign computer and communication links.
- Bonding into larger organizations through strong cultural bonds.

Strong cultural bonds? As in the academic guild, the invisible college? – the 'old boy' network. That sounds like the enterprising academy and so the wheel comes full circle. If the entrepreneurial academy can do better than its ivory-towered predecessor in exploiting the potential for synergy in campus co-location, the university may well continue its long historical record of adaptive genius which has allowed it to outlive most institutions outside the Icelandic Parliament, the monarchy (in some countries) and the Catholic church (ditto).

References

Clark, B.R. (1983) *The Higher Education System: Academic Organisation in Cross-national Perspective.* Berkeley, University of California Press.

Committee of Vice-Chancellors and Principals (1985) *Report of the Steering Committee for Efficiency studies in Universities.* (The Jarratt Report.) London, CVCP.

Deal, T.E. and Kennedy, A.A. (1988) *Corporate Cultures: The Rites and Rituals of Corporate Life.* London, Penguin.

Fielden, J. (1975) 'The decline of the professor and the rise of the registrar' in G.F. Page, (ed.) *Power and Authority in Higher Education.* Guildford, SRHE.

Freire, P. (1972) *Cultural Action for Freedom.* London, Penguin.

Gilliland, N. (1993) 'Training to win', *Training and Development* (February).

Handy, C. (1993) *Understanding Organisations.* London, Penguin.

Kogan, M. (1984) 'Models and structures', Block 3, E 324, *Management in Post-Compulsory Education.* Milton Keynes, Open University Press.

McGregor, D.V. (1960) *The Human Side of Enterprise.* New York, McGraw Hill.

McNay, I. (1994a) '"To see the world in a grain of sand?" The risk of closure and reductionism in open learning initiatives' in M. Thorpe, and D. Grugeon, (eds) *Opening Learning in the Mainstream.* York, Longman.

McNay, I. (1994b) 'The future student experience' in S. Haselgrove, (ed.) *The Student Experience.* Buckingham, SRHE and Open University Press.

McNay, I. (1995) *The University as an Organisation* (module for MA Higher Education by independent study). University of Middlesex.

Miller, H.D.R. (1994) *The Management of Change in Universities*. Buckingham, SRHE and Open University Press.

Mintzberg, H. (1989) *Mintzberg on Management: Inside our Strange World of Organizations*. New York, Free Press.

Moodie, G.C. and Eustace, R. (1974) *Power and Authority in British Universities*. London, Allen and Unwin.

National Advisory Body (1987) *Management for a Purpose*. London, NAB.

Neave, G. (1988) 'On the cultivation of quality, efficiency and enterprise: an overview of recent trends in higher education in Western Europe', *European Journal of Education*, 23(1/2).

Otter, S. (1991) *What Can Graduates Do?*, Leicester, NIACE.

Schein, E.H. (1980) *Organizational Psychology*. New York, Prentice Hall.

Schuller, T. (1992) 'The exploding community? The university idea and the smashing of the academic atom' in I. McNay, (ed.) *Visions of Post-compulsory Education*. Buckingham, SRHE and Open University Press.

Shattock, M. (1994) *The UGC and the Management of British Universities*. Buckingham, SRHE and Open University Press.

Tasker, M. and Packham, D. (1993) 'Industry and higher education: a question of values', *Studies in Higher Education*, 18(2).

Thomas, H. (1995) 'The Development and Consequences of the University of Bristol's Resource allocation System 1986–90, with Special Reference to the Faculty of Engineering and to Comparator Universities.' PhD thesis, Anglia Polytechnic University.

Toyne, P. (1991) 'Appropriate Structures for Higher Education Institutions.' Paper to British Council International Seminar: Management in Universities, cited in Miller (1994) q.v.

Warner, D. and Leonard, C. (1992) *The Income Generation Handbook*. Buckingham, SRHE and Open University Press.

Weick, K. (1976) 'Educational organisations as loosely-coupled systems' *Administrative Science Quarterly*, 21(1). (Reprinted in A. Westoby, (1988) *Cultures and Power in Educational Organizations*, Buckingham, Open University Press).

Williams, G. (1992) *Changing Patterns of Finance in Higher Education*. Buckingham, SRHE and Open University Press.

10

Pay as You Learn? Students in the Changing University

Christine King

Over the past decade, it has not been difficult to identify a number of quite significant developments in higher education. These include, most obviously, changes in organization and governance, in sources of income and in the way in which universities are now required to describe and justify their role in society. A new language and science of educational planning and marketing has emerged. Budgets are no longer simply allocated – they are devolved; income is no longer collected – it has to be earned. Students are 'clients' or 'consumers' and courses are 'programmes of study'.

It could be argued that some of these changes are largely cosmetic and subject to the vagaries of fashion. There are both individuals and institutions who are keeping a low profile, hoping that it will all go away and that university life will return to 'normal'. The media flirts with issues of principle like 'academic freedom' and reports on lecturers resisting new contracts of employment. Students continue to be represented as school leavers with 'A' levels, moving away from home to a university of their choice. The very real problem of student poverty, recognized in the House of Lords (Hansard 1993) is largely ignored by the media. A recent issue of a *Home Decoration* magazine carried a feature on the renovation by experts of some student accommodation. The student in question happened to be at an Oxbridge college and the arrangement of the 'typical student's room' had to ensure that there was a proper place for his grand piano!

Behind the media confusion and all the structural and other changes lies one key factor: the number, age, social, economic and ethnic background of students is changing dramatically. The most dominant influence is the growth of the size of the student body. By the year 2000 the decade will have seen up to a 50 per cent increase in the number of applications for places within higher education (CBI 1994). This increase is not made up solely of more applicants from that group popularly perceived to be 'representative', the school leaver with 'A' levels. As more mature students enter the system and more programmes for access are set up, both the age profile and the socio-economic balance is changing.

Even though the growth in applications from 18-year-olds is dominated by the children of the middle classes, there are already significant changes in the social composition of student campuses. Over half of all students in higher education in the UK are 'mature' at the point of entry. The definition of 'mature' normally covers students who are over 21 years at the commencement of their studies. However, increased opportunities for those in their twenties, thirties and well beyond, mean that the word is increasingly taking on a wider range of meanings.

A high proportion of these mature students are entering programmes of study without the traditional 'A' level qualifications and are coming via access or foundation courses at universities or further education colleges. Even amongst 18-year-old school-leavers, there is evidence of the entry of a small but increasing proportion of those for whom this is the first generation in the family even to stay in education beyond the age of 16 years. People with disabilities are beginning to find more opportunities as are part-time students, whether they are in employment or not. Some well-qualified young people, studying full-time, are beginning, largely for financial reasons, to live at home. Numbers of full- and part-timers are spending two or more years at their local further education college before finishing their programme at their regional university, and with collaboration, the divide between college and university is diminishing.

For those institutions with a strong commitment to widening participation, it has not been realistic for some time to describe a typical student path as one in which the student lives away from home, on campus or in the neighbourhood, studies for three years from the age of 18 or 19 years, has his or her fees paid, lives on a maintenance grant and goes into graduate level employment at the end of the programme. Both the realities and the opportunities are more complex. Students can and do study full-time, part-time or by a mixture of both at undergraduate and postgraduate level. They cannot survive on maintenance grants and supplement this in various ways, including the Government's loan scheme and the small Government hardship funds. Most end their programmes with an overdraft and many go into non-graduate employment or to a period of unemployment.

What students need and want from a university and what they bring to it, from school, employment or life experiences is also changing. Whilst universities cope with the logistics of increased numbers and decreasing public funding, they are also having to take careful cognizance of these changes. Currently, the UK system offers diversity and choice. However an institution sees its mission to students, it is clear that the quality and usefulness of a student's time at university must be an adequate return for the investment of time, money and for the support of the state, families and sponsors. Students and those who are paying for their studies are increasingly aware of their rights, enshrined in student charters, and of the need for a university to offer a package which fits their varying needs (Robertson 1994).

Growth or consolidation?

Whichever political parties form the government of the future, it is unlikely that education will slip from the political agenda. The mass higher-education system has been created to help the UK compete internationally in industry and must remain a key factor. Different governments and different parts of the education system will offer varying solutions to this problem, yet overall the need for an educated workforce will remain. There may be talk of consolidation and further reductions in funding, perhaps of a radical nature, but the aspirations of institutions for flexibility and growth, is likely to ensure that at least some parts of the system maintain the trend of the past decade. Assuming a demographic decline in the number of 18-year-olds until the late 1990s, it is clear that mature students, often studying part-time, will constitute a critical part of this expansion.

In support of this trend is the strong historical and ideological commitment of some institutions to a socially representative student body. Whilst the Conservative Government since 1979 has offered its political support to the concept of widening participation into higher education, it has been, in practice, a large number of institutions of further and higher education working together which have effected the changes. Through initiatives designed to raise aspirations amongst those who had either missed opportunities the first time round or who came from families where post-16 education was not the norm, a demand has been created. The goal set in the Lancaster speech of Kenneth Baker, the Secretary of State for Education, in 1986 of a one in three participation rate amongst school-leavers by the end of the century, has been met well ahead of time. Aspirations, once raised, are likely to continue and to be communicated to friends and neighbours, as a first generation of graduates and new role models is created. These will fuel a demand for increased opportunities as will the idea of life-long learning, of flexible study and of the value of an education post-16 for employment and other aspects of life.

The public's recognition of the accessibility and usefulness of many universities, and perhaps particularly of their local university for themselves and their children, remains a strong political lever for increasing opportunities for study. A recent CBI report gives this trend its backing and calls for a 40–50 per cent graduation rate in higher education amongst school-leavers simply to allow the UK to catch up with its international trading and industrial competitors (CBI 1994). The report argues that places in higher-education institutions should be available for all who are qualified and able to benefit. Popular demand, coupled with industrial pressure is likely, therefore, to ensure an expansion of further and higher education in the next ten years and beyond. The universities, many of them having acquired entrepreneurial skills and clarified their mission to their regions and to a representative student body, will find ways of opening doors to the new kinds of students. One way or another, the UK will see in the twenty-first century not only a continued demand for places at university but an even greater cross-section of the community spending time in university study.

Today's students

There is a motto used by the trainers of women managers (Josefowitz 1983):

We are
Today's women
Born yesterday
Dealing with tomorrow

Today's students are caught in the middle of a whirlwind. They suffer the difficulties brought about by recent expansion, like, for example, the high demands on library books and other resources. They take large lectures for granted and are, on the whole, sympathetic to the problems lecturing staff have in making time for them since they are still largely dependent on staff for their progress. They have only hazy points of comparison with a time when student life was easier, and accept and cope with, in most cases, the extreme financial hardship they face. Yet they are taught and work in an environment, both physical and cultural, which was constructed for a different scenario; one where the passing on of knowledge was largely at a personal level, where there were fewer students and more resources and where facilities, from catering to the students' union were built and organized for the 18-year-old living away from home.

Like staff, except that they are not paid for this, students adapt and survive. They are quick to use any of the tools, from modularity to mixed-mode study, which help them achieve their goals. Whether or how much they take part in the social life of the campus depends on their circumstances and the relevance or otherwise of what is on offer. In a time of financial pressures, contemporary students are notably more single-minded than many of their predecessor generations. Financial pressures are not the only reason why it is hard to persuade UK students to travel under European exchange schemes as fully as their European counterparts: many simply want to complete their studies as quickly and as cheaply as they can.

These students, however, have come to university with a mixture of skills and experiences which are not always formally recognized, and often not recognized at all. The 51 per cent who are 'mature' bring, for example, a vast range of different life experiences. Most staff are very aware of the commitment and ability of the mature students and research indicates high success rates, both in absolute and 'added value' terms, of this group of students. Their place in most students' union buildings is less clear and in any case, many are living at home and managing families with little time for Saturday night events.

School-leavers are the product of an education which is very different from that which most university staff experienced as undergraduates. The introduction of GNVQs and a vocational route for 16–18-year-olds is producing cohorts with distinct experiences and skills (Deere 1993). A large number of school-leavers are computer literate and will have a second modern language. Some, coming from schools with more pressure on staff time, will have a standard of grammar and spelling which needs improvement but which does not necessarily reflect on their ability. Many will have developed a number of explicit 'transferable skills', detailed in the records of achievement which overworked admissions tutors seldom have time to read. Those from ethnic-minority homes may have yet another range of varied experiences and values. Experienced and committed staff, who represent the majority, recognize and use these strengths and work to support weaknesses even though their own time is under a great deal of pressure.

Tomorrow's students

Tomorrow's students will be more likely to be self-financing, studying part-time or in mixed mode. A high percentage will be registered at their local university and will expect to use distance-learning packages and facilities at their local colleges to support their own campus study. They will be largely or wholly self-financing, and, aware that the job market will not guarantee a 'graduate job', will study a mixture of subjects which will allow them flexibility and transferable skills as well as serving their personal interests. They are likely to be very aware of themselves as the 'purchasers' of higher education and to be clear of what they want and expect in terms of content, timing and quality.

Particularly in universities which choose and market this route, students will come from the immediate region. They will live either wholly at home or go home for part of the time. They may have family responsibilities, or take this path simply for financial reasons. If they are school-leavers, they may be first-generation undergraduates and have come by way of their local college or through a special compact with the university.

Considerably more students will study part-time or in a mixed mode, so that they can work to finance their studies or to manage domestic circumstances. They will expect to be able to undertake a large proportion of their work at home, by means of distance-learning packages and may need local access to computers, phones and faxes.

A proportion of students will be in employment and will study 'in-company' with university staff working with them in their place of employment. They will want professional updating and recognition of their skills and experience. To turn 'training' into a broader experience, some may receive sponsorship for a campus-based 'sabbatical' in order to undertake a period of intense study of professional 'conversion' or postgraduate updating. Some will receive sponsorship from the state in the form of scholarships or from private sources for a period of study spent in a college with some time at the local university. Such a programme might result in an Honours degree, or, more likely, a two-year diploma or the proposed 'Associate Degree' (Robertson 1994).

A generation of 'higher-age' entrants reflecting an ageing population and a younger retirement age will be those who have retired from full-time employment and are seeking a structured learning and social experience. Most will study part-time, collecting credits as they go. They will be self-funding. This group will also want to be able to undertake some part of their work at home as well as having personal contact with staff and other students.

Many women students will be in self-employment or in small- or medium-sized businesses. They will be seeking high-level specific skills training as well as the opportunity to acquire a portfolio of knowledge and transferable skills.

Finally, students will be aware of the need for flexible and up-datable skills in their university programmes. With credit accumulation and modularity standard throughout Europe and throughout the whole education system from nursery school onwards, students will construct packages which serve a number of their interests and needs. Enthusiasm for the Arts and Social Sciences will continue and, whilst there may be financial incentives to study Engineering and other currently less-popular subjects, only those with a more flexible content and mode of delivery will be able to increase their take-up rate.

Some common factors

It is legitimate to ask whether the diversity, of which the UK higher-education system is proud, will survive the onslaught of mass higher education, especially in its current forms. Many universities, particularly the 'new' universities, already target and cater for students of a wide range of ages and backgrounds. The educational and cultural benefits this deliberate mix provides may, as well as the more pragmatic issues of the 'market', lead others to review their own recruitment policies. Whether some universities will wish and be able to attract almost exclusively school-leavers with traditional entry requirements is an interesting question. Even if this is a real choice, these universities, along with all others, will need to work with nationally recognized credit systems which operate throughout the whole education system from school onwards (Robertson 1994). The divide between further and higher education will become eroded and further and higher education institutions within a region will need to cooperate to provide resource centres and two-way ladders between their programmes or face some potentially destructive competition. All institutions will need to take account of the diversity of their student population and to cater for this with great care. At a university which has campuses around the region, which is partially electronic and where most students do not reside within walking distances of its main centre, not only teaching and learning arrangements but a range of other needs will have to be catered for in more creative ways than at present.

Questions students will ask – and some possible answers

Why should I study?

To improve career prospects, to develop personal skills and for enjoyment.

Offering the incentive of better employment or even employment at all has been problematic during the recession of the 1980s and 1990s. What has become apparent, to employers and to students, however, is that skills acquired along with knowledge are crucially important. This is unlikely to change. In the future, graduates may well change career direction a number of times and find themselves moving towards a portfolio of commissions which they manage on a self-employed basis. Others will need highly specialist skills and knowledge, for example in medicine, although such students will need, as much as any others, the ability to think flexibly, manage a wide portfolio of responsibilities and learn new techniques speedily. Increasingly, all graduates will need a range of sophisticated skills in word-processing and computer literacy. They are likely to demand, instead of an in-depth knowledge of modern languages, the ability to 'get by' and manage the courtesies in a number of European and non-European languages. They will need to manage money, understand marketing and have good interpersonal skills. Those wishing to attract to their programmes those who are not in employment, will need to demonstrate the value of study as both a valid interest/leisure pursuit and a possible tool for future employment.

There will be a larger generation of parents who are themselves graduates and who will wish to see their children at university. It may be that the personal and social value of an education and the benefits of life-long learning are more firmly rooted in a wider section of the population than has been the pattern in the past, although there is a strong risk that aspirations will fade as public-funding diminishes.

As a school-leaver, a 'second time around' returner, an employed person updating skills or a higher-age recreational student, the reasons for taking up a university place will be different and this will need to be recognized in issues such as opening hours, flexible learning and distance-learning packages, access to study centres and a diverse and varied university cultural and social life.

How long will it take?

As long as you want it to. You can get a degree in two years or take much longer working at your own pace and at the rate you can afford to finance. There is no need to worry about 'dropping out'. Your work will be credited and you can 'cash in' your credits in the future, or transfer them to another institution.

The answer is likely to be that the time taken to study for a degree will vary enormously. The minimum and norm for what are currently called full-time students will be two calendar years, with four terms in each year, but for many, credits will be built up over a longer period of time. The 12-hour full-year timetable will be the norm and some facilities may open on a 24-hour basis.

What will it cost?

Each credit will be costed at a fee level determined by the university. You pay as you learn. You will also need to support yourself financially and buy or rent necessary materials.

Each module or part of a programme studied will be costed by the providing institution. There may well be competitive price structures from rival universities, or an attempt to undercut by further education colleges. Regional voluntary consortia will be the best protection and best means of assuring a variety of provision at a quality level. Core facilities at the university and constituent college campuses will be included in this fee.

How will I pay for my study?

It depends where you are in your life and career. If you are a school-leaver you may be entitled to vouchers to put towards your studies. Otherwise you will need to be self-financing or have sponsorship, for example, from an employer or a charity or business. If you are studying in a national priority area, like engineering or some of the sciences, a future employer may be prepared to sponsor your studies in return for a commitment from you to work for that company for an agreed number of years.

For most, the answer will be that the cost of fees and maintenance will fall on them and their families. For school-leavers there will be support in the form of vouchers towards, but not representing, the whole cost of a programme of study. For some, on low income, there will be state scholarships and for others sponsorship from employers. Others will take out student loans or sign up for a graduate tax and those studying out of interest may pay towards a 'friends' membership scheme which allows them access to programmes and events in return for voluntary services to the institution, such as examination invigilation.

There is likely to be no distinction, from the student's point of view, between full-time and part-time study. They will pay for each module or credit-based unit. Above all, students will be looking for value for money and for speedy or flexible provision.

What will I study?

Most subjects will be available to you, and in flexible combinations. You will want to satisfy yourself that your interests are met and that your programme is flexible enough, if you are seeking a career, to take you not only into your first but into subsequent career changes. You will collect credits as you go. You should recognize that this may just be the first stage of a lifetime of further study. You may opt for a degree in a mixture of subjects which interest you and develop your general skills and then undertake specific postgraduate professional training.

However acquired, core skills of literacy, visual literacy, numeracy and computing skills will be necessary. The acquisition of these will be explicit and noted in some form for employers to see and test. Along with these basic skills, the graduate will need to demonstrate communication skills, and work skills in addition to specialist skills and knowledge.

It is likely that the Arts and Social Sciences will remain popular, especially with mature students, but that they will be studied in combination with other subjects to give the maximum flexibility in terms of a skills and knowledge portfolio.

Where should I study?

Consider what you need. If you are studying to get a job or to develop new skills, your local university is probably ideal for you. If you want to study at that university and spend part of your time in another university, remember that your credits are transferable and that your university, along with others in Europe and throughout the world, will have schemes which allow you to spend some time in a new environment, whilst still collecting credits towards your qualification.

The choices will be available for those able to travel, either to attend a formal or one of the new private universities offering overseas degrees. Within the region the choice will be between local college and university, but as regional post-16 provision develops, this choice will become less meaningful. Some universities will have a reputation for being at the cutting edge in research and these institutions will be the destination of those aiming for a particular research-based career.

Where will I live?

You have options, depending on your circumstances and what you can afford. You can live at home and study at your local university and this may be the most cost-effective or convenient route. Your university will maintain a number of bookable rooms on campus for the occasional overnight stay. Alternatively, you can live on campus in special student accommodation, which is simple but convenient, or rent privately.

Increasingly, the answer will be 'at home', not only for mature students with local roots and commitments, but also for many school-leavers for whom the luxury of moving away from home will not be financially possible. Since institutions have a commitment to broadening a student's outlook and experience as part of their education, it is important that everyone at university has some chance to travel and study away from their home region, either through national or international exchanges. or periods of study/work placement. Similarly, universities will want to build a mixed community so that local students meet those from further afield and visitors from all over the world. It may be, to this end, that international students are recruited at a reduced-fee level and that in the UK interuniversity exchange programmes are organized.

What will my social life be like as a student?

Your university and its partner colleges will be the centre of a number of arts, sporting and other activities in the region. You may already have had contact with these as a local inhabitant or through your school or college.

The campus itself will be less of a focus. Work at home and at the work stations of local colleges and schools will provide a great deal of the resource-based learning experience. For those who follow a 'specialist' route, this will be interspersed with work-based practical experience, somewhat like the current 'sandwich' arrangements.

For most, there will be times at the central campus and the social and cultural life of the region will be closely tied into the college and university campuses. Social contact will be a valued balance to the isolation of learning and institutions and students' unions will need to cater for the full range of members. There will be need for support in caring, whether of children or elderly relatives, and it is possible that a number of these agencies, together with catering and welfare, will be handed over to the students' unions. Networks will increase in importance, both for social and professional contacts, and alumni associations will help to provide the structure for this.

What will I have at the end?

Evidence for employers that you have a number of skills and a specific knowledge base. You will also have acquired leisure and personal skills which will enhance your life.

A certificate, diploma or degree, which is credit-based, and the expectation that this will be 'topped up' at a later stage will be the most common outcome of a period of study. Degrees will be of a variety ranging from the current Honours to the proposed 'Associate Degree' gained after the equivalent of two years' study.

How do I get a place?

Universities are now much more flexible than they used to be. Especially if you are self-financing, you will find that the accreditation of your learning and life experiences so far may give you credits to start with. You may wish to enter from school by way of the usual route, but this is now just one of many.

With flexible modes of study, and 24-hour campuses, open all year, there will be places for the majority of those who wish to, and can afford to, study. Where scholarships exist, they will be competitive and means tested, otherwise financial arrangements will be between each institution, which can use its government grant in a number of ways, one of which might be to sponsor certain categories of student to ensure a balanced community. There will be flexible exit and entry times and students will be able to tailor their studies to their own needs and circumstances.

Institutions will have targets for categories of students and develop specialisms and resources to attract these. 'A' levels or their equivalent will maintain currency, although their content and style will more flexible, crossing the vocational/academic divide. Other students, both from the region and outside, will come through a number of compacts, transferable around the country, but which ensure that the school-leaver's educational experience is continuous and holistic. Similar schemes will exist for returners coming through further education colleges.

How will I judge the quality of the education and experience I am buying?

The responsibility for learning is yours and only you can judge, using the codes of practice you are given, whether the help you are receiving from those who are employed to facilitate your learning is what you want and need and if it is up to standard.

Students will be involved in a serious way in the quality-assurance processes and monitoring, with both compulsory and credit-rated periods of responsibility for this within the university's systems. Peer-group academic help and study groups will exist on a mutual basis and some students will be employed as assistants.

Issues of quality will be of even greater importance to institutions as the power to 'purchase' a place comes to rest in the hands of students, given that they will be seeking qualifications which have currency and value in the labour market.

Two scenarios

The bad news

Only the rich and the very poor and bright will travel away from home to study, supported by their families or by a few highly competitive means-tested government scholarships. Money will thus allow freedom of choice only to those who can afford it. These students will have access to a small group of élite universities which have a greater income, more resources and which may offer better prospects to the undergraduate as well as more opportunities for research. Out of this might well come an ossification of a 'tiered' system and a schism between education and training, with the latter being seen as the provision of 'enough' education to produce, as in the Industrial Revolution, efficient workers, whilst the élite have time to ponder.

The good news

Whereas the current system is built on the assumption that higher education is a race in which few have been selected to enter and even fewer are able to jump the hurdles and win, the new mass system will be based on different premises. These will be largely non-competitive and predicated on the provision, à la Robbins and the CBI report, of opportunities for everyone who can benefit, with this interpreted in the widest sense.

The good news is therefore that opportunities will be available to far more people and barriers of age, disability or background will be somewhat eroded. The challenge to achieve effective policies to widen participation remains enormous. Unlike the expansion of the early 1990s which has benefited largely the middle classes, with children from professional and managerial families being four times more likely to apply to university, a genuinely expanded system will need to be serious about its target groups. It will also need to have clear strategies to enhance quality whilst offering an individual the chance for intellectual and personal development.

In order to fulfil the demands of the public for more opportunities, industry for a better educated work force and to deal at source with issues of social unrest, an ageing population and changes in the ways in which people work, the challenges will have to be met. The cost of not meeting them is great, both financially and socially. The large and flexible new universities, which could constitute some 95 per cent of the system, will have a vibrant regional base, provide relevant education and training and offer an academic, social and cultural package to students which will serve them well and keep the majority committed to continued learning throughout their lives. Research opportunities will be available widely in graduate schools attached to most of these universities.

Within this scenario, students will themselves choose a range of flexible ways of studying which fit their lives. They may go to a local college for all or part of their degree work or to undertake their post-college studies by distance learning from another institution. These are the students who will satisfy employers that they have the relevant skills.

Just as the writing of history can never be free from the concerns and prejudices of the time in which it is written, so predictions of the future, in the form of discussion documents or science fiction, are saying as much about the present as the future. Issues of the quality of the student experience within a mass system, funding and the implications for staff, for teaching and learning are all currently being faced by the providers of post-16 education. Students are our business and students remain our prime concern. To give the largest number, from the widest possible spectrum of backgrounds, the best possible education that we can provide, is the challenge which will not go away.

References

CBI (1994) *Thinking Ahead: Ensuring the Expansion of Higher Education into the 21st Century.* London, CBI.

Deere, M. (1993) *Guidance to Higher Education on GNVQs Level 3.* London, SCVE UCAS.

Hansard (1993) *Student Financial Difficulty.* London, HMSO.

Josefowitz, N. (1983) *Is This Where I Was Going?* London, Columbus.

Robertson, D. (1994) *Choosing to Change.* London, HEQC.

11

Changing the Culture of Scholarship to the Culture of Teaching: An American Perspective

Stephen Brookfield

This chapter examines the cultural changes that have altered how American public and private universities' view what counts as 'proper' scholarship. In the UK, university teachers currently feel overwhelmed by what they regard as an American style emphasis on equating scholarly competence with the number of research papers published. However, this is a somewhat distorted picture of how one's fitness for university teaching is viewed in universities across the USA. Whilst the publish or perish syndrome is still evident in the larger and more prestigious research universities, many campuses within the state university system, as well as numerous smaller public and private universities, have moved to a more reflective approach to evaluating faculty performance (Centra 1993, 1994). In books by Halpern *et al.* (1994) and Katz and Henry (1993) we can see how teachers' ability to reflect on teaching and learning has emerged as a focus for employment and promotion decisions, for professional development, and for assessing scholarly competence. The appearance of the Carnegie Foundation's report *Scholarship Reconsidered* (Boyer 1990) has prompted new conceptualizations of what it means to be a university scholar (Richlin 1993), including a recognition and honouring of teaching as a scholarly act (Ronkowski 1993). An engagement in what is generally described as 'reflective practice' has been invoked as the conceptual cornerstone in building a case for broadening how scholarship is conceived and for making changes in how faculty are appointed, promoted and tenured. A consistent commitment by lecturers and professors to teaching more reflectively is now an important indicator in many universities for deciding how to award merit payments, travel money, and other professional perks. In the following paragraphs I examine the concept of reflective practice, reframing it with a critical edge, and speculating on how university cultures and reward systems would have to change if scholars' engagement with critical reflection on teaching became the chief professional behaviour that administrators wished to encourage. Building on some ideas discussed by Duke (1992) in *The Learning University*, I conclude with a scenario of how a staff development project would look if it took critical reflection as its organizing idea.

The concept of reflective practice

Reflection as an organizing idea for educational practice has captured many people's imagination, partially because of its apparent conceptual malleability. It seems to be able to mean all things to all people. Newman (1994: 236) describes its chequered history as follows:

> the meaning we have given to reflection has undergone a number of changes. It started as a concept very much within the liberal tradition of education, was injected with a charge of high emotion from the field of psychotherapy, was politicised, was gradually wrested back by the humanists, and is currently in danger of being taken over by latter day behaviourists.

Reflective practice has its roots in the Enlightenment idea that we can make rational decisions that are in our own best interests and that we can come to a clearer understanding of what we do and who we are by freeing ourselves of distorted ways of reasoning and acting. There are also elements of constructivist phenomenology in the understanding that identity and experience are culturally and personally sculpted rather than existing in some kind of objectively discernible reality. American pragmatism is also present in the reflective tradition's emphasis on making practice attentive to context, and in its disdain for standardized models of good teaching. Schon's work on the reflective practitioner (1983, 1987) and the reflective turn (1991) has been crucial to bringing this train of thought to the attention of educators. In recent years, books on reflective practice have burgeoned and an impressive number of studies have been conducted on the ways that teachers learn to reflect on what, why and how they teach. John Smyth (1988, 1992) is one of the few writers who has crossed the frontier of reflective practice to explore its interconnections with critical theory. Although his work seems on the surface to be grounded in the reflective practice paradigm, he draws consistently and explicitly on the Frankfurt School tradition.

Reflective practice theorists are interested in helping scholars understand, question, investigate and take seriously their own learning and teaching. They argue that professional education has taken a wrong turn in seeing the role of staff and faculty developer as being to interpret, translate and implement theoretical insights. They believe instead that practitioners, including university faculty, must research their own work sites, must recognize and generate their own theories of practice rather than importing them from outside, and must develop the capacity for a kind of continuous investigation and monitoring of their efforts. Good teachers, according to this tradition, are in the habit of identifying and checking the assumptions behind their practice and of experimenting creatively with approaches they have themselves evolved in response to the unique demands of the situations in which they work. In Smyth's (1988: 32) words, they perceive themselves as 'active' learners, inquirers and advocates of their own practices . . . critical theoreticians in their own teaching and the structures in which they are located.

The critical edge: reframing reflection as critical reflection

The idea of reflective practice has informed discussion on the scholarship of teaching and has provided the justification for the use of the teaching portfolio on North American campuses. This idea is not without its problems. It is noticeable that the literature on reflective practice is strong on suggestions for classroom practice but pays much less attention to the social and political purposes of reflection. Reflection is in real danger of becoming a buzz word denuded of any real meaning, of acting as a premature ultimate. A premature ultimate is a concept that, once it is invoked, stops any critical debate dead in its tracks. 'Reflective' may well simply become a word that we attach to any teaching that we happen to like. As Smyth (1992: 285) writes,

> reflection can mean all things to all people, and because it is used as a kind of umbrella or canopy term to signify something that is good or desirable to do in respect of teaching, it runs the real risk of being totally evacuated of all meaning.

In reframing reflection as critical reflection, we need to define exactly what it is that makes reflection critical. As an intellectual activity, reflection involves three distinct but overlapping processes: (1) becoming aware of the assumptions that inform how we think and act; (2) learning how to check these assumptions for their accuracy and validity in different contexts; and (3) taking different perspectives on familiar ideas and actions. The point of reflection is the taking of informed actions in the world.

The reflective process becomes critical when it has four distinct concerns:

1. The first is the concern to illuminate how the variable of power is manifest within, and influences, all educational interactions. This includes processes in which there exists power *with* as well as power *over* learners (Kreisberg 1992).
2. The second is the concern to focus on the intended and unintended repressive dimensions to educational ideologies and practices. By 'repressive dimensions' I mean the ways in which educational practices and ideologies impede the realization of democratic forms and values. Reforms such as centrally prescribed curricula that are embraced because they seem to make a teacher's life easier, can obscure their undemocratic nature and consequences.
3. The third is the concern to be aware of the ways in which assumptions and practices that seem to be for teachers' own good actually work against their own long-term best interests. For example, learning to play the scrambling, frenetic, politically fraught game of getting tenure may seem to be a wonderful short-term goal for a university teacher. In the long run, however, the experience

can leave teachers exhausted and compromised with a burden of self-loathing that is never unloaded. A better use of their time might be to work collectively for ways of altering or abandoning the tenure system, or to challenge the premises on which it is based.

4. The fourth is the concern to study the reflective process itself. Critical reflection regards reflection as a problematic activity in which is embedded the possibility for self-deception and for authoritarian practice. A critically reflective teacher realizes that critical reflection itself constitutes an ideology that has sprung from a particular group, time and place. It is not viewed as a universal form of consciousness or a divinely ordained intellectual process, but as an ideological formation representing a certain set of interests.

Creating a reward system for critical reflection

Reward systems drive faculty behaviour. Consequently, the most important place to start creating structures and procedures which imply that critical reflection is a normal and desirable institutional habit is by changing the reward systems that are in place within universities. If we log the ways in which lecturers spend their days on campuses where the 'publish or perish' syndrome reigns, the greater part of their energy is devoted to scholarly research and writing. If we compile a similar record of teachers' behaviours in colleges that prize good teaching, we find, not surprisingly, much more emphasis on teachers participating in faculty development, in their designing new materials, and in their experimenting with different pedagogical approaches. We also find that students' evaluations of teachers' abilities are taken very seriously when promotion and re-appointment decisions are being made.

A reward system that encouraged critical reflection would make a demonstrable commitment to this process the chief professional behaviour that was rewarded. An eagerness to become critically reflective – and a minimal understanding of what this involved – would become an important criterion for whether or not candidates were appointed to lectureships in the first place. Those who could document a more or less continuous effort on their part to question assumptions and explore alternatives would be the ones who would be most likely to be promoted, given merit payments and honoured with 'Teacher of the Year' awards. Teaching-evaluation forms completed by students at the end of a course would be redesigned to take account of the cognitive and emotional complexities entailed in teachers becoming critically reflective. Instead of lecturers being evaluated only on how or if they pleased students (through forms that ask students whether or not they liked the teacher or the class) there would be items on course evaluations that would probe the extent to which students felt they had been stretched, challenged, questioned and introduced to alternative perspectives.

Job descriptions would name critical reflection as the professional attribute most sought after in candidates. Application forms would ask for evidence of past engagement in this process and for a statement of how it would be pursued in the position being sought. Involvement in faculty critical reflection groups would be institutionally supported through faculty being given release time to participate in such groups during the normal work day.

A reward system for critical reflection would also encourage lecturers and professors to engage in the kind of professional development experience in which they agreed to learn something new and difficult on a regular basis as a means of gaining new insights into their teaching. Making the deliberate attempt to view their own practice through the lens of learning would become the norm for faculty-development activities. An attempt to help colleagues negotiate their own critical journeys – to be critical friends or reflective mirrors – would be regarded as the most collegial kind of behaviour possible. At the end of each year (or at other points of faculty review and appraisal) lecturers would be asked to submit a critical reflection portfolio (Seldin 1991, 1994). This portfolio would constitute the major piece of evidence used to determine promotion and tenure. It would document not only teachers' personal involvement in critical reflection, but also their efforts to encourage this in colleagues through various forms of mentorship. Items to be included in the portfolio might include extracts from teaching journals, letters of thanks from colleagues, video vignettes from classroom teaching, taped discussions from critical reflection groups, statements of purpose and rationale in course outlines, examples of how syllabuses for the same course had changed over the years to take account of new theoretical formulations or research findings, narrative evaluations given to students on their work in progress, and so on. As a way of the administration showing its commitment to this activity, sufficient release time would be granted for the preparation of these portfolios. Honours recognizing pedagogic excellence (such as 'Teacher of the Year' awards) would be bestowed on those individuals who had owned up to what they saw as their own failures and mistakes and who had demonstrated how they had learned from these. Those willing to make their struggles public, rather than those who seemed to have resolved all possible problems, would become acclaimed professional exemplars.

Modelling critical reflection

In studies of how teachers change their practice, teachers time and time again stress that the factor most likely to encourage them to risk being critically reflective is seeing this behaviour modelled by the senior administrator who has the greatest control over their futures. It takes a while for lecturers to trust administrators (just as it does for students to trust teachers) but once those who have the most to lose in terms of their reputation, status and prestige are seen to be inviting and welcoming a critical scrutiny of their actions, the effect is undeniable. One way administrators could send a message concerning how seriously they took critical reflection would be for them to make their perceived readiness to engage in this process, the chief indicator of administrative effectiveness. In institutions where administrators regularly invite faculty to appraise their work, asking the faculty how well the administrator was exemplifying critical process would ensure that there was no perception of a double standard where teaching and administrative effectiveness was concerned. Both groups would be shown to be held to the same criterion of good, critically reflective practice.

If they took modelling critical reflection seriously, deans, department chairs, and even chancellors and Chief Executive Officers would find themselves going public with their own learning. In college newsletters, faculty meetings and in public speeches they would recreate in public the private reasoning behind their decisions, paying particular attention to times when events had caused them to re-think their basic assumptions or to see things from an entirely different viewpoint. They would invite critique of their actions and, when this critique was not forthcoming (as it would not be at first given the level of mistrust in most educational institutions) they would play the role of devil's advocate in offering alternative perspectives on what they had done. They would take pains to ensure that their words and actions were perceived as being as consistent as possible by soliciting regular anonymous commentary on how they were doing (the anonymity being crucial to make faculty feel safe in being honest) and by then making this commentary public. Several times a year, faculty would receive written summaries of the anonymous comments they had given, and they would be invited to discuss these at a faculty meeting. Administrators would also do their best to build a case for critical reflection by using their autobiographies to illustrate the benefits of the process in their own lives. They would start faculty-development days by talking about the role that critical reflection was playing in their own practice and they would invite faculty and administrators from other institutions where critical reflection was valued to come and talk about its importance.

Scenario

In this scenario I imagine that a university chancellor has provided funding for a staff development effort designed to foster lecturers' critical reflection on the experience of teaching.

MEMORANDUM

To: All Faculty
From: The Chancellor
Re: The ELICIT Programme

Most staff development is done *to* teachers by people defined as outside experts around a problem that these experts have selected. What I want to do this year is find a way to make the 'content' of our staff development your own experiences as learners and teachers. The following four projects – all of which I have authorized funding and release time for – are aimed at getting you to take your experiences seriously.

ELICIT: Experiential Learning to Improve
        Classroom Inquiry and Teaching

A Staff Development Project

Becoming learners

In the first project for the coming academic year I want each of you to learn something new and difficult, to analyse carefully how this feels, and to talk with each other about the implications these experiences as learners have for your work as teachers. As outlined below, the project is arranged to run from the start of term until Christmas.

1. For the Autumn Term, each lecturer and professor will be granted some remission of their normal work load (a course less, being able to resign from certain committees, and so on) to enable them to participate in this scheme. I want you to use the time that has become available to learn something that is new, unfamiliar and difficult for you. The only conditions I place on this effort are that it must be learning that occurs in a group setting where someone (it does not have to be just one person) is identified as the leader or teacher.

2. In the second week of term we will hold an introductory session. Classes will be cancelled so that all staff can meet for a half day in which we will try to accomplish four things. First, we will describe to each other the various learning activities we have each chosen to pursue. Second, we will write down as many of the thoughts we have about the learning that awaits us. I want you to document how it feels to be a neophyte, what kinds of things you hope will happen at the first class and beyond, and what characteristics you would most like to see in the teachers you will soon be meeting. Third we will talk about how we might best be able to keep a learning journal of our experiences. I want you to note down at the end of each class the moments in the class during which you were most engaged, the moments when you were most distanced, the actions that anyone in the room took that were most helpful and affirming for you, the actions that anyone in the room took that were most puzzling to you, and anything that surprised you about your experiences in the class that week. Fourth, we will start to talk about the assumptions and beliefs we have about what constitutes good teaching.

3. In the first week of October you will each begin the learning activities you have chosen. Once a week – from the first class onwards – you will meet to talk to each other about whatever you have written in your learning journals. As you listen to each other's stories you should start to look for common themes. For example, what happened on the first class meeting that most of you disliked or were affirmed by? What did you feel it was important to know about, or to accomplish, that first night? What did you sense that was missing?

4. In the first week of November and again in the first week of December classes will be cancelled for a half a day each time so that you can devote ourselves entirely to an in-depth interim analysis of the themes that have emerged from your analyses of your learning. I want you to talk about the assumptions and beliefs about good teaching that you voiced at the

first session and to compare these to what good teaching now looks like from the vantage point of your having reflected purposefully on your own experiences as learners.

5. In the last week of the term (just before the Christmas break) classes will be cancelled for a whole day so that we can undertake a cumulative analysis of the experience so far. I want you to identify the common themes that have emerged from your weekly debriefing sessions. I want you to make explicit how your basic assumptions, beliefs and models of teaching and learning have been changed, modified, confirmed or broadened by your experience of learning. Finally, I want you to talk about how your own teaching will change in the future as a result of this experience.

6. We will find a way to write up the discussion and insights that emerge in the cumulative analysis during this last meeting. This material will be published as the lead article in the next issue of our newsletter.

Teaching Logs

For the rest of the academic year (that is, from next January onward) I want you to compile a weekly Teaching Log. A Teaching Log is a weekly record of the events in your teaching that have impressed themselves most vividly on you. Each week I would like you to think about the things that happened to you that caused you some particular pleasure, stress or puzzlement. Keeping a log of your private reactions to – and interpretations of – these events, is one way of helping you realize several things about yourself. As you review your jottings over a period of time you'll see that they comprise a record of your preoccupations, obsessions and commonly experienced problems. Reading your log you'll start to see patterns of inclusion and exclusion – things that keep cropping up and consuming your attention and emotional energy and things that are conspicuous by their absence. You'll become more aware of some of your habitual practices, you'll get a more accurate reading of the dilemmas (ethical and methodological) you encounter on a regular basis, and you'll begin to notice typical triggers to your emotional peaks and to periods of self-doubt.

The log will also help you develop insight into your own emotional and cognitive teaching rhythms. By this I mean that you will become more aware of how you go about organizing your teaching, what kinds of teaching tasks you are drawn to, what teaching styles you find most congenial, what tasks you resist and seek to avoid, what conditions encourage you to take risks, what warning signals indicate that you are hitting an emotional low, and what factors tend to keep you going through the 'quitting times' of low morale, depression and loss of confidence. You will also become aware of the framing assumptions you have as a teacher, and of how these can be analysed critically.

Keep this log on a regular weekly basis, spending maybe 15–20 minutes a week on writing your entries. To give you ample time for the reflection and writing that this task entails, all staff will have their weekly teaching loads reduced by two hours from January onward. Use the time that will be made available to jot down some brief responses to any of the following questions that seem appropriate:

- What was the moment (or moments) this week when I felt most connected, engaged or affirmed as a teacher – the moment(s) I said to myself, 'This is what being a university teacher is really all about'?
- What was the moment (or moments) this week when I felt most disconnected, disengaged or bored as a teacher – the moment(s) I said to myself, 'I'm just going through the motions here'?
- What was the situation I faced that caused me the greatest anxiety or distress – the kind of situation that I kept replaying in my mind as I was dropping off to sleep, or that caused me to say to myself, 'I don't want to go through this again for a while'?
- What was the event that happened this week that most took me by surprise – an event where I saw or did something that shook me up, took me off guard, put me off my stride, gave me a jolt, made me unexpectedly happy?
- What were the most significant events or moments I passed through this week in my life as a teacher?
- Of everything I did this week in my teaching, what would I do differently if I had to do it again?
- What do I feel proudest about regarding my teaching activities this week? Why?
- What do I feel most dissatisfied with, regarding my teaching activities this week? Why?
- What teaching tasks gave me the greatest difficulties this week? What made them so tough?
- What teaching tasks did I respond to most enjoyably and easily this week? What made them so pleasurable?

Feel free to ignore these questions, to suggest your own, and to record any other entries that scream for inclusion but that don't fit one of the questions above. Don't worry if your answers to these questions overlap or if you feel one question has already been answered in your responses to an earlier question. Do try and write something, however brief, in response to each question. Even noting that nothing surprised you, or that there were no high or low emotional moments in your teaching, tells you something about your teaching and the conditions under which you work.

As you read your weekly entries over the weeks and then months of a term or semester, you'll notice certain patterns emerging in your responses. You may well start to see a range of typical situations that create pleasure or pain for you. The frequency with which these occur will give you clues as to the sources of energy and strength that need to be guarded in your practice. It will also alert you to the energy draining, debilitating situations that need changing, or at least keeping to a minimum. Your responses over time to the question 'What gave me my greatest surprise?' should give you clues to some of the tangles and dilemmas you face for which you don't have a ready explanation or pre-set instinctive response. Recognizing these unexpected dimensions of your practice should help you develop a sense of where your blind spots might be; it will alert you to some assumptions about teaching that you might need to question and to areas in which you might need to become more skilful. Having this information should help you make better informed decisions about the faculty development activities in which you want to become involved, or the kinds of professional conferences and workshops you want to attend. It will also help you structure any time you have for your own professional reading or for any other development efforts on which you want to work.

If possible, I encourage you to share your log with a colleague. If you feel uncomfortable about having someone read your entries you could arrange a time (lunch, over coffee) to talk in general terms about what you've written. Colleagues can act as useful reflective mirrors; they can spot patterns of behaviour we exhibit and assumptions that inform our practice that are too close to our experience for us to be able to see clearly.

Staff meetings

At our weekly two-hour staff meetings I am proposing that we invert the normal running order so that 'Any Other Business' is the first, not last, item on the agenda. We will spend one hour on this item. All other agenda items will have to be discussed during the second hour.

References

Boyer, E.L. (1990) *Scholarship Reconsidered: Priorities of the Professoriate*. Princeton, Carnegie Foundation for the Advancement of Teaching.

Centra, J.A. (1993) *Reflective Faculty Evaluation: Enhancing Teaching and Determining Faculty Effectiveness*. San Francisco, Jossey Bass.

Centra, J.A. (1994) The use of the teaching portfolio and student evaluations for summative evaluation, *Journal of Higher Education*, 65, 555–570.

Duke, C. (1992) *The Learning University: Towards a New Paradigm?* Milton Keynes, Open University Press.

Halpern, D.F. and Associates (1994) *Changing College Classrooms: New Teaching and Learning Strategies for an Increasingly Complex World*. San Francisco, Jossey Bass.

Katz, J. and Henry, M. (1993) *Turning Professors into Teachers: A New Approach to Faculty Development and Student Learning*. Phoenix, Arizona, The Oryx Press.

Kreisberg, S. (1992) *Transforming Power: Domination, Empowerment, and Education*. Albany: State University of New York Press.

Newman, M. (1994) 'Response to understanding transformation theory', *Adult Education Quarterly*, 44, 236–242.

Richlin, L. (ed.) (1993) *Preparing Faculty for New Conceptions of Scholarship.* San Francisco, Jossey Bass.

Ronkowski, S.A. (1993) 'Scholarly teaching: developmental stages of pedagogical scholarship', in L. Richlin (ed.) *Preparing Faculty for New Conceptions of Scholarship.* San Francisco, Jossey Bass.

Schön, D.A. (1983) *The Reflective Practitioner.* New York, Basic Books.

Schön, D.A. (1987) *Educating the Reflective Practitioner.* San Francisco, Jossey Bass.

Schön, D.A. (ed.) (1991) *The Reflective Turn: Case Studies in and on Educational Practice.* New York, Teachers' College Press.

Seldin, P. (1991) *The Teaching Portfolio: A Practical Guide to Improved Performance and Promotion/Tenure Decisions.* Boston, Anker Publishing.

Seldin, P. (1994) *Successful Use of the Teaching Portfolio.* Boston, Anker Publishing.

Smyth, W.J. (1988) *A Critical Pedagogy of Teacher Evaluation.* Victoria, Australia, Deakin University Press.

Smyth, J. (1992) 'Teachers' work and the politics of reflection', *American Educational Research Journal,* 29, 267–300.

12

Funding a Changing System

Gwynneth Rigby

Introduction

This chapter argues that unless government and the academic community can come together to rework the basic principles and practices which have governed the funding of higher education since the Robbins expansion of the 1960s, higher education in the UK will suffer an unacceptable decline in quality and academic standards. The hard-won and dramatic increase in participation and access may go into reverse, and the system will fail to prepare individuals and society adequately for life and work in the competitive world economy of the twenty-first century. It argues that the costs of continued expansion must be met by a new balance between public and private investment, and that the funding regime for institutions must have sufficient flexibility to facilitate in practice the diversity of mission which government, institutions and organisations such as the CBI and the World Bank all now promote as a desirable strategic goal.

Accelerating change and financial pressure

Universities in the UK have already undergone fundamental and accelerating change in recent years. The move from an élite to a mass system now seems a *fait accompli*. The student population has not only expanded beyond all expectations but has become more diverse in terms of its socio-economic and age profile. There are beginning to be changes in the way students qualify for entry to higher education, in what they learn while at university and in the ways in which they learn. There is a better understanding of the importance, in a society in which knowledge and applied intelligence are central to economic success and personal and social well-being, of the need to encourage continued life-long learning. The value of looking at all post-compulsory education and training as part of a continuum of learning is increasingly accepted. The balance between full-time and part-time study is shifting and the advent of modular courses and credit accumulation and transfer schemes has the potential to make such distinctions outmoded. The supremacy of the three-year classified Honours degree is being challenged in favour of a system of cumulative and staged awards. Universities are no longer the sole providers of higher education and now compete with the further education sector and with private providers, including large employers.

Much of this change is very positive. But it has placed a considerable strain on public funding. While the Government claims the credit for increased participation and its expenditure plans refer comfortably to productivity gains 'accompanied by maintained or increased quality' (DFE 1994: para. 167), the impact at institutional level has been severe. The total amount of public funding devoted to higher education has grown rapidly in recent years, with an increase of 23 per cent since 1989–90 (CBI 1994, para. 110), but this has largely been accounted for by growth in the student support and welfare element in the overall budget. The reality for institutions has been one of cuts, with a fall of over 30 per cent in the public funding they receive per student since 1980 (Williams and Fry 1994). Moreover, further efficiency gains of 10 per cent are to be imposed in the next three years on the amount per student received from the funding councils, with continued downward pressure thereafter.

Cuts have been deeper for some institutions than others, but most university managers have tried to find ways of maximizing income from alternative sources, thereby placing new and often unwelcome responsibilities on both teaching and research staff. Conditions of work for both staff and students have deteriorated as human and physical resources have become increasingly over-stretched. At the same time, increasingly complex formula funding and demands for greater accountability have led to the introduction of mechanisms which link funding to performance, and have brought in their wake a range of externally imposed, rigid, and administratively demanding procedures for assessing quality both in teaching and research. While reluctant to admit to any erosion in academic standards, the Committee of Vice-Chancellors and Principals (CVCP) has been provoked into stating publicly that the 'student experience has been qualitatively impaired' in recent years, as institutions have tried to do more with less (CVCP 1994).

Expansion threatened

As the costs of expansion have increasingly become a matter for public debate, government has reined back on numbers, cutting the level of public funding channelled to institutions via student fees to discourage institutions from recruiting at the margin. At the same time, there has been questioning of the value and usefulness of continuing to produce ever-increasing numbers of graduates especially during a recession, and with indications of rising graduate unemployment. Changes in the structure of the labour force and the organization of work are leading employers and careers advisers to dampen student expectations of automatic entry to a high-powered job with a fast track to the top (Goodman 1993). For prospective students, the traditional 'glittering prizes' associated with higher education begin to look a little tarnished as graduate status becomes much less exclusive, and full-time study entails ever higher levels of indebtedness (Coldstream 1994). Just as the battle to change attitudes towards higher education seemed to be drawing to a successful conclusion, there is now a new fear that people from backgrounds where the expectation of higher education is not firmly entrenched will once again be deterred because they see places being rationed, short-term costs rising and long-term benefits receding.

Government funding

Government funding for higher education in the UK is not ungenerous by international standards. International comparisons are always difficult and up-to-date figures are not available, but figures produced by the DES in 1991 show that UK higher education expenditure in 1986 fell into the middle range of 13 industrialized countries which were compared. Although a number of recent reports have pointed to the 'funding gap' which expansion has created, and expressed concern about the need for increased resources, there has been no persuasive argument that higher education should receive a higher proportionate share of public funding at the expense of other sectors of education, or indeed other public services. Interest has instead focused on the balance between public and private investment, and on the way in which public funds are applied (CIHE 1992; CBI 1994). The World Bank has recently made the same point from an international perspective. Commenting that investment in higher education is 'in crisis in industrial as well as developing countries throughout the world' it goes on to say (World Bank 1994: 16, 50)

> if public higher education institutions wish to increase their overall level of financing or improve their financial stability, mobilising a greater share of their revenues from non-governmental sources will be essential . . . eliminating non-instructional subsidies, introducing (or increasing) fees, pursuing donations, and undertaking income-generating activities will provide institutions with a more diversified and stable funding base.

A more detailed look at the 1986 figures for the UK shows that within the total expenditure, the UK had the highest expenditure on student support and welfare and, together with France, the lowest expenditure per qualifier (DES 1991). In other words, investment in non-instructional subsidies is high but investment in institutional costs – people, buildings, equipment, libraries – is low by international standards. Since those figures were prepared, moreover, rising student numbers and falling unit costs have tipped the balance further towards student support.

Student support

Under the present arrangements, home students who gain a place on a designated full-time course at a higher or further education institution are automatically entitled to a mandatory award covering tuition fees, and to a means-tested maintenance allowance and access to the Government's Student Loan Scheme. Where students choose to study at an institution outside their home locality, a higher level of maintenance is payable. Expenditure plans for 1996–7 show that of the £6.68 billion expenditure on higher education £2.91 billion will be devoted to student support, of which £1843 million (maintenance grants £945 million, loans £898 million) will be for non-instructional purposes (DFE 1994, Table 1).

A number of aspects of this system are worth commenting on. First, support is targeted almost exclusively towards full-time students. The steadily rising numbers of part-time students have no mandatory fee entitlement, and the vast majority are dependent on private funding to get them through their studies. Nearly one million people who attend continuing education and vocational short courses in higher education institutions must seek out their own sources of funds. Second, it means that full-time students make no contribution at all to the costs of their courses, regardless of financial circumstances, as the fee element is not means-tested. Third, generous though it is in respect of full-time students, the system is no longer providing them with an acceptable standard of living. There is ample and growing evidence from the banks and from institutions' own surveys of student hardship and indebtedness. Linking the means-testing of the maintenance element of the grant to parental income often exacerbates the situation as a surprisingly high number of parents are unwilling or unable to make their contribution.

Finally, as the National Commission on Education has demonstrated, the system is socially inequitable (National Commission on Education 1993: 258–261). Full-time places in higher education in the UK have always been occupied by a disproportionately high number of people from families in the upper income brackets, and the pattern of participation seems to have changed little since 1945 in spite of the recent expansion. Research into benefits in kind across families with different income groups shows that households in the top income bracket, on average, receive subsidies that are ten times greater than households in the bottom income bracket (Evandrou *et al.* 1993)

To summarize: the system is no longer working for those at whom it is targeted; it excludes those who seek to study cost effectively in a part-time mode; and it siphons scarce resources away from institutional support into inequitable personal subsidies. As the National Commission on Education (1993: 261) put it:

> The time has now come for a radical change in the way we fund students in higher education. A new balance between public and private funding is needed, so that as a nation we are able to devote a greater proportion of GDP [gross domestic product] to continuing education and training in all its forms. If we are not to inhibit the welcome increase in participation in higher and further education, nor to starve universities and colleges of the funds necessary to provide both a high quality teaching environment and an appropriate research effort, there must be a shift in funding towards private sources.

Private finance

There are a number of options for raising private finance, whether from the capital markets, through a capitalized vehicle company, as recommended in a recent report (Bain 1993), through income-generating activity (conference lettings, intellectual property rights, consultancy, short coursework, etc.), or direct fund-raising from alumni and industrial sources. Some universities have been successful in diversifying their funding base by such measures. However, the funds actually released for general running costs by such activities are often relatively small, as the activities themselves often require new investment to get them up and running, and may even be a drain on other institutional resources – for example, in the case of research contracts where it can be difficult to recover full overheads. Potentially, the most productive source of additional funding is the one which there is the most reluctance to tap – those who benefit most directly from higher education, the students themselves.

There is, however, a growing consensus on the need for a greater contribution from students. However, battle rages over how to secure it. The Government presents its Student Loan Scheme as a contribution to this end. By 1996–7 the shift in the values of the maintenance grant and the loan will be complete with the two being broadly equal. This will 'share the cost of student maintenance more equitably between taxpayers, parents and graduates themselves' (DFE 1994: para. 174). The Government's scheme is expensive, however, and it will be many years before administrative costs are covered and significant repayments feed back into the system. Moreover, serious arguments have been advanced that under the present arrangements 'new and disguised forms of government subsidies or grants are quickly emerging and are taking the form of increasing costs associated with the present loan structure' (West 1994). Most importantly perhaps, it applies only to maintenance, which is a relatively small element in the budget as compared to tuition costs.

Contributing to fees

There is little sign of the Government moving in the direction of a contribution to tuition costs, and technical Treasury objections to the associated loan arrangements which would be necessary have yet to be countered to the Government's satisfaction. The Government's reluctance to lead on this issue is understandable, given its likely political sensitivity with middle-class voters, and it is not out of line on this with the official policies of the other parties. The principle of free tuition is strongly defended from many quarters, not just within the universities, where a consultative exercise by the CVCP in 1992 showed that 'many objected fiercely to the CVCP even asking such questions' (CVCP 1992). The CBI, which strongly backs expansion, and is in favour of routing the taxpayer contribution to higher education via the student in the form of a financial credit while reducing the bill for maintenance by significantly sharper targeting, draws the line at requiring a contribution to fees from full-time students (CBI 1994). The Royal

Society in its recent report on higher education is equally strongly opposed (Royal Society 1993).

University vice-chancellors, however, are reluctantly recognizing the inevitability of a move in the direction of some form of fee contribution. The CVCP's examination of a range of options for raising additional private funding (was based on a review carried out in 1993 by consultants London Economics. The options considered in the original report were: a graduate tax, fee contribution plus income contingent loan, maintenance and income contingent loan and top-up fees. A supplementary report produced in July 1994 examined two further options (vouchers and state scholarships). The examination seems to be coming out in favour of a contribution scheme associated with an income-contingent loan. In a recent address, the chairman identified the criteria which any such scheme must satisfy as follows (Edwards 1994):

- That it be fair and equitable.
- That it should not deter students from entering higher education.
- That it should enable students to devote their time at university to their education.
- That it should be simple and therefore inexpensive to administer.
- That it should create genuinely additional funds over and above those provided by government.

This raises one of the major and very real concerns of those who oppose a fee contribution – that it will deter those from poorer backgrounds. There is not yet a lot of evidence from other systems around the world where income-contingent loan schemes have been introduced of the impact on access, but the World Bank report has looked at schemes in Australia, Sweden and Ghana, and concludes (1994: 50)

> cost-sharing (through income-contingent loans for tuition) coupled with student financial assistance (for maintenance for poorer students) is an efficient strategy for achieving expanded coverage and better quality in higher education with a given amount of government resources while protecting equity of access.

There is at least a prima facie case, therefore, that a well-constructed scheme need not impede access, and every reason why government should now agree to look seriously at this option in conjunction with universities and other interested bodies.

Proposals for change

Considerable effort has already been put into examining how a contribution scheme might operate in this country, notably by researchers at the London School of Economics, who have campaigned for many years for the introduction of an income-contingent loan scheme administered through the tax system. The National Commission on Education drew on that and other research in putting forward its proposals for a higher education contribution scheme. This advocates an annual flat-rate contribution to fees, payable up-front at a discounted rate or, after graduation, through an income-contingent loan system funded by the financial institutions but guaranteed by government and recovered through the National Insurance machinery. This has the potential to raise very considerable new funds for investment in the infrastructure of an expanded system, while at the same time extending an entitlement to support to part-timers and those in higher level courses in further education (National Commission on Education 1993: 262–269, Appendix 2).

If the stakeholders in the higher education system have the will to think what for many has been unthinkable – that free tuition for full-time study is not necessarily an entitlement which must be preserved at all costs – and to stop using arguments about access to put up an automatic barrier to a deeper look at the options, then there are a number of ways forward, and the technical difficulties remaining will have every chance of being overcome. Inevitably, some will lose a privileged benefit but, overall, high-quality higher education provision will be secured for the future, and be accessible on a more equitable basis to a wider constituency.

Flexible funding

If the higher education system is to continue to expand without an unacceptable drop in quality a rebalancing of funding contributions, with a greater proportion of public funds directed towards institutional rather than student support costs, is a key requirement. However, it is equally important that individual institutions be given greater freedom to apply public funds in the development of their specific corporate goals. As financial pressures have become tighter, institutions have been forced into an increasingly constricting strait-jacket of formula funding linked to performance assessment which is in danger of forcing a stifling conformity, at a time when innovation and imaginative thinking about the role of higher education institutions and the needs of students is required. The point was put trenchantly in a recent article by the new vice-chancellor of Exeter, who draws on the unique perspective of his former position as permanent secretary at the Department for Education. While making the point that universities had only got themselves to blame for poor financial control in the past, he said (Holland 1994):

> We are in grave danger of going beyond the bounds of sense in terms of the elaboration of the funding model . . . If higher education is about anything it is about new developments, the unexpected and exploring ways that have not been explored. I am dismayed that, seen from the other end of the telescope, we are in danger of becoming ever more restricted in innovation opportunities and flexibility.

Differentiation and diversity

Institutional diversity is now promoted as a highly desirable feature of the higher education scene. It is an ever-present theme in government policy documents. Numerous reports both from the business and the academic communities have seen this as essential if the system is to provide the type of opportunities for learning after the compulsory phases which society needs, and to continue to support research which is excellent by international standards. What is envisaged is not a diversity produced by each institution trying to carry out all the different roles which are now envisaged for universities. That would imply the development of institutions of a much larger size than even the biggest of existing institutions. What is envisaged is functional differentiation. Institutions are encouraged to develop their own missions, based on an examination of their customer base, an assessment of changing student needs and their wider role in a knowledge-based society. They must consider whether to focus on developing closer relationships with their local and regional economies or to try to compete in the wider national and international research community. They must identify academic strengths and weaknesses and decide on the areas of expertise which merit development, and those which may need to be dropped or redirected.

As yet, however, there is still considerable conformity of institutional aspiration within the system, and 'the trend is actually toward convergence with almost all universities trying to expand their presence in both research and access courses and to increase their range of subjects and facilities' (Williams and Fry 1994). Because of the inevitable tendency of institutions to act in their own financial self-interest they devote their energies, wherever possible, to those activities which are perceived not only to have greatest financial rewards, but also the greatest prestige. Even though the operation of the highly selective research assessment exercises have in practice led to the emergence of an élite group of institutions in which research resources are increasingly concentrated, this has not led the less successful institutions to abandon aspirations in research, which most still see as the distinguishing characteristic of a 'real' university.

Formula funding

The allocation of resources by the present funding formula exacerbates the problem of conformity by perpetuating traditional patterns. It is based upon the concept of the full-time student following a traditional three-year course. Student numbers are subject to a mechanism which is designed to produce convergence on the Average Unit of Council Funding (AUCF). It assumes that 'the interaction between the student, a course and an institution is fairly stable and immobile' (HEQC 1994). This traditional relationship is, however, being significantly modified in practice, as modular courses, credit accumulation and transfer arrangements and part-time and distance learning assume an increasingly important role. As a result the formula may be incapable of recognizing and rewarding adequately the variety of activity undertaken by some institutions, and create negative incentives through its normative impact. Moreover, the current use of assessments of quality to generate differential factors to feed into the funding model are in danger of producing a bland orthodoxy, particularly in teaching, as institutions seek to conform to the received ideas of quality in order to protect their academic reputations and maximize their income.

If the call for diversity in a unified system is to be more than rhetoric, therefore, universities need financial flexibility and appropriate incentives plus the freedom to move resources around in support of their strategic objectives. Financial flexibility must, however, go hand in hand with accountability at institutional level, and combining these two objectives is a challenge which the funding councils must face, but one that they will have difficulty in meeting successfully if present funding arrangements continue.

Breaking out of the strait-jacket will remain problematic as long as such a large proportion of public funding flows to institutions through the funding councils. The Government's action in cutting the value of the tuition fee routed through the local authorities has only intensified the problem, by transferring a greater proportion of public funding for allocation by the councils. The average annual cost per student of an undergraduate degree course, exclusive of any maintenance or loan support, ranges between about £4200 and £8000 depending on the relevant fee banding. The fee element, reduced by 45 per cent in each band for 1994–5, accounts for only about 20 per cent of instructional costs. Although it is public money, the fact that fee income flows through different channels has given institutions some flexibility in the past, and indeed regulating the level of fee income up or down has been the Government's most effective method of stimulating or depressing institutional competitiveness – itself a key factor in promoting diversity.

Market mechanisms

If diversity and institutional differentiation is the way in which the system should be moving, the most effective means of achieving this is likely to be through market forces. This would mean giving students genuine purchasing power by routing all or some of state funding for tuition through them in the form of vouchers or credits, as advocated for example by the CBI, and evaluated in London Economics' report for the CVCP (mentioned earlier in this chapter). Such an approach could easily be combined with the introduction of a fee contribution, and moreover could open the way to making financial arrangements for students more flexible as course structures and modes of study move in new directions. The recent report of the HEQC CAT Development Project (HEQC 1994) – which deserves fuller discussion than it has so far been accorded – points to the potential for the future funding of a modernized higher education sector of a combination of credit-based funding through the funding councils and credit-led educational vouchers.

Any move towards a 'social market' in higher education would call into question the role of the funding councils. A fully 'privatized' and deregulated system where the whole of the public contribution to instructional costs of tuition were routed through the student and institutions were free to charge, whatever fee the market would bear, would leave no role for the councils and be unlikely to appeal to the Government, which would lose too much control. Moreover, it would be most unlikely to promote equity and access, and would inevitably lead to the development of a socially exclusive group of universities where ability to pay the fee governed access. A central steer to ensure that public funds are used to further public objectives will continue to be needed, and some form of intermediary body to channel funds between institutions, students and government, will be needed to mitigate the full-blown impact of market forces.

Action now

What is needed now is for joint public debate of the options for institutional funding to take place in tandem with discussions on the introduction of a private contribution to fees. If all parties – politicians, academics, current and prospective students, and the business community – face up to the issues involved and take action now, we may yet escape the depressing and damaging fate for higher education envisaged in the introduction: impaired quality, failure to keep up with international standards of excellence, a step backwards from the recent high rates of participation and a society ill-equipped to face the economic technological and social challenges of the twenty-first century.

References

Bain, A. (1993) *Private Sector Funding in Higher Education*. Bristol, HEFCE.

CBI (1994) *Thinking Ahead. Ensuring the expansion of higher education into the 21st century*. London, Confederation of British Industry.

Coldstream, P. (1994) 'Life beyond the glittering prizes'. *Times Higher Educational Supplement*, 2 September.

Council for Industry and Higher Education (1992) *Investing in Diversity*. London, CIHE.

CVCP (1992) *CVCP News*, No. 17, June.

CVCP (1994) 'The Case for Increased Public Investment in Universities: A Statement of Key Funding Needs for 1995–6 and Beyond'. London, Committee of Vice-Chancellors and Principals.

DES (1991) *International Statistical Comparisons in Higher Education: Working Report*.

DFE (1994) *The Government's Expenditure Plans 1994–5 to 1996–7*. London, HMSO.

Edwards, K.J.R. (1994) 'The CVCP Perspective'. Speech to a conference at CBI headquarters, 6 June 1994.

Evandrou, M. *et al.* (1993) 'Welfare benefits in kind and income distribution', *Fiscal Studies*, 14(1).

Goodman, C.J. (1993) *Roles for Graduates in the Twenty-First Century*. London, The Association of Graduate Recruiters.

Higher Education Quality Council (1994) *Choosing to Change: Extending Access, Choice and Mobility in Higher Education*. London, HEQC.

Holland, G. (1994) 'Gamekeeper turned poacher'. *Times Higher Educational Supplement*, 3 June 1994.

National Commission on Education (1993) *Learning to Succeed*. London, Heinemann.

Royal Society (1993) *Higher Education Futures: Report of a Royal Society Study Group*. London, The Royal Society.

West, E.G. (1994) *Britain's Student Loan System in a World Perspective: A Critique*. London, Institute of Economic Affairs.

Williams, G. and Fry, H. (1994) *Longer Term Prospects for British Higher Education. A Report to the Committee of Vice-chancellors and Principals*. London, Institute of Education.

World Bank (1994) *Higher Education: The Lessons of Experience*. Washington DC, World Bank.

13

Thinking European: Is UK Higher Education Out of Step?

John Field

Since 1985, the European Union (EU) has made itself a force to be reckoned with in higher education. In implementing the Single European Act, the EU developed a series of higher education programmes which are now extremely well established. Through the Treaty on European Union, it also acquired new competences and responsibilities in respect of education policy. It is timely and appropriate to consider the impact that moves towards European integration are having on national higher education systems, and although the Maastricht Treaty explicitly blocked any attempt at harmonization, it also seems sensible to ask whether the distinctive nature of the UK higher education system is now placing its future at risk.

If the future of higher education lies in closer European integration, should we not be seeking to ensure that the organization, curriculum and research systems in UK universities become more rather than less similar to those of universities in other member states? On balance, perhaps not. Arguably, Europe's universities now stand at the threshold of a new relationship between higher education, civil society and the state. In their modern organizational forms, Western universities are essentially Enlightenment creations, embraced and managed after the Second World War within the wider ambit of the welfare state. For a variety of reasons, universities now face a series of challenges which are bound to place their present role, and relations with the public sphere, under challenge. Among other forces which are reshaping the university and its immediate environment are the institutions, programmes and policies of the EU. It is still far from clear, though, that the EU's approach to higher education is, either in itself or in combination with other independent factors, sufficiently forceful to override other considerations at international, national and regional level.

Perhaps this seems a little cavalier. Yet it is easy to forget that European policies and activities are a relatively recent phenomenon. So accustomed have higher education managers become to overseeing European activities of various kinds that they seem to have been part of the game for decades. Still, until as recently as the mid-1980s, the European Community had nothing remotely resembling a policy towards higher education, and its few programmes in the area were relatively small scale, and – for good measure – of dubious legality. That situation has now been transformed, under the combined pressure of moves towards European integration, the slow but steady evolution of an international graduate labour market, and piecemeal enlargement of the definition of European citizenship and its associated entitlements. Under these pressures, the EU has embarked on a far more ambitious attempt to extend what it calls the 'European dimension' within the higher education curriculum, to fund selectively transnational research activities, and increase the pace at which new knowledge and ideas are brought into the marketplace.

Is the UK increasingly out of step with these developments on the European plane? If it is, how much does it matter? This chapter provides a historically-informed context to the current round of policies and programmes. The intention is to sketch out a background against which to assess the extent to which one can now speak of, and if necessary therefore plan academically for, the Europeanization of higher education. The argument is essentially that although the EU has some ambitious ideas about higher education, its specific policy measures are rather modest; furthermore, the extent to which graduate labour markets are really Europe-wide in scale tends to be exaggerated. In these circumstances, the pressures on universities to undergo thoroughgoing institutional change, as opposed to marginal and mainly administrative readjustment, are negligible. If EU policies on higher education are much more significant for universities than they were in the mid-1980s, they nevertheless have some way to go before they have a significant impact on institutional practice.

Education and the policy process within the European Union

European Union policies and programmes for higher education have developed rapidly since the passing of the Single European Act. From 1986 onwards, a number of distinctive programmes were adopted which affected the teaching of undergraduate and postgraduate students in universities. With the completion (if partial) of the Single Market programme, and the ratification of the Treaty on European Union, new or revised policies and programmes have now been devised for education, training and research, all of which are already having a noticeable impact upon universities.

Historically, though, the EU has only had an interest in higher education for a very short time. Under the Treaty of Rome, the Commission's competencies in the field of education were narrow. Apart from a somewhat vague enjoinder in respect of developing European citizenship, the Treaty restricted the Commission's powers to the field of vocational training. In the early years, this was understood chiefly as referring to special training for marginal groups, and particularly migrant workers; with the growth of youth unemployment in the 1970s, member states increasingly permitted the Commission to use its regional policies as a framework for supporting upskilling programmes for the unemployed. Although the comparability of vocational qualifications was also a legitimate area of interest, progress was painfully slow, and in the view of most of those concerned, the results were disappointingly modest. For the first thirty years of its existence, then, the EU's interest in education was effectively restricted to the arena of vocational training for the unemployed.

Curiously enough, it was thanks to the European Court of Justice that the EU's modern higher education policies came into existence. Court rulings are almost invariably concerned with specific instances; their implications, though, have frequently been general (Meehan 1993, 52–54). For example, a 1985 Court ruling in favour of a French arts student admitted to a course in Belgium was primarily concerned with discrimination against EU nationals in the level of registration fees charged; the Court ruling, though, was based on a view of higher education as constituting, in part at least, a form of vocational training. This view was confirmed in a 1986 judgement involving veterinary students from outside Belgium (Meehan 1993: 92). Subsequently, in 1989 the Court reached judgements in cases involving the ERASMUS and PETRA programmes which had further implications for policy development in the EU. In the case of ERASMUS, the Commission had complained that the Council had used its powers under Article 235 of the Treaty of Rome unreasonably, so as to weaken the programme; the PETRA case was brought following a complaint by the UK. In both judgements, the Court of Justice left no doubt that it believed that Article 128 to the Rome Treaty allowed the EU to bring forward action programmes in vocational education and training. It also required that programmes be realized in cooperation with member states – a requirement which inevitably meant that programmes developed incrementally (Ofenbach 1992, 10). Subsequently, the Treaty on European Union enshrined this principle into legislation, placed a clear block on harmonization of education systems or teaching content, inserted the right of the Parliament to exercise a negative veto over incentive measures for education, and introduced a requirement for cooperation with the Parliament in the field of training measures (CEC 1992, 47–48). The effect of the Treaty was therefore ambiguous: on the one hand it blocked harmonization and introduced the largely-untested European Parliament into the decision-making process; on the other hand, it clarified the basis on which EU policy could be made, and extended it unambiguously to encompass the entire field of education as well as training.

As well as incrementalism, fragmentation has also continued to characterize the educational policies of the EU. Education and training policies are not developed only within the Commission's Task Force on Human Resources, Education, Training and Youth, itself answerable to Directorate-General V (Employment, Social Affairs and Education) until 1995, when it assumed the title of DG XXII. They are also central to the work of DG XVI (Regional Policy) and DG XII (Science, Research and Development). Thus the 55 million ECU allocated to the development of flexible and distance learning within the Research and Technological Development Programme in 1993 represents quite a significant investment compared with the relatively modest sums allocated through the Task Force. Yet other sections of the EU also have an interest in education and training, whether in their own right or as complementary measures developed in order to support other policy objectives. An outstanding example of the confusion which can result is the creation of the Jean Monnet programme, which included the creation of a number of prestigious academic chairs in European Integration, by DGX (Information, Communication and Culture) in 1990, without consulting the Education Committee (Preston 1991: 36).

Of course, it is hardly to be expected that policies will develop with any great clarity within an intergovernmental body. Moreover, the EU was founded only in the 1950s; power is shared between a Council made up of ministers from the various member states, a Commission nominated for fixed periods by member states, and a Parliament still uncertain how best to exercise new powers, many of which are negative rather than positive; the EU's membership has changed significantly over recent decades. The policy process itself is convoluted. Policy developments are initiated by the Council of Ministers, whose proceedings continue to be held in secret; they are then brought forward by quite a different body, the Commission, which is often in conflict with the Council and the Parliament. Under the terms of the Treaty on European Union, the Commission must then seek the support of the European Parliament for any new education proposals; the Commission is also required to consult the Economic and Social Committee (ECOSOC) and the newly-established Committee of the Regions, which shares a secretariat with ECOSOC and resents its status and resources. Any new policy initiative is subject not only to predictable processes of negotiation and amendment; it then repeatedly has to be held up while it is translated by linguist-jurists into all the official languages. In the background, as Guy Neave has noted, is 'a noise of lobbies and vestigial groups in and around Brussels whose links with higher education are amazingly elastic' (Neave 1994: 131). If higher education policy within the EU is fragmented and sometimes contradictory, this should not be too surprising.

Nor is it in itself necessarily damaging that policy should lack coherence. As a positive influence on practice, policy consistency is probably overrated. Certainly it is rare in advanced nations for different ministries to coordinate systematically their policies for higher education, advanced training and the highly-skilled labour market. Even in Japan, often held up as an example to the rest of the capitalist world, there is felt to be a pronounced lack of policy coherence (McCormick 1989). In seeking to reform such conservative institutions as universities, though, it is probably necessary to have either an internal consensus in favour of change, or to possess externally a strong will for reform among political leaders. Neither currently exists in the case of the reform of the European universities. Yet conviction that reform is highly necessary certainly exists.

European Union policy and the universities

Since 1986 and the passing of the Single European Act, higher education has become a major area of policy development for the EU. With the move towards a single internal market, and the removal of internal barriers to trade and labour migration, attention steadily shifted towards other perceived weak spots in Europe's economic engine. Throughout the late 1980s, the Commission had in Jacques Delors a dirigiste President who was deeply committed to protection of 'the European model' of 'economic well-being, social cohesiveness, and high overall quality of life which was achieved in the post-war period' (CEC 1994a: 7). In addition, policymakers throughout Europe were increasingly concerned by the competitive threat which they perceived to this blend of social solidarity and prosperity, as a consequence of the extraordinary economy dynamism of the Asian Pacific economies. After the peaceful revolutions of 1989, it also dawned on the policy community in western Europe that, as well as Japan and the 'little dragons', the nations of central and eastern Europe offered a well-educated workforce, deregulated markets, and low labour costs – hourly labour costs in Poland and Hungary in 1992 were estimated at around one-third of those in Singapore or South Korea, and well under a tenth of those in the German *Länder* (*Die Zeit*, 10 September 1992; Field 1994: 43–44). Europe's potential capacity to innovate, to bring new knowledge and know-how to the market, and to develop cost-effective applications quickly enough to make a difference, were identified as central to its future success. An evident failure to achieve these critical steps resulted in increasingly ambitious proposals for higher education reform.

In 1994, the Commission set out details of the new programme for education. In the Socrates action programme, the Commission set the parameters for its education policies for the second half of the 1990s. While Socrates does include important new measures for schools, its implications for universities are rather more limited. First, there is what Socrates has not done. In the *Memorandum on Higher Education* issued in 1991, a number of ambitious proposals were aired in anticipation of the new education programme to be adopted from 1994. In general terms, the *Memorandum* called for universities to 'support an expanding knowledge-based economy'; they should contribute to the 'single labour market for highly qualified personnel' which it claimed now existed, widen access to higher qualifications, offer opportunities for regular updating and renewal, and ensure that research contributed to technological renewal in the economy through the formation of 'partnerships with economic life' (CEC 1991). Among the specific proposals identified were a number of measures such as the extension of the European dimension across new subject areas, collection of information on national systems, an EU interest in quality issues, continued attempts to ensure mutual acceptance of academic and professional qualifications across borders (CEC 1994b), and above all an expansion of continuing education and advanced training. On this latter theme, the *Memorandum* was unambiguous. In the words of the executive summary (CEC 1991, III), 'Given the pace of technological change a new balance between initial and continuing education becomes an absolute requirement for the future.'

Subsequently, the implications of this 'absolute requirement' were spelt out (CEC 1991: 23):

These challenges imply a shift in policy terms in the balance of attention, investment and organisation as between initial and continuing education with an increased importance being attached to the latter.

Nor was this simply a short-term view. Three years later, the White Paper on Growth and Competitiveness called for member states to 'reorganise educational resources'. It also announced that within the EU (CEC 1994a: 136–137),

All measures must therefore necessarily be based on the concept of developing, generalising and systematising lifelong learning and continuing training.

Whether these ambitious proposals were ever realistic in the first place is somewhat beside the point; the fact is that they are nowhere reflected in the Socrates action programme, whose main thrust in higher education really amounts to little more than a new way of administering student mobility programmes.

Student mobility and institutional change

Student mobility is, of course, well established within the European university system. Even so, its impact on higher education systems has been limited, for three main reasons. The first reason is that student mobility is relatively small scale. Under its ERASMUS action programme, itself constructed on the basis of a smaller temporary mobility programme, the EU has supported student and staff mobility since 1987. The outcomes have been somewhat disappointing: although a target was set at the time of ERASMUS' launch of giving 10 per cent of all Community students the chance to study in another member state, the actual figure achieved *on the most optimistic estimate* was around 4 per cent (CEC 1991: 28).

The second reason is that of all the measures which an intergovernmental organization might adopt in order to influence university policy, student mobility provides far less leverage than most. In the first place, most mobility can be dealt with under existing arrangements, with universities accepting incoming students and staff on a 'knock-for-knock' basis. Other than minimal adjustments for language preparation, accommodation and other practical arrangements, nothing much needs to change. Secondly, incoming EU students have to take their place among a burgeoning number of foreign students from outside the EU. Indeed, both the Irish and UK governments have actively sought to market their traded educational services outside the EU, as these are income-bearing while incoming EU students are unfunded and represent a net drain on resources (Rialta na hÉirann 1992: 233–234).

The third reason is that there is no political will, either in government, within the EU or in universities themselves, to rock the curricular boat. Indeed, the EU itself recognized this fact of educational life some time ago. When it adopted the First General Directive on the Mutual Recognition of Qualifications in 1988, the Commission effectively accepted that, despite enormous differences in the length and intensity of university courses across the EU, it was unable to make any judgement on the quality of national higher education systems or on the graduates who emerged from them. A degree is a degree, in other words, and has to be treated as such by employers and member states. A similar outcome emerged from the pilot stages of the European Credit Transfer Scheme; after considering a number of alternatives, it was decided to develop a credit system based on units of study time. Even were there a political will to intervene, the subsidiarity principle as applied to education (the Treaty on European Union specified that the content of study is a matter for national government) would pose a significant barrier to curriculum reform at the European level.

Finally, if the goal is to secure a 'new balance' between continuing and initial education, student mobility is the least appropriate lever to use. As the Open University in particular has repeatedly emphasized, mobility programmes are highly selective. They best suit the young, full-time student who has few other commitments (and inevitably, they also best suit those whose families can afford to top up loans and grants). They least suit those whose studies are combined with work, family or other commitments. If important in sensitizing the individual students involved to cultures and practices outside their own nation, mobility programmes have limited value in developing a European dimension in university teaching and learning.

How atypical are UK universities?

Domestic critics of the UK higher education system sometimes draw an explicit contrast with the reportedly superior practices and policies of other European national systems. Yet firm evidence that the UK university system's structures and quality are either seriously out of step, or that if they are the consequences are predominantly damaging, is hard to come by. In particular, it does not seem that UK universities are suffering unduly from unfavourable national conditions. The reasons for this are at different levels. Some affect primarily the circumstances facing UK universities; others are more broad in nature. This can be illustrated by reference to the performance of UK institutions within European networks and consortia, particularly those established under the aegis of the EU programmes.

Certainly UK universities seem to find little difficulty in gaining access to transnational mobility consortia. Indeed, within the EU it is quite disproportionately involved in all the current mobility programmes. For example, the UK is by far the largest single national destination for European students involved in the EU mobility programmes. This may be partly explained by reference to the appeal of the English language rather than UK universities; however, the UK also supplies a disproportionately large number of lead institutions in transnational consortia. In 1993–4, for instance, UK institutions provided the coordinators of 31 per cent of ERASMUS interuniversity collaboration programmes (ICPs) and 43 per cent of LINGUA programmes. This pattern is not only visible within mobility programmes. For example, 12 of the 42 university-level institutions involved in the Research and Technology Development programme for flexible and distance learning in 1993 came from the UK (CEC 1994c: Annex A). The peculiarities of the UK system do not seem to prevent UK universities from playing a quite disproportionate role within consortia established within the framework of EU programmes.

However, even if UK universities were not substantially involved in EU mobility and research and development programmes, would it matter? From a number of points of view – financial, educational and historical – it may be prudent to maintain existing relationships with other parts of the world rather than worry unduly about the rest of the EU. Looked at from a strictly financial point of view, UK universities lose more than they gain from their involvement in EU mobility schemes, because they are almost invariably net importers of students. Incoming students from nations outside the EU are another matter, though. Most university managers are far more interested in students from Taiwan or Malaysia than from Finland or Greece. Financial reasons probably explain most of this interest, but educationally, non-EU students bring very different perspectives, and many come from nations with far more successful recent economic track records than any in western Europe, and therefore represent a perfectly sound strategic investment. However, there are other more structural reasons why the importance of involvement in the EU mobility schemes should not be exaggerated.

The graduate labour market in Europe remains strongly marked by national boundaries. One recent overview of intra-EU mobility concluded that 'the Single European Act has not greatly increased intra-EU migration' (Koslowski 1994: 374). Despite a notably fierce line from the European Court of Justice against governments who hide behind the national security provisions of the Treaty of Rome, there remains little mobility within the private sector, where traditional labour market barriers combine with ignorance of European legislation to ensure that most recruitment, especially at graduate levels, is among nationals of the member state concerned (Saunders and Davies 1994: 246–247). As Marsden notes, flows in internal labour markets are relatively unaffected by developments in national training systems, nor are they greatly influenced by the nature or currency of qualifications. It is to be expected that the importance of such internal labour markets will increase as firms adjust their operations to benefit from the Single Market, but as yet this process is in an embryonic stage; the human resource implications may, moreover, prove to be fairly minor and easily met by in-house training (Marsden 1994: 90).

If there is little sign that a general EU-wide graduate labour market is emerging, then it is of little importance whether UK universities are out of step or not. Yet the evidence clearly supports those who argue that the UK higher education system is already able to fit into the wider, loose and voluntaristic European system that is slowly starting to emerge.

There is no doubt that UK universities continue to appeal to students from other EU member states. UK academics appear to be as active as most of their continental colleagues in establishing and running scholarly associations at the European level. There is also plenty of evidence of curriculum development, if inspired at present more by entrepreneurialism than the ideal of serving Europe's corporate growth. Students in UK universities are able to choose from a range of European Studies courses (including a reasonable number located in departments that are top ranked for research and highly regarded for their teaching). Albeit somewhat uneven in coverage and quality, modern European language teaching is increasingly available to undergraduates across a range of courses; the more challenging but possibly appropriate task of teaching foreign topics in foreign languages has yet to make any headway, but in this the UK rather than being odd one out is typical of the larger European member states (Rigby and Burgess 1992). Perhaps the question might be turned around: does the UK system resemble the conventional western European university system too much rather than too little?

Institutional change or minor adjustment?

Is there any remaining reason why universities should regard the European dimension as a further factor in an increasingly turbulent environment that requires wholesale institutional change? No. No such pressures come from, or are likely to come from, the EU. Its policies are constrained by the terms of the Treaty on European Union; ambitious rhetoric has a habit of turning into cautious implementation; its efforts are concentrated on the visible but institutionally unchallenging activity of supporting student and staff mobility, and on the matter of ensuring mutual recognition of qualifications so as to help create 'a European area for the professions and for training' (CEC 1994b: 1).

Far from showing that a modest investment has produced significant leverage, the EU's education programmes have created a marginal administrative burden at institutional level, but produced very little in the way of leverage effect at system level. Mutual recognition of qualifications has proceeded slowly, and has avoided such tricky questions as how one makes a qualitative judgement about different national qualifications systems, or indeed whether it might make sense in some circumstances to seek to harmonize qualifications (Field 1994: 29–32).

Nor is there any evidence from studies of senior management that they find themselves under pressure to adapt the university to the needs of the new Europe. Quite the reverse. In two recent collections of essays on the processes of institutional change by senior and middle managers in UK universities, the policies and programmes of the EU simply do not feature (Weil 1994; Slowey 1995). Possibly this gap simply represents the blinkered perspectives of a narrow academic culture, concerned exclusively with Britain's parish pumps? Conceivably so, though it would be unusual for twenty vice-chancellors, principals, deans and heads of departments to ignore something as large as the EU if it really did exert significant leverage over their daily activities. Would the picture have been radically different had the perspectives originated elsewhere? At institutional level, the process of Europeanisation is limited in scope and shallow in depth. This said, it would be wrong to suppose that no institutional adjustments whatever are needed in the light of moves towards European union. So far as the management of EU programmes are concerned, there are clearly challenges which have not yet been fully addressed. An evaluation of the COMETT programme, for example, identified a number of weaknesses in project management, including the existence of 'sleeping partners', inter-organizational conflicts within consortia, tensions between institutional and departmental goals, and widespread lack of clarity on objectives (Prosser and Durando 1992, 339–341). Similar management issues arise with respect to other EU programmes, as with externally-funded projects more generally.

However, only in a handful of institutions is EU-derived income a significant proportion of all non-mainstream funding; in the minority where EU funding is at a significant level, this is accounted for by research contracts. Most universities have found it helpful to place their European office (usually one or two people) under the shelter of other income-earning activities, usually in an external liaison or industrial development office. In other words, activity arising out of the EU's programmes is being managed largely as a subset of those activities.

Implications for institutional change are, then, limited. If this seems somewhat parochial, it has to be said that the counterevidence is weak. For all the staff and management mobility of the last decade, there has been very little serious investigation of cross-cultural influences within the European higher education system – or, for that matter, of the education policies and programmes of the EU. The study of educational policy, so it is said, has recently come of age (Troyna and Halpin 1994b). Yet the volume of methodological papers which are cited in support of this claim (Troyna and Halpin 1994a) is typical of the somewhat introverted nature of much UK educational research. While the intellectual influences seen in the volume are suitably cosmopolitan, education policy scholarship seems unregenerate in its focus on the single nation state as the macro-level focal point of its analysis. What may justly be said about the best of policy analysis holds true even more strongly for other fields of educational study. If European universities are indeed on the verge of a massive mutual transformation, it seems odd that no one is apparently collecting and publishing the evidence. Until they do, it seems more sensible to assume that the such pressures as exist towards a marked Europeanization of higher education are readily manageable through marginal adjustments to existing curricula and systems of administration.

References

Commission of the European Communities (1991) *Memorandum on Higher Education in the European Community*. Luxembourg, Office for Official Publications.

Commission of the European Communities (1992) *Treaty on European Union*. Luxembourg, Office for Official Publications.

Commission of the European Communities (1994a) *Growth, Competitiveness, Employment: The Challenges and Ways Forward into the 21st Century*. Luxembourg, Office for Official Publications.

Commission of the European Communities (1994b) *Communication from the Commission on Recognition of Qualifications for Academic and Professional Purposes*. Luxembourg, Office for Official Publications.

Commission of the European Communities (1994c) *Research and Technology Development of Telematic Systems for Flexible and Distance Learning: DELTA 1993*. Luxembourg, Office for Official Publications.

Field, J. (1994) *Educational and Vocational Training Policy*. Spicers European Union Policy Briefings. Harlow, Longman.

Koslowski, R. (1994) 'Intra-EU migration, citizenship and political union', *Journal of Common Market Studies*, 32(3), 369–402.

McCormick K. (1989) 'Towards a lifelong learning society? The reform of continuing vocational education and training in Japan', *Comparative Education*, 25(2), 133–149.

Marsden, D. (1994) 'Skills and the integration of European labour markets', *Social Europe*, Supplement 1/94, 77–109.

Meehan, E. (1993) *Citizenship and the European Community*. London, Sage.

Mulcahy, D.G. (1992) 'Promoting the European dimension in Irish education', *Irish Educational Studies*, 11, 179–190.

Neave, G. (1994) 'The politics of quality: developments in higher education in Western Europe, 1992–1994', *European Journal of Education*, 29(2), 115–134.

Ofenbach, B. (1992) 'Die "europäische Dimension der Bildung" als zentrale Herausforderung', in *Bildung in Europa*. R. Lassahn and B. Ofenbach (eds) Frankfurt-am-Main, Peter Lang.

Preston, J. (1991) *EC Education, Training and Research Programmes – An Action Guide*. London, Kogan Page.

Prosser, E. and Durando, M. (1992) 'European Community experiences from the coalface: some lessons from the COMETT programme', *European Journal of Education*, 27(4), 333–347.

Rialta na hÉirann (1992) *Education for a Changing World: Green Paper on Education*. Dublin, The Stationery Office.

Rigby, G. and Burgess, R.G. (1992) *Language Teaching in Higher Education: A Discussion Document*. Sheffield, Employment Department.

Saunders, M. and Davies, S. (1994) 'The impact of European Community mutual recognition of professional qualifications on local authority recruitment', *Local Government Studies*, 20(2), 241–256.

Slowey, M. (ed.) (1995) *Implementing Change from Within Universities and Colleges*. London, Kogan Page.

Troyna, B. and Halpin, D. (eds) (1994a) *Researching Education Policy: Ethical and Methodological Issues*. Lewes, Falmer Press.

Troyna, B. and Halpin, D. (1994b) Policy studies have come of age. *Times Higher Education Supplement*, 25 November 1994, 13.

Weil, S. (ed.) (1994) *Introducing Change From the Top in Universities and Colleges*. London, Kogan Page.

14

Funding, Access and Teaching: The Canadian Experience of a Mass System of Higher Education

Hans Schuetze

Introduction

Canadian higher education has changed quite dramatically over the last four decades. This is most visible with respect to the growth in student numbers and to new types of institutions that have emerged, partly in response to the growing demand. This phenomenon of expansion and change is not specifically Canadian, but has occurred in virtually all industrialized countries. Although enormous expansion gave rise to a new sector of non-university post-secondary education, the change affected, and continues to do so, the universities in a major way.

Canada has gone further than any other country except the USA in developing a mass system of higher education. According to the OECD, 66.5 per cent of the Canadian population in the typical age group are enrolled in tertiary education, the same as in the USA, as compared to 38.6 per cent in Japan, 39 per cent in France, 27.5 per cent in Germany and 26 per cent in the UK. Canada spends more as a percentage both of its gross domestic product and of total public expenditures on public tertiary education than any other OECD country (OECD 1993). The gradual change from an élite to a mass system of higher education is a result of two major trends: first, the adoption of egalitarian policies aimed to expand education opportunities for returning veterans, and later, the population at large. The aim was to make society more just and fair, to reduce the wastage of talent, and to improve economic performance. Second, programmes and curricula expanded to accommodate emerging professions such as social work, teaching, commerce and business administration, nursing and pharmacy, and to meet the demand for the variety of specialized skills which became too complex to be taught in the secondary sector

The 1960s saw a number of important changes in the relationship between universities and governments. A period marked by student disruptions and demonstrations in North America and western Europe, the decade was one of unprecedented expansion of higher education. Between 1956 and 1968, the number of university-level institutions grew from 40 to 59 and now stands at 69. There occurred an almost fourfold increase in the number of full-time university teachers, from approximately 4350 to 16 000. From a university enrolment of 90 000 full-time students at the beginning of the 1950s, Canadian university enrolment expanded to over 500 000 in 1990, not counting more than 300 000 part-time students.

The expansion of educational opportunities and the development of the requisite facilities were regarded as a necessary social investment for future economic growth. This philosophy, coupled with a buoyant economic climate in the 1960s, saw many provinces in Canada develop publicly funded community college systems, construct other new institutions of post-secondary education, expand the numbers and scope of programmes offered at the post-secondary level, and provide financial assistance to less advanced students. As in most other countries, this climate of optimism and the phase of unprecedented growth came to an end in the 1980s.

Today the situation is characterized by a growing public concern with the enormous size of public debts – both provincial and federal – and a concomitant consensus that public budgets must be reviewed. At the same time, earlier expectations that enrolment levels would shrink as a result of demographic developments have not materialized; on the contrary, demand for post-secondary education, and for university education in particular, is still growing. This increase in demand is no longer coming from the population of the traditional age (18–22 years), but from non-traditional groups, for example adults and racial and ethno-cultural minorities.

The expectation is thus that post-secondary education in the future will need to do more with less public resources – and that institutions will need to reorganize to meet this goal. This is part of a more general scrutiny of the public sector overall and a growing public demand for greater effectiveness and efficiency of the public sector in general, in the universities in particular.

Against this backdrop, this chapter will address three themes that are part of the debate about and within universities in Canada, indicating the scope and the direction of change. The first theme is the manner in which issues of accessibility, equity and institutional responsiveness have been tied to the restructuring of financial support for higher education. The discussion will concentrate on two recent government proposals for changing funding mechanisms. Both the federal government and the largest of the provinces, Ontario, have announced large-scale changes in the present policy of university financing, and discussions are going on in other provinces that suggest that the entire Canadian university system is in for a major funding review. This will have – intended or not – a major impact on university structures, programmes and curricula as well as on the way services are delivered.

The second theme concerns the segmentation of the higher education system, one of the results of the rapid growth of the post-secondary education sector in the 1960s and 1970s. A good deal of the growth in post-secondary enrolment has been absorbed by the newly established and fast-growing community college sector. Unlike most of the community colleges in the USA, which followed a comprehensive or 'multipurpose' model, offering vocational courses and qualification as well as the first two of the four-year university first degree (or undergraduate) programmes (OECD 1991), community colleges in most provinces in Canada do not have an explicit university transfer or university preparation role (Skolnik and Jones 1993). Increasingly, the existence of two distinct sectors, and the lack of efficient coordination between them, has given rise to policy concern. This is, of course, particularly apparent in those provinces where community colleges do have an explicit university transfer role, i.e. Quebec, Alberta and British Columbia, but increasingly the need for inter-sector coordination is also being articulated in the others, in particular as the sectors compete for shrinking public funds. This has a direct bearing on universities in several respects, and two ways in particular that tend to threaten their traditional autonomy. First, any coordination between the two sectors will entail a decision, on which sector can best accommodate students in those programmes, such as nursing, industrial accounting or medical technologies, which are offered by both universities and non-university institutions. Secondly, in systems where an explicit or implicit university transfer role is given to the college system, the question of academic standards is at stake, as is the power of the universities (or the respective faculties, departments or programmes) to select applicants according to their own criteria.

The third theme, the quality and the importance of teaching in universities, does not seem to be directly linked with the two earlier issues. While primarily an academic matter that deals with the principal function and the original mandate of universities, the question has more than marginal links with issues of efficiency, quality, funding, public accountability, responsiveness to students, and the adequate preparation for cultural, social and working life. The question of quality of teaching and of the emphasis that is given to teaching in comparison with research, is not an entirely new topic, but it is only recently in Canada that it has advanced from the back-burner to a more prominent place in the political soup kitchen.

Doing more with less: changing funding mechanisms and their impact on universities

Both the federal government (which has no constitutional power in educational matters but has for a long time financially supported higher education) and the provinces have started a discussion about the need to restructure so that institutions can do more with less. Thus, for instance, the Ontario Ministry of Education and Training, in a recent letter to the Province's Council on University Affairs – a buffer body with the responsibility of advising the provincial government on university matters – made clear that serious budget constraints entail that 'Ontario's public institutions cannot continue to do business the same way' as at present, that demand for university services will grow faster than public resources and that therefore 'universities will have to find new ways to provide improved services' (OCUA 1994). The same message, although with a slightly different emphasis, owing to the absence of federal powers to directly mingle with university matters, comes from the Federal Minister of Human Resources Development in his plan to discontinue (indirect) funding of post-secondary institutions and instead to set up a new student loan fund that would enlarge access for new groups of students, ineligible under the current system, such as adults who want to upgrade their professional skills or change their careers (HRDC 1994)

The federal proposal: moving to the market model

The federal government has supported universities substantially yet indirectly in the past, partly through a system of a block funding programme (the so-called Established Programme Financing Scheme, EPF), consisting of transfers to the provinces of cash and so-called tax points (a percentage of the federal income tax), partly through a Canada-wide student loans programme,[1] and partly through support for academic research, channelled directly to the institutions, mainly in the form of grants from the three Research Councils.[2] The entire federal support package for the post-secondary education system is presently worth some $8 billion per year, accounting for around 50 per cent of the total operating cost. Of this, the largest amount is given in the form of EPF, i.e. cash transfers in the order of $2.6 billion and tax points that presently account for approximately $3.5 billion.

In view of the enormous debt load, the federal government had decided in early 1994 to freeze the current transfers to the provinces for post-secondary education at 1993–4 levels. As the tax points transferred to the provinces as part of the EPF scheme are increasing in value, provinces are increasingly getting a larger share of their transfers for post-secondary education in the form of money raised through the tax points, and correspondingly an ever smaller amount of cash transfers. With the freeze of the overall transfers in place, the federal government is projecting that, in about ten years, the cash component of the entitlement will be running out and the EPF will be entirely paid in the form of tax foregone by the federal government and accruing to the provinces.[3]

While the freeze has been bad news enough for the provinces which are confronted with both a continuous demand for study opportunities in post-secondary education and with rising costs, the federal government is now proposing to discontinue the cash transfer altogether. Instead, it is proposed that cash funds presently going to the institutions via the provinces be turned into a system of expanded student loans to individuals. The stated objective of the government proposal is to widen access to individuals who wish, or need to, upgrade their earlier education by re-entering, or entering for the first time, college or university. Post-secondary education institutions, it is argued, would be able to compensate for smaller institutional grants by raising tuition fees, and students would be able to pay higher fees through the proposed new loan scheme. Repayment of the student loans would be administered through an income contingent repayment scheme which means that individuals would repay as they develop the financial capability to do so (HRDC 1994: 62–64).

For the institutions the proposals, if enacted, will mean the loss of some $14 billion in cash grants over ten years, which the provinces, equally hampered by heavy debts of their own, will most certainly not be able to replace by provincial funds. This major loss of revenue from the public purse will force institutions to a major increase of tuition fees which presently account for approximately 15–20 per cent of university income. Thus universities will be passing the burden onto the students who will have to pay student fees that will, as it is estimated, probably more than double that of the present level (AUCC 1994).

This shift from cash transfer to the provinces to a student loan scheme will certainly attain the first, but not openly stated, objective of the intended reform: it will privatize the public debt, a policy that is seen by many (Stager 1989; Kesselman 1993; West 1993) as offering a clear advantage over other means of financing public capital expenditures. However, it is much less certain that the second objective, namely to increase accessibility to post-secondary education for adults and generally opportunities for life-long learning, will likewise be met.

It is often argued that ordinary, mortgage-type loans for post-secondary education discourage potential participants from investing in their education, and in particular students from non-traditional backgrounds. Income contingent repayment loans are seen to address this particular problem as borrowers would only need to repay loans if, and to the extent to which, their income after completion of their studies exceeds the income prior to them. Students who did not succeed with their studies or who do not earn a better income than before would not be obliged to repay the full amount of the loan (Schuetze and Istance 1987: 150).

However, there are two questions to be asked with regard to the suitability of a loan scheme for older students, i.e. mid-career adults. The first is whether income contingent loans would be attractive for this group as the time span for repayment is shorter, and private returns smaller as they are incurred over a shorter period than in the case of younger students. The second question concerns the living costs of adult students with families or dependants at their charge, which are significantly higher than those for younger students. Unless they are to continue working full-time during their studies, how is income maintenance financed under such a scheme? If adult students were to borrow the full amount needed for tuition fees, income maintenance and incidental cost, for, say, two years of full-time study, this would amount to a very sizeable loan indeed, which could be expected to act as a major disincentive. The present proposal is extremely vague on this point, and – in spite of the language of the discussion paper which explicitly talks about a new approach to financing life-long learning – it appears that the new scheme is primarily designed for borrowing money to cover tuition fees. Only if this interpretation is correct would the same amount of funding overall be available to universities as it is under the present scheme of institutional grants.

The question remains as to what effects on the universities the change in funding from indirect institutional support to a system of extended loans to students is likely to have. Giving public funding for post-secondary education to students, rather than to the institutions, has been discussed for a number of years. Proponents argue that a voucher system for higher education would have the main advantage of providing a strong stimulus to competition among educational suppliers. The example in the USA of such a voucher system was the so-called

GI Bill, which had its equivalent in Canada, providing war veterans with educational benefits, including tuition fees for accredited training and educational programmes. Competition among institutions for students and their fees would enhance diversity among the institutions. Such diversity is seen (Stager 1989: 58) to be the core of accessibility,

> because individuals are more likely to find a match between their preferences and abilities and a university's programmes and admission standards. The more likely such a match will occur, the greater the actual accessibility and participation in the university system.

Elements of choice and competition are in fact already present under the current system. Students as Canadian universities pay tuition fees, and even if most institutional funding comes from the provincial governments (part of which is funded in turn by EPF), it is the enrolment numbers that provide the basis of such funding (West 1988: 99–100). However, institutions are not free with regard to the level of fees, as these are typically controlled by provincial governments, allowing for very little variation from the 'set formula fee' set forth by the responsible ministry, nor are institutions free to influence the number of enrolments that determine the size of a government grant.

The role fees play in the financing of universities, and the effect that the present system has upon diversity and innovation in programme structure and delivery, have been the subject of discussion for some time in Canada. Among the most critical voices has been a Royal Commission which looked broadly into the main factors and prospects of economic development in Canada (Royal Commission on the Economic Unity and Development Prospects for Canada). The Commission, clearly not impressed with the present state of higher education, deplored the lack of innovative spirit in the institutions and argued in favour of a greater variety in tuition charges across programmes and institutions which in turn would result in 'a much more heterogeneous post-secondary system, efficiently serving the highly varied needs of different students' (MacDonald Commission 1985: 749). It is this direction of change, advocated ten years ago by the MacDonald Commission, which was appointed by a liberal prime minister, that a new liberal government, which came to power after nine years of Conservative rule, is now putting back on to the political agenda.

With the drop of federal transfers that go to the institutions via the provinces and with an extended student loan system that is guaranteed by public funding, the Canadian system of financing would start resembling more than presently the US higher education system – one which provides approximately 20 per cent of the total support of higher education, almost all of it for research and for student aid (Trow 1992: 72). The example of the USA clearly suggests that such a system of funding does not prevent higher education from flourishing. Yet, it is questionable whether to emulate such a system is adequate for Canada, given Canada's traditions and policies of a more egalitarian society as well as the structure of a university system which is not only very little diversified but predominantly public, with a much smaller private sector than the US.

The Ontario proposal: Government policy and university autonomy

Almost simultaneously, but unrelated to the federal proposal, the government of Ontario, the most populous province with the greatest number of universities and university students, has also suggested major changes in the funding of universities. Universities are requested to seek new ways to provide more cost effective education, increase accessibility for students – in particular from non-traditional age groups, the poor and minority populations – put a stronger emphasis on teaching, engage in programme co-operation and restructuring and develop mechanisms for greater accountability.

In response to this request, the Ontario Council of University Affairs has drawn up three alternative models for the distribution of government funding to the Ontario universities (OCUA 1994). The first model resembles, but modifies the current system which bases funding on so-called 'enrolment corridors', by removing the present requirement of additional funding when enrolments are above the defined corridor. The second model would eliminate the corridor system and base funding on either a slip-year, five year moving average of enrolments or on a combination of such an enrolment sensitive method and a basic funding grant that would be insensitive to enrolment change. While both mechanisms would take account of the need to accommodate additional numbers of students without increasing overall funding, both models would leave the decision to the universities as to how to accommodate student numbers among programmes and how to allocate funds internally for teaching, research and service activities.

The third model would largely do away with the autonomy of universities to make such allocation decisions. The so-called 'purpose of service' scheme is a contractual funding system whereby the provincial government would purchase from the individual university a defined level of teaching, research and service, based on a negotiation of specific terms and conditions. Such negotiated terms would not only specify number and measures of quality, but could also concern institutional practice and compliance with particular policy objectives such as equity employment, rationalization or particular innovations such as the extension of distance study, external degrees and specific admission rules for mature students without proper academic access credentials. This third model, while not radical by international standards, would mean a significant departure from the funding traditions in Canada in that it would significantly impinge on institutional autonomy and flexibility.

This infringement of autonomy is the main focus of opposition to the proposal from the university community. Most critical voices, while emphasizing the role and importance of universities for the public, have been alarmed by the view that universities should be conceived as instruments of public policy. Thus, for instance, the fixation of the Ontario Government on expansion of student numbers admitted to universities has been criticized as myopic, given the present high enrolment rates and the difficulties university graduates have finding a job commensurate with their qualifications. The tendency to confuse accessibility and equity, which the Government is accused of by many critics, is seen to be grounded in the fact that expansion is politically popular.

Responsiveness and funding

Who should make decisions about enrolment numbers and capacity, the weight of teaching and research activities and the balance between them, and to what the current role of universities is, and should be, in a changing democratic society and a modern economy? Both the federal and the Ontario proposals for changing the allocation mechanisms of funding are based on the belief that universities are not responsive enough to the demand and pressures from society and that the 'public [is] frustrated by the current system' (OCUA 1994: 24).

Both proposals use funding allocation as the lever to make universities more responsive, efficient and accountable, by introducing an element of market allocation in the funding system which has been unknown to Canadian universities. Conceptually they differ in their approach, however. The federal proposal regarding the disposition of its share of funding, would let the market decide which institutions would draw support, and a major part of their revenues, from the consumer, i.e. students through payment of tuition fees. By contrast, the Ontario approach would entail a more regulated market in which government, as the main purchaser of university services, would place constraints on market competition by linking provincial funding to the compliance by institutions with government objectives (OCUA 1994: 21). However, both proposed funding mechanisms will secure a much greater say from the public as to where universities will place their priorities and how they will design and deliver their services.

It is not clear yet whether any of the proposals will be implemented, and, if so, what the specific features will look like. As the financial predicament that is at the origin of the proposals will not go away, it is safe to predict however that the present system of considerable university autonomy of Canadian universities will be greatly abridged, and that the Canadian system will follow others, notably the USA and more recently the UK and Australian systems, on their move to a more market-oriented order.

Increasing student mobility

To call the Canadian higher or post-secondary education system a 'system' is stretching the meaning of the term. If a system is defined as a set of institutions that form an integrated whole, working together within well-defined relationships, governed by established rules, and coordinated in a consistent fashion, then there are no actual provincial 'systems' of post-secondary education in Canada, perhaps with the exception of Quebec. Instead, there are 12 provincial and territorial quasi-systems which, while having a few comparable features and using much of the same terminology, have quite different rules and arrangements concerning accessibility, curriculum, student mobility and planning, making the Canadian 'system' one of the most diversified in the OECD countries (Dennison 1995). The principal reason for this wide variety is the constitutional distribution of powers, which gives the provinces the exclusive authority to regulate all matters of education. This is in contrast with other federal systems, such as Germany, in which the federal government has a formal role in setting forth the organizational framework, i.e. the basic rules and structures within which provincial systems operate, providing nation-wide standards in relation to such matters as admission, transfer of credits, recognition of degrees, etc. (Cameron 1992b; Teichler 1992).

Accessibility to post-secondary education institutions has been discussed above in the context of funding mechanisms and in particular student assistance. Another growing policy concern is student mobility between the different institutions within the same province and between regions. There are three reasons why this is a problem in Canada. First is the almost complete lack of standardization which would facilitate portability of credits from one institution to another. The autonomy that institutions, in particular, universities, enjoy includes the right to define criteria and standards of their own for admission, to design programmes and curricula, including the prerequisites required to enrol in programmes and courses.

The second reason is the lack of clearly established rules for transfer between the different parts of the post-secondary education system and of effective coordination mechanisms in the provinces. The former is the result of the often unplanned and uncoordinated ways the post-secondary sectors grew in the 1950s and 1960s. With the exception of Quebec and the provinces of British Columbia and Alberta, the various categories of institutions – the universities, the community colleges, and a third category comprising institutes of technology, agricultural colleges, colleges of art and design, etc. – were set up and developed independently from each other. Thus, Canadian higher education is characterized by at least two and, in some provinces, three distinct sectors, governed by different laws and funded according to different formulas. While the main features of universities are identical or similar across the provinces, the role and mandate of non-university institutions vary, and only in the three provinces mentioned above, do community colleges have an explicit role in preparing students for university or providing the first two years of four-year degree programmes (Skolnik and Jones 1993: 59). While students who have been successfully enrolled in such transfer programmes can go on to universities in their respective provinces, this is much more difficult in other provinces with a college system without an explicit or recognized transfer function.

Coordination among the different institutions in most provinces so far has been 'spasmodic at best and in some regions virtually non-existent' (Dennison 1995: 123). Some provinces have set up special coordination mechanisms or bodies, such as the Councils of Admission and Transfer in British Columbia and Alberta. These bodies have no regulating powers and their role is thus limited to informing, articulating and convincing institutions to negotiate what is considered as 'credit equivalents'. They also prepare transfer guides, containing a list of all courses and programmes that have been negotiated as being equivalent between sending and receiving institutions or their relevant academic departments. Given the strong tradition of institutional autonomy, any arrangement of credit transfer needs to be voluntary (Dennison 1995: 124). This makes the process both cumbersome and very time-consuming in spite of the fact that the principle of credit transfer and student mobility among institutions is generally recognized.

The third aspect concerns the barriers to student mobility across provincial borders. While it has been pointed out that this might be of less importance in Canada, compared to Europe where distances are much shorter (Cameron, 1992a: 37), the problem is of growing importance in Canada as well, as general mobility is increasing. Unlike Germany, where regional barriers to access to both higher education or to the exercise of one's profession are seen as violating the constitutional right of every citizen, in Canada provinces are free in principle to erect such barriers by, for instance, levying higher tuition fees from students from another province. Although this right is not exercised in any of the provinces – unlike in the USA where some states require higher fees for out-of-state students – the lack of agreements between provincial governments concerning credit equivalence and transfer constitute difficulties. Some institutions have taken initiatives to address the problem. Thus 28 universities across Canada have formed a University Exchange Consortium, and the ten largest research universities have established an Exchange Programme which ensures that students receive full recognition by their home institutions for the credits earned in one of the other institutions of the Consortium. In addition, the Council of Ministers of Education has called upon universities to agree to a pan-Canadian recognition of credit transfer for the first two years of undergraduate study by September 1995. The Council (CMEC 1994: 3) points out that

> the lack of consistency in the rules and procedures governing credit transfer among the universities, and at times within an institution, at best leads to substantial confusion for the student and at worst results in inconsistencies in the recognition of credits and in injustices to students.

Aware of the academic autonomy concerning admission, curriculum, and academic standards the Council pointed out (CMEC 1994: 5–6):

> . . . the Ministers of Education wish to reassure the universities on the following points:
> 1. The protocol in no way infringes on the academic autonomy of the university;
> 2. the protocol applies to transfer students who are deemed admissible by a university. It does not reflect on the policies and practices used by the universities in deciding upon the admissibility of students who apply for admission with advanced standing; and
> 3. the protocol is consistent with the integrity of university programmes and the right of universities to determine programme design and delivery, to determine academic prerequisites and to establish admission criteria and certification requirements of academic achievement.

The Council's reassurance of universities as to their autonomy is quoted here in full to demonstrate to what extent governments in Canada have so far been unwilling to legislate, or regulate through other instruments, such as funding, to bring universities to recognize course credit from other universities. This reluctance is remarkable, particularly when it is considered that transfer based on course credits as a common academic currency is recognized in principle, and often in practice. Moreover, the present protocol concerns transfer among universities only, and not the more difficult issue of college-to-university-transfer, which is, as we have seen, problematic even within a province.

It is fair to predict, however, that public frustration with the present state of affairs and pressures from a variety of quarters, will translate into terms and conditions of university funding which will speed up universities' willingness to become 'part of an integrated educational system which permits easy movement from one sector to another' – one of the policy objectives of the Ontario Minister of Education (OCUA 1994: 24).

The new emphasis on teaching

Seemingly in contrast to the concern discussed so far about accessibility, competition and diversity, student mobility, accountability and efficiency of the university system as a whole, a major discussion presently ongoing concerns the role and quality of teaching and its relationship with research. This discussion has several roots. One of these is a direct consequence of the proposed change in allocating federal funds to students rather than to the institutions. The recognition is growing that, if students are given more of a consumer's choice and more influence through a greater reliance by universities on income generated from student fees, programmes and curricula must be not only seen to be relevant but also delivered in ways that are valued by the students.

There is, however, another source of the growing concern for the role and quality of teaching, beside market influence and consumer choice. It comes from recognition both from within the professoriate and the public, 'that the teaching and learning mandate of the universities is taking second place to other activities on the part of the faculty' (Commission of Inquiry on Canadian University Education 1991: 33), and in particular research activities. After collecting evidence through consultations with the main representatives of universities and a series of public hearings, the Commission of Inquiry on Canadian University Education reported in 1991 that, in spite of the efforts of academics and numerous initiatives by some universities, teaching in universities was generally undervalued, and made a number of recommendations addressed both to governments and universities. The report noted, in particular, the strong trend towards putting clearly more emphasis on research than on teaching activities when it comes to hiring, tenure or promotion decisions. The revealing language of 'research opportunity' and 'teaching load' and the fact that a growing part of undergraduate teaching is left to part-time faculty, sessional lecturers and teaching assistants are indications of this imbalance.

At the base of the Commission's critical appraisal of the present role and esteem held of teaching is a strong belief that quality instruction is at the very centre of the university's mission (Commission of Inquiry on Canadian University Education 1991: 31):

> Universities are believed to be institutions of teaching and learning wherein research is performed and wherein the teaching is done by persons who are engaged in continuing scholarly activities. This arrangement persists because it is felt to be desirable that teachers and students both be in the learning mode with an enthusiastic desire to expand their understanding. There must be no mistake about this, however. If university professors are being paid to improve their own knowledge and to engage in scholarly activities, it is primarily so that the teaching they offer to successive generations of students will be enriched, and only secondarily because society perceives a need for the research findings themselves.

Thus, the hiring of part-time faculty to do the teaching (1991: 55)

> challenges the basic idea that faculty must do both research and teaching. By letting active researchers teach so little, and putting sessional lecturers in their places, universities are putting at risk not only the quality of university education but also the very system itself.

This view, although it may reflect a strong tradition of thought, has recently been challenged by the Ontario Council of University Affairs (1994: 14). Based on a review of literature, the Commission found that

> there is little evidence of necessary links between effective undergraduate teaching and research. Excellent researchers may well be excellent teachers but there is nothing to suggest that one is a prerequisite for the other. Similarly, there may be superb teachers who have little or no engagement in . . . research.

Whatever the views about the relationship between research and teaching and the proper balance between these two principal academic missions, interest in teaching has moved centre stage in the current discussion about universities. This discussion can be viewed from the perspective of a new understanding of scholarship, as suggested by a number of US authors (Lynton and Elman 1987; Boyer 1990; Rice 1992). These authors have redefined scholarship to include not only research as the discovery of new knowledge, but also teaching, practice in the form of application of knowledge, and the integration or synthesis of knowledge. Among these four different, yet related forms of scholarship, which are equivalent in their importance to society, research is but one kind of scholarly activity, and not the only or single most important goal of universities.

The Commission Report's recommendations to improve the conditions and the appreciation of, as well as the rewards for, university teaching, take account of this multischolarship concept of distinguished yet equivalent functions of the professoriate, as the following three examples illustrate:

- The definitions of scholarship should be stated clearly at each university and should include much more than the publication of research articles.
- Professors who undertake technological or other innovation in university pedagogy should be recognized for the scholarly contribution they are making.

- Every faculty member, on hiring end at the start of each evaluation period, [should] be given the opportunity to decide . . . whether his/her evaluation will be based primarily on research (or some other form of scholarship) or teaching. Promotion to every rank should be based on excellence in the chosen category, along with competence in the other.

Individual institutions, in particular research universities, have started to realize that undergraduate students had been shunted to the margins of the institutions' concern and were not receiving the attention and the resources they deserve. Many of these institutions have begun to revitalize teaching in numerous innovative ways. A few examples will suffice here.

Most universities have adopted an official policy that teaching and research will be given equal weight when it comes to hiring, promotions or tenure. This principle does not always translate into practice but there are institutions, individual faculties or departments that have begun to give teaching equal or greater importance in tenure or promotion decisions. Furthermore, prizes for excellence in teaching have been instituted in most institutions which carry palpable rewards such as sizeable cash grants, as well as a fair amount of prestige. Many institutions have introduced mandatory student ratings for all courses which are administered by an independent office whose mandate is the instructional development of faculty members whose rating is below average. Such Instructional Development Offices offer seminars and workshops for faculty members on pedagogical principles and teaching practice. In some universities, all new faculty and professors with poor teaching records are required to attend such workshops. Some universities have introduced so-called 'teaching dossiers', consisting of a file with teaching materials such as course outlines, reading lists and other teaching materials, and evaluations by students and peers. Such peer reviews are required in many institutions as a regular part of a promotion or tenure procedure. Some universities have established teaching innovation funds that award grants to faculty on a competitive basis for the development of innovative courses or ways of delivery, for example developing innovative learning materials designed to enable students to learn 'by objectives' in a self-teaching situation.

The emphasis on all of these measures is on good practice of teaching students, many of whom being adults, not only by the standard of legal age but also in terms of life experience. Most of this is based on grass-roots experience and development and very little on programmes with a claim to sound theory. The emphasis on practice relevance is probably the reason why staff on the whole seems very cooperative, interested and engaged in the process. This observation might find its explanation in the fact that Canadian universities have, unlike the research universities in the USA, Germany or France, a tradition of being primarily teaching institutions, and emphasis on research has been relatively recent.[4]

Summary and conclusion

This analysis of the changing university in Canada cannot provide a full picture. Obviously, the selection of the issues discussed here has been somewhat arbitrary and the interpretation of their impact on the university speculative. This is particularly so with respect to those political proposals that are presently under intensive discussion, but not yet put into effect, primarily the proposed changes in the funding system.

What binds the three topics together are the two poles, their relationship and the tension between them, that are at the heart of the matter of current change. One is the traditional institutional autonomy which is probably more pronounced in Canada than in any other OECD country. The other is the fact that Canadian universities have started preparing seriously for markets – half pushed by governments or intermediate funding and planning bodies, half pulled by internal forces such as students, some of the faculty and university management. The ongoing change process is one that can be observed, and is, in fact, being eagerly observed by Canadians, in other countries where this move to the market and the discussion about the actual impact on institutional change is further advanced than in Canada.

Notes

1. Only the Province of Quebec and the North West Territories have set up their own loan schemes, to which, however, the federal government has contributed funding.
2. The Medical Research Council, established in 1969, the National Sciences and Engineering Council, and the Social Sciences and Humanities Research Council, both set up in 1978.
3. There is disagreement between the provincial and the federal governments on the question whether the revenue from the taxes should be rightfully considered provincial or federal. The original transfer of tax points was agreed almost thirty years ago and tax revenues derived from this source are now seen as part of the regular provincial tax revenue. However, federal law requires the Minister of Human Resources Development to report annually on federal and provincial expenditures for post-secondary education, including the imputed yield from the tax transfers as federal expenditure (Cameron 1992a: 54).
4. Although several Canadian institutions of higher education are among the oldest in North America, the concept of the research university is a later one in Canada than in the USA. Few doctoral degrees were awarded by Canadian institutions prior to the Second World War (Fisher *et al.* 1994).

References

AUCC (1994) *Notes for a Presentation to the the House of Commons Standing Committee on Finance* (brochure). Ottawa, Association of Universities and Colleges of Canada.
Boyer, E. (1990) *Scholarship Reconsidered: Priorities of the Professoriate*. Princeton, NJ, Carnegie Foundation for the Advancement of Teaching.
Cameron, D. (1992a) 'Higher education in federal systems: Canada', in *Higher Education in Federal Systems*, D. Brown, P. Cazalis and G. Jasmin (eds). Kingston, Ontario, Institute of Intergovernmental Relations at Queen's University.
Cameron, D. (1992b) 'Higher education in seven federal systems: A synthesis', in *Higher education in Federal Systems*, D. Brown, P. Cazalis and G. Jasmin (eds). Kingston, Ontario, Institute of Intergovernmental Relations at Queen's University.

CMEC (1994) *Pan-Canadian Protocol on the Transferability of University Credits* (draft brochure). Toronto, Council of Ministers of Education, Canada.

Commission of Inquiry on Canadian University Education (1991) *Report* ('*The Smith Report*'). Ottawa, Association of Universities and Colleges of Canada.

Dennison, J.D. (1995) 'Organisation and function in higher education', in *Challenge and Opportunity – Canada's Community Colleges at the Cross-roads*, J.D. Dennison (ed.). Vancouver, UBC Press.

Fisher, D., Rubenson, K. and Schuetze, H.G. (1994) *The Role of the University in Preparing the Labour Force – A Background Analysis*. Centre for Policy Studies in Education, Vancouver, University of British Columbia.

HRDC (1994) 'Improving Social Security in Canada – A Discussion Paper'. Ottawa, Ministry of Human Resources Development, Canada.

Kesselman, J.R. (1993) 'Squeezing universities, students, or taxpayers? – Issues in designing a Canadian income-contingent loan program', in *Ending the Squeeze on Universities*, S. Easton (ed.). Montreal, Institute for Research on Public Policy.

Lynton, E. and Elman, S. (1987) *New Priorities for the University – Meeting Society's Needs for Applied Knowledge and Competent Individuals*. San Francisco, Jossey Bass.

MacDonald Commission (1985) *Royal Commission on the Economic Union and Development Prospects for Canada*, Report, vol. 2. Ottawa.

OCUA (1994) 'Sustaining Quality in Changing Times: Funding Ontario Universities – A Discussion Paper'. Toronto, Ontario Council on University Affairs.

OECD (1991) *Alternatives to Universities*. Paris, Organisation for Economic Co-operation and Development.

OECD (1993) *Education at a Glance – OECD Indicators*. Paris, Organisation for Economic Co-operation and Development.

Rice, R.E. (1992) 'Toward a broader conception of scholarship: The American context', in *Research and Higher Education – The United Kingdom and the United States*, T. Whiston and R. Geiger (eds). Buckingham, Society for Research into Higher Education and Open University Press.

Schuetze, H.G. and Istance, D. (1987) *Recurrent Education Revisited – Modes of Participation and Financing*. Stockholm, Almquist and Wicksell International.

Skolnik, M. and Jones, G. (1993) 'Arrangements for coordination between university and college sectors in Canadian provinces'. *Canadian Journal of Higher Education*, 23(1), 56–73.

Stager, D. (1989) *Focus on Fees – Alternative Policies for University Tuition Fees*. Toronto, Council of Ontario Universities.

Teichler, U. (1992) 'Higher education in federal systems: Germany', in *Higher Education in Federal Systems*, D. Brown, P. Cazalis and G. Jasmin (eds). Kingston, Ontario, Institute of Intergovernmental Relations at Queen's University.

Trow, M. (1992) 'Origins and development of federalism in American higher education', in *Higher Education in Federal Systems*, D. Brown, P. Cazalis and G. Jasmin (eds). Kingston, Ontario, Institute of Intergovernmental Relations at Queen's University.

West, E.G. (1988) *Higher Education in Canada – An Analysis*. Vancouver, Fraser Institute.

West, E.G. (1993) 'Ending the squeeze on universities', in *Ending the Squeeze on Universities*, S. Easton (ed.). Montreal, Institute for Research on Public Policy.

15

The Social and Political Vocation of the University in the Global Age

Radim Palouš

The drama of our times is the exodus from particularity and the advent of universal community. Mankind must relinquish individual and social games on separate playing fields. The second half of the twentieth century is an entrance onto the scene, where people take part in the common performance of the drama, the 'world'. Leaving egoistic cells and prisons and entering worldwide openness can be called education (from the Latin *educatio*, 'to take out, to bring out, to lead out').

In the modern, civilized era there exist educational institutions at lower and higher levels, from the basic, such as the nursery school, to the university. What is the basis of the distinction between 'lower' and 'higher' in the educational system? What is 'higher' about institutions of higher education? The characteristics involved in 'higher' education are complex. One shall be the subject of focus here: education in transcendence. 'Transcendence' in this context is 'a stepping beyond' which presupposes academic openness.

It was the universities which were historically the first to emerge as institutionalized and educative agencies. The middle-school system of the gymnasium type was instituted later, and only toward the end of the eighteenth century and in the course of the nineteenth did an elementary school system appear. For instance, this three-level structure of education was legislatively confirmed in the Czech Republic (formerly part of Czechoslovakia) in 1869, and so the 'tripartite' tradition, i.e. elementary schools, middle schools and schools of 'higher education' has already lasted for well over a hundred years. All levels of education were originally founded, not principally as ways of meeting the productive needs of society, but for pious purposes (that is, for preparation in religion) and they were generally of a meditative character. This opened up the way to the world of disputation and learning.

During the nineteenth and twentieth centuries the educational system became even more 'practically' and pragmatically oriented. The main reason for this development was evidently the penetration of academic thinking into the sphere of production. The experience to be gained in the common work of father and son in the family field or in the mutual participation of master and apprentice in a trade workshop became ever less adequate. The school – as it does today all over the world – began to take an ever greater role in inducting people into the mechanisms of civic and productive social life. In this way, the school becomes a tool for instruction – how to understand this or that – instead of a means of asking major questions of life and searching for a life orientation. The greater the amount of instruction which indoctrinates people in this or that way, the less the school is 'high'. The institutions of higher education keep their dimension of openness, that is of academic disputation and learning, by preserving academic tasks which the teachers are supposed to perform. University teachers must not only teach 'passing on knowledge and skills' but should be at the same time and inseparably still open in their field of inquiry, problematics and controversy. They should be versed not only in their own field but also in research which crosses the borders of their fields. They should cultivate this transcendence not only in research but also in teaching.

Thus we are offered a means of distinguishing between lower and higher education: for the lower type, a more intensive form of instruction is typical; the higher we go, the more academic doubt and research is added. This is not to say that the capacity for intrinsic human openness and reflection should or could be absent at schools of lower levels.

What is happening now in the field of higher education is critical: both the number of schools of higher education and the students attending them is growing rapidly but we are witnessing the hypertrophy of pragmatic instruction and the disappearance of scholarly transcendence. The character of schools of higher education is changing: universities are becoming outnumbered by 'professional' schools of higher education.

It is not the mission of the universities to be 'professional' schools. Of course, they must not allow themselves to fall behind in their professional standards and so slip into dilettantism, but nevertheless their character as universities leads them to a broader perspective. Their universality consists not, therefore, in amassing pieces of all and everything but primarily in responsibility for a wholeness which was always, but is now especially capable of realization only through the mutual opening of special disciplines. For all the importance of professional qualifications, it is still basic scholarship and the original conceptualization of problems which again and again shatters the intellectual chains which hold mental life in closed caves. It is this which opens the path to the greater universe within which we move whether as scientists or as citizens, as members of the world community or even as beings among other beings and therefore as people – sojourners in the created and creating universe.

Universities and institutions of higher education, in general, have their own significant role in a global coexistence, and this in their responsibility for introducing their graduates to the movement of self-transcendence described; this means that they must lead them to openness. Of course this is the task of all kinds of schools, but the higher their status, the more it is their mission.

The political trend in the modern world is characterized as one of democratization. This is an expression of human humility: no person rules absolutely and totally. It is crucial in the modern world, and crucial for the mere preservation of human society, its material needs and the very existence of man, that a relatively large proportion of the population should have a high level of education. This is implicit in the scientific and technical character of contemporary civilization. On the European scale, we are talking about the target of 50 per cent of the population having a higher education.

On the other hand, however, the word 'university' according to Comenius's interpretation of the word *universum* points toward the expression *ad unum vertere*, that is, 'to turn to the one'. This orientation had deeply transcendent character. Integrity then rests first of all on the acceptance of responsibility for the meaningful existence of the whole, by the individual parts in which it consists, even if the price is self-sacrifice or some loss. Without some such dedication and willingness on all sides, the whole community is in mortal danger. If someone wants to take part in university life, then he or she must also accept its framework and the responsibilities and limitations which go with it. As a *civis academicus universatis* he or she is, however, above all called to participation in the spiritual mission of the university. The most significant element of this mission is openness and transcendence and in no way submission to pragmatism or to totalitarian or consumerist manipulation. The mission of universities today is of the highest significance. In the next century it will be still more significant. If universities do not fulfil their tasks in the spirit of their intrinsic responsibility, they will not be the only ones to suffer injury (indeed, from the purely material point of view they may not outwardly suffer at all!). It will be the world that suffers.

Index

The Society for Research into Higher Education

The Society for Research into Higher Education exists to stimulate and coordinate research into all aspects of higher education. It aims to improve the quality of higher education through the encouragement of debate and publication on issues of policy, on the organization and management of higher education institutions, and on the curriculum and teaching methods.

The Society's income is derived from subscriptions, sales of its books and journals, conference fees and grants. It receives no subsidies, and is wholly independent. Its individual members include teachers, researchers, managers and students. Its corporate members are institutions of higher education, research institutes, professional, industrial and governmental bodies. Members are not only from the UK, but from elsewhere in Europe, from America, Canada and Australasia, and it regards its international work as among its most important activities.

Under the imprint *SRHE & Open University Press*, the Society is a specialist publisher of research, having some 45 titles in print. The Editorial Board of the Society's Imprint seeks authoritative research or study in the above fields. It offers competitive royalties, a highly recognizable format in both hardback and paperback and the world-wide reputation of the Open University Press.

The Society also publishes *Studies in Higher Education* (three times a year), which is mainly concerned with academic issues, *Higher Education Quarterly* (formerly *Universities Quarterly*), mainly concerned with policy issues, *Research into Higher Education Abstracts* (three times a year), and *SRHE News* (four times a year).

The Society holds a major annual conference in December, jointly with an institution of higher education. In 1992, the topic was 'Learning to Effect', with Nottingham Trent University. In 1993, it was 'Governments and the Higher Education Curriculum: Evolving Partnerships' at the University of Sussex in Brighton, and in 1994, 'The Student Experience' at the University of York. Conferences in 1995 include, 'The Changing University?' at Heriot-Watt University in Edinburgh.

The Society's committees, study groups and branches are run by the members. The groups at present include:

Teacher Education Study Group
Continuing Education Group
Staff Development Group
Excellence in Teaching and Learning

Benefits to members

Individual

Individual members receive:

- *SRHE News*, the Society's publications list, conference details and other material included in mailings.
- Greatly reduced rates for *Studies in Higher Education* and *Higher Education Quarterly*.
- A 35 per cent discount on all Open University Press and SRHE publications.
- Free copies of the Proceedings – commissioned papers on the theme of the Annual Conference.
- Free copies of *Research into Higher Education Abstracts*.
- Reduced rates for conferences.
- Extensive contacts and scope for facilitating-initiatives.
- Reduced reciprocal memberships.

Corporate

Corporate members receive:

- All benefits of individual members, plus
- Free copies of *Studies in Higher Education*.
- Unlimited copies of the Society's publications at reduced rates.
- Special rates for its members e.g. to the Annual Conference.

Membership details: SRHE, 3 Devonshire Street, London, WIN 2BA, UK. Tel: 0171 637 2766 Fax: 0171 637 2781
Catalogue: SRHE & Open University Press, Celtic Court, 22 Ballmoor, Buckingham MK18 1XW. Tel: (01280) 823388

HOW TO GET A PHD (2nd edition)
A HANDBOOK FOR STUDENTS AND THEIR SUPERVISORS
Estelle M. Phillips and D. S. Pugh

This is a handbook and survival manual for PhD students, providing a practical, realistic understanding of the processes of doing research for a doctorate. It discusses many important issues often left unconsidered, such as the importance of time management and how to achieve it, and how to overcome the difficulties of communicating with supervisors. Consideration is given to the particular problems of groups such as women, part-time and overseas students.

The book also provides practical insights for supervisors, focusing on how to monitor and, if necessary, improve supervisory practice. It assists senior academic administrators by examining the responsibilities that universities have for providing an adequate service for research students. This is a revised and updated second edition; it will be as warmly welcomed as the first edition:

One way of providing a more supportive environment for PhD students is for supervisors to recommend this book.

(*Teaching News*)

Warmly recommended as a bedside companion, both to those hoping to get a PhD and to those who have the responsibility of guiding them, often with very little support themselves.

(*Higher Education Review*)

This is an excellent book. Its style is racy and clear . . . an impressive array of information, useful advice and comment gleaned from the authors' systematic study and experience over many years . . . should be required reading not only for those contemplating doctoral study but also for all supervisors, new and experienced.

(*Higher Education*)

Contents

224pp   0 335 19214 9 (Paperback)

THE FUTURE OF HIGHER EDUCATION

Tom Schuller (ed.)

Increasingly, the social and economic well-being of the country depends on the educational qualities of the population. Education has risen swiftly to near the top of the political agenda. Yet in education, as in so many other areas of policy, the debate in Britain has lacked a longer term perspective. This volume addresses itself to that lack in relation to higher education. Its contributors cover an enormous range of experience in teaching, research and management, in universities, polytechnics and colleges.

The Future of Higher Education focuses on three key themes:

- Access. There is widespread consensus on the need to expand the system, but how is this to be achieved and what are the implications for the structure and content of higher education?
- Governance. Change is essential at institutional and system level, but of what kind and how is it to be brought about?
- Quality. Remarkably, fundamental questions remain to be answered about what we mean by quality in higher education, and how it is to be maintained.

The volume challenges all those concerned with education to debate the priorities for the future of higher education.

Contents

Reassessing the future – Finished and unfinished business – Widening the access argument – Access and institutional change – Access: an overview – Governance and sectoral differentiation – Governance: the institutional viewpoint – Governance: an overview – The future and further education – Quality in higher education – Quality and qualities: an overview – Access, quality and governance: one institution's struggle for progress – Appendix – References – Index.

Contributors

Sir Christopher Ball, Tessa Blackstone, Colin Flint, Andrew McPherson, Pauline Perry, Elizabeth Reid, Michael Richardson, Tom Schuller, Peter Scott, Michael Shattock, William H. Stubbs, Gareth Williams.

144pp   0 335 09793 6 (Paperback)   0 335 09794 4 (Hardback)